WHAT WE'RE UP AGAINST

The Destructive Force At Work In Our World —and How We Can Defeat It

ANDREW BARD SCHMOOKLER

Press the Battle
PRESS

Press the Battle Press
Broadway
Virginia

10–9–8–7–6–5–4–3–2–1

First Edition: September 2015

Book Design: Steve Busch & Greg Correll
Cover illustration: Greg Correll

Cataloging Data
Schmookler, Andrew Bard.
What We're Up Against: The Destructive Force At Work in the World, and How We Can Defeat It / Andrew Bard Schmookler.
p.–cm.
bibliographical references and index.
isbn 978-0-9963013-0-5 (pbk. : alk. paper)
1. Good and Evil. 2. American Politics.
3. Social Evolution. 4. Historic forces.

What We're Up Against

CONTENTS

INTRODUCTION

Both as Americans (in our present national crisis) and as part of humankind (with the uncertainty about whether civilization on this planet will ultimately prove viable) we are up against a force we urgently need to understand.

Who is the "we" in this book's title, "What We're Up Against"?

First, the "we" is we citizens of the United States in this time of darkness and danger in America. We face a national crisis as profound as any in our history (with the exception of the crisis over slavery in the middle of the 19th century). The crisis is manifesting in the ugliness and dysfunction in our political arena, but the problems go far deeper than politics.

Second, the "we" is humankind, with its increasingly powerful system of civilization on this planet. History continues to accelerate toward an outcome that, looking to the centuries to come, increasingly congregates toward the extremes of catastrophe or utopia, with the middle ground of "muddle through" affording less and less viable space. How long can civilization survive if the war system remains intact with weapons as powerful as those we have, and perhaps still more destructive weapons ahead? What kind of future can civilized humankind have if we fail to create a civilization in harmony with the only planet we've got?

The prospects—both for America in its present crisis, and for humankind as history accelerates into the future—while far from hopeless, are deeply worrisome.

In America, developments over more than a decade have greatly increased the probability that the nation in the future will be one where the many are dominated by the few, the mass of the population will be "informed" by propaganda masquerading as news, and the government will exploit rather than serve the people.

Part of the crisis is that many of us are blind to the nature of the force we are up against, and as a result of this blindness we are failing to respond appropriately to protect what has been best about America.

Meanwhile, for humankind as a whole, it is far from clear whether this experiment that life-on-earth is conducting with this new form of a living system—civilization—will turn out well or badly.

Our global civilization is already on a course toward environmental disruption of a serious and perhaps catastrophic magnitude. Our species—with the exponential growth of our numbers, the take-off in the power of human technology, and the demands on the planet from the unprecedented levels of affluence in much of the world—has become a bull in the biospheric china shop.

To this is added that danger still posed by nuclear weapons, a danger magnified by the continued levels of disorder in the international system and the ever-present possibility of war.

If we as a species could better understand the forces—both constructive and destructive—at work in the system of human civilization, we would be more able to guide civilization's evolution toward the better outcome.

What are we up against?

This book will show that there is a meaningful sense in which the answer is the same for both senses of "we." Both the immediate crisis in the United States and the long-term challenge facing human civilization require much the same of us.

Of these two important dramas, it is the crisis in the United States that must be our most urgent concern—for two reasons.

First, the American crisis is the more acute. Less than a generation ago, the balance of power between constructive and destructive forces was significantly more positive than it has become. The disorder in civilization generally is as old as history. Acute pathologies require the most urgent attention.

Second, for the foreseeable future, a positive course for civilization as a whole depends on having a United States that is governed by a positive, constructive spirit. For three generations now, with all our nation's missteps, the role of America in leading human civilization forward has been indispensable. And there is no sign of another source of leadership available if the United States should continue to become more part of the problem and less part of the solution.

If America cannot shift greater power back to the nation's better elements, the chances will be greatly diminished that humankind will be able to navigate successfully through the perils it faces, to achieve a more humane, viable, and just civilization in the future.

The choice to focus on the American crisis, however, by no means implies a neglect of the long-term challenge facing civilization. As this book will demonstrate, understanding what we are up against in America leads directly into understanding the essential challenge humankind has faced for some 10,000 years, ever since our species took the unprecedented step of creating an altogether new kind of living system on earth.

The American crisis fits into a bigger picture. The destructive force that's been degrading America in recent years is part of a drama that is central to the human story: here you will find presented a secular, rational, and empirical understanding of a dynamic at the heart of the civilized human world, a dynamic that warrants being called, "the battle between good and evil."

I will show how the lack of understanding of this dynamic—a rejection by many intelligent, secular Americans of the whole idea of good versus evil—is an important part of why the forces of destruction have lately gained such power in our nation. There is a battle between the forces of wholeness and those of brokenness, and the stakes could not be higher.

Will American democracy survive and revive? Or will we continue down the road to plutocracy? Will the lie continue to defeat the truth in our national discourse? Or will the founders' vision of a healthy "marketplace of ideas" prevail? Will the divisions among groups or factions of Americans continue to widen? Or will the bases for cooperation and common purpose be rebuilt?

Favorable answers to those questions depend on our understanding what it is that we are up against—a force that fosters injustice, that deals in deception, that employs a strategy of divide and conquer, etc. etc. One despicable move after another.

And understanding that force—how it works in the human world to spread its pattern of brokenness, how it gains power, how it arose in the first place—will illuminate the meaning of the human saga, and the fundamental challenge we as a species confront.

Will humankind learn to live in harmony with the biosphere on which we all depend for our survival? Will our kind manage to create a world in which disputes are settled peaceably and justly? Will humanity create an order that reliably serves human fulfillment? Or will the forces of brokenness—in war, in ecological destruction, in cultures hostile to human needs—lead to misery, to a dark age, or even to extinction?

This book will provide an answer to the question, "What are we up against?" by asking first the question, "What's gone wrong in America and how can it be set right?"

That will lead to a truth that can become powerful in the battle that must be fought and must be won in America today.

Part One

Our National Crisis, and Liberal America's Role in It

Preface to Part One

What America's Shameful 2014 Elections Make Indisputably Clear

All the main parts of the American political world are showing serious pathology. Because the cure of this pathology will have to start in Liberal America, sparking that change is the purpose of this book.

The 2014 congressional elections in the United States should remove all doubt that a serious pathology afflicts virtually every component of the American body politic. These shameful elections also make clear an urgent need for fundamental change in America's political dynamics. Sparking that change is the goal of this book.

First, the pathology. Consider these three facts:

- In the 2013-14 Congress, Republicans violated fundamental norms of American democracy, deliberately keeping government from addressing the nation's pressing problems, showing an utter lack of concern for serving the public good.
- After this travesty went on in plain sight for nearly two years, the American electorate rewarded the Republicans by handing them even more power.
- Democrats coasted into electoral disaster without even trying to focus attention on the Republicans' unprecedented abuse of the system our Founders gave us.

Plenty of shame to go around.

Republicans' conduct in Congress was disgraceful, of course. They deliberately disabled our government: making this past Congress the least productive in history; passing bills that they knew had zero chance of being enacted; focusing on provocative but useless gestures such as voting more than 50 times to repeal the health care law; refusing to bring to the House floor an immigration bill that had passed the Senate by a more than 2 to 1 margin; never proposing serious solutions of their own.

And they did all this out in the open, for all to see. It could hardly have been clearer that these Republicans were even worse than indifferent to the good of the nation, as they had calculated that making government fail was their best ticket to partisan success.

Shame on the American electorate for proving them right. That the people would hand still more power to a party that had chosen to betray the nation should ring alarm bells in every caring American.

But responsibility for this shameful spectacle rests not on the voters alone. The voters apparently needed help to see how seriously the conduct of the Republicans had violated this nation's basic democratic values. Who ought to have supplied that help?

The press? For well over a decade, our press has ignored one of the major stories of American history—the rise to power of a force more consistently destructive and dishonest than anything seen before at center stage of American politics (except perhaps for the decade leading up to the Civil War).

But what about the Democrats, whose political interests, and even survival, depended on the electorate's seeing how the other party had betrayed the nation? If Democrats wouldn't bring that issue forward, who would? And if not in a national election campaign, then when?

Since the election, President Obama has become feisty about using the power of his office to get something accomplished despite the Republicans' do-nothing obstructionism. That's good. But why didn't he get feisty *before* the election—when the people were still deciding to whom to give power—and show the electorate how the Republican Party was trampling on the traditions of our democracy and harming America?

This should have been the central issue of the 2014 campaign. What could be more pertinent to a congressional election than how to get a Congress that will do the people's business?

But from the Democrats on this issue, including the president, hardly a peep. That left the American electorate hating Congress for failing them but nonetheless inclined to hand still more power to the party that deliberately made Congress the dysfunctional mess they hate.

And whatever is wrong with the Democratic Party is amiss also with the larger culture of Liberal America to which the Democrats give political expression. During the campaign, the liberal grassroots never rose up, in any effective way, to demand that their candidates call out the blatant Republican trashing of our democratic ideals. Nor has that failure figured prominently in liberal post-election analyses.

Although a sickness evidently pervades the entire American body politic, initial focus should be on the pathology on the liberal side. It is only from that side that the impetus for rescuing America can come. The Republican Party—embedded in the rigid political culture that the right has created over the past generation—is not going to change until it is compelled to from outside.

We should be asking: What must change for Democrats to be able to provide that impetus? What is the reason for the weakness or blindness of the Democrats (and Liberal America generally) that was demonstrated so dramatically by the 2014 election? And what can be done about it?

It is the purpose of this book to provide answers to those questions—answers that can help begin a process that remedies the dangerous pathology that has taken hold of the power system in America.

Chapter One

You Can't Hit What You Can't See: The Role of Liberal America in Our National Crisis

Approaching Our National Crisis from Two Directions

Two very troubling things are true: America's political world has been seriously degraded over the past generation, and too much of America fails to notice the disturbing picture right in front of our eyes.

For well over a decade now, America has been mired in a dangerous crisis. Here's one way of glimpsing this crisis.

In our era, there has been a dangerous shift in the power of various elements in the American system. Over the past decade-plus, in terms of the forces determining the course of our nation:

- The power of greed has increased.
- The power of the lie has increased.
- The power of blind rage has increased.
- The power of the spirit of conflict has increased.
- The power of the lust to dominate has increased.

(I've been chronicling these developments for a decade now, and could abundantly document them here. See the more than 3000 postings from the past decade on www.NoneSoBlind.org. But I am addressing here those readers for whom all these assertions ring true, who do not need them to be substantiated before we can proceed.)

These adverse shifts have already inflicted significant damage on the United States as a civilization, and especially as a polity:

- Our public discourse—our capacity as a nation and a people to discuss issues constructively—has degenerated.
- Plutocracy—the rule of the billionaires and of the mighty corporate system—has gained ground.
- Our ability to use the instruments of government, bequeathed us by our Founders, to navigate our way wisely and constructively through the challenges we face has declined precipitously. (And these unmet challenges includes the potentially catastrophic threat of climate disruption.)

These forms of degradation have called into serious question our ability, as a nation, to maintain a democracy based on those basic values that inspired our founders.

A Rip Van Winkle who woke up now after, say, a quarter-century slumber would be incredulous to witness what happens almost daily now in the American political arena. Of all the possible scenarios one might have envisioned a generation ago, the one that has actually unfolded would be far down toward the bottom end, where worst-case possibilities dwell.

This is far from American politics as usual. Much that we have seen has been unprecedented in our national history.

- Unprecedented that we have seen a program of torture, coming from the very White House.
- Unprecedented that we have seen a major American party turn its back on science—and more generally on the norms of responsible ways of knowing—in the face of the most serious alarms being raised by an entire scientific field, from all over the world.

- Unprecedented that even as the American and global economies were on the edge of an abyss, that same major American political party decided that its top priority would be to make a new president fail—even though the failure of the president would inevitably mean the failure of the nation, and suffering for tens of millions of Americans.

The list of shocking developments of the "who would have believed?" variety could easily be expanded.

(For an expansion of the idea that the conduct in recent times of this major American political party—the Republicans—has been unprecedented, see* "The Unprecedented in Our Times.")

[NOTE: Asterisks here will refer to a collection, called "More Depth," of articles expanding on the ideas presented in this book. These additional pieces are posted at the website at www.whatweareupagainst.org]

So much of what we have lately seen is so extraordinary—and so destructive—that hardly any American would have seen it coming. But while it's regrettable not to have seen it coming, it is downright calamitous that even now all too few Americans yet recognize the "it" that has come.

And that blindness, too, is part of the problem. This crisis is the product not only of the destructive force that has gained power and that is systematically inflicting great damage on the nation, but also of the failure of the rest of the American body politic to comprehend the gravity of the threat and to respond accordingly.

This two-sidedness of our national crisis—the destructive force and the blindness to it—leads here to the two-part nature of this book: in part, this book sounds a call to action, a call to battle against this destructive force; but in part also, this book provides a picture of how destructive (and constructive) forces arise and operate in civilized societies, and how some kinds of "blindness" can provide a force of destruction an opening to gain power.

The hope behind this book is that an understanding of the deep forces at work in our civilization will fortify our ability to take action to turn back the force that is degrading the prospects for our children and grandchildren.

The Two-Sided, Asymmetrical Dynamic at the Heart of America's Crisis

America's crisis grows out of this combination: the right has become almost purely destructive, while the liberal side has become woefully weak.

For years, unusually high percentages of Americans have told pollsters that they feel the nation is "heading" in the wrong direction. These big majorities have certainly been correct in their concern, but one can draw only limited comfort from this widespread recognition that *something* has gone awry.

Many of those people, one may assume, are people whose sense of the "wrongness" of the nation's direction focuses on such falsehoods as the supposed threat of "sharia law" being imposed on the nation, or the danger that our nation is speedily heading down the road to socialism, or the travesty of a man illegitimately occupying the presidency because of his having been born in Kenya, or the issue of climate change being engineered through a scientific hoax as a way to assault American capitalism, or that a war is being waged against Christmas, etc. etc.

Those people's concerns—all based on falsehood—will do nothing to move us toward the "right direction." Indeed, these concerns are an important manifestation of the force that's driving America in the wrong direction. And those people are not the intended audience for this book.

The people who align themselves with the right, and who act politically on the basis of a false picture of the world being peddled by the force that's taken over the once-conservative Republican Party, are important. Many of them are good people. And America will never be truly healthy until a goodly number of those good people are giving their support to a force that better represents their better angels.

But the necessary transformations will not begin with them, ensconced as they are in a rigid right-wing system so well organized to prevent challenges from within. The impetus for the necessary change on the right will have to come from outside that right-wing system.

But that points to another profound problem in the American body politic. The grotesque developments on the right are imperiling this nation only because they have arisen in combination with a serious defect on the left side of America's political divide. In this era, what I am calling here "Liberal America" has seriously failed the nation.

The rescuing of America, I will argue, must begin on the liberal side of our broken polity. Making the necessary transformations in Liberal America can provide the impetus to turn around the whole destructive dynamic that is now degrading the nation.

It is, therefore, to my fellow liberals (or progressives, as some prefer) that I am speaking in this work.

Which brings us to the first iteration of the two-sided dynamic at the heart of America's present profound national crisis:

- The political right—and its political arm, the Republican Party—has become an extraordinarily destructive force in the American body politic.
- Meanwhile, the political left, taken as a whole—and its political arm, the Democratic Party—has shown extraordinary weakness in the face of the threat posed to the nation by that destructive force.

[NOTE: This is not in any way to deny the passion and hard work of many activists on the liberal side. But if we focus on the *overall* conduct of the Democratic Party, and of Liberal America generally, in response to the extraordinarily destructiveness of today's right, what we find has been an almost incomprehensible failure to rise to meet the threat.]

The big question, "What has gone wrong in America, and how can it be set right?" directs us to ask two important subsidiary questions:

- How are we to understand the rise of this destructiveness on the right? And what will it take to drain away from this force the power to destroy what's best in America?
- What are the sources of the weakness displayed in our times by Liberal America, and what can change the liberal part of the American body politic into a force capable of fighting and defeating the ugly thing that has taken over the right?

The raison d'être for this book is that I have answers to those questions. And I've been aflame with those answers for more than a decade.

A Crisis of Asymmetry

Although both sides play a role in this crisis, the usual "both sides do it" way of seeing that is fundamentally mistaken. The "polarization" we see is not of two sides similarly "extreme" on the issues but as opposites with respect to some basic human qualities of the spirit—for example, one side's insistence on fighting and the other side's unwillingness to fight.

It is the right that has become grotesque, as if possessed by a daemonic force of the kind that surfaces in history's most nightmarish episodes. But both sides of our divide are failing the nation.

There are helpful but also some profoundly unhelpful ways of seeing how both sides (and indeed the entire American cultural system) are implicated in our present crisis.

It is, for example, a complete misunderstanding of our present political dysfunction to see it in terms of the symmetry of "both sides do it."

What we have is not a pathology of symmetry but one of asymmetry.

Have you heard the one about how we've got a problem of "polarization," with the "extreme right" and the "extreme left" creating our political dysfunction?

Yes, it is true that our politics manifest the brokenness of "polarization," but it is not at the level of the issues. That is, the problem is not that one side has staked out an extreme position in one direction and the other has taken an equally extreme position in the other direction. In today's political dynamic, the right has shown that it will not take "yes" for an answer, attacking even proposals that not so long before had been their own.

There is nothing remotely extreme—either in the context of generations of mainstream American policy or in the context of the decisions made by other advanced societies—in the agenda of today's Democrats. (And I would also argue that it is off target to characterize what's driving the right in terms of its "extremism" on the issues.)

(On this topic, see the opinion piece* "The Myth of the Two 'Extremes'" I published in the *Washington Post* when I was a candidate for Congress.)

The kind of "polarization" that afflicts the American power system is at a deeper level than the issues. It is with respect to some basic human qualities of the spirit that the two sides have divided, with one side being "all" and the other "none." The result is that the two sides show imbalance of opposite sorts, and the two sides together lack fundamental areas of overlap.

We have, for example, one party (the Republicans) that has insisted on making a fight over *everything*, even when the good of the nation desperately needed for the two sides to work together for the public good. And meanwhile, the other party (the Democrats) has been reluctant to fight over much of *anything*, even when the protection of the nation required it to stand and fight. (Fortunately, there are signs this is becoming gradually less true.)

It is polarization at that level—not at some parallel level of "extremism," or "unwillingness to compromise," or indifference to the general good—that has allowed a force of brokenness to attack the foundations of American civilization with a wrecking ball.

> [NOTE: I am *not* maintaining, it should be noted, that there is anything grand about today's Democratic Party. The rise to prominence of unusually "bad guys," does not, unfortunately, imply the rise on the other side of especially "good guys." What I would say about the Democratic Party is that—other than in its blindness and weakness in dealing with what has arisen on the right—it is a *normal* major American political party. It is the usual mixture of constructive and self-serving that, over the course of American history, has sufficed for a record of national progress that constitutes one of civilization's more positive stories.]

If the "both sides do it" fallacy comes from the precinct of those mild liberals eager to demonstrate their "fairness" and to be "nice" to the other side, there's another kind of error of "symmetry" one hears from the more disaffected further to the left. This is the "not a dime's worth of difference" school of thought. According to this view, the two sides are both so fully corrupt, it makes no sense to differentiate them. Both are feeding out of the same plutocratic troughs, it is said, and some even go so far as to say that the apparent conflicts between the major parties are staged—like some professional wrestling bout—and the two sides are actually in cahoots.

Without going into any depth here in refuting this view, I will just note that while it is true that some of the problems involved in our crisis—

such as the role of big money—are not confined to one side, the situation is not identical on both sides. Where the political battles occur, without exception it is the Republicans who are pushing things in the direction of the interests of the mightiest and the richest, and the Democrats who are pushing toward the interests of the average citizen.

And as for the idea of "staged" battles, to believe that is to believe not only that the actors in our political arena are engaged in a kind of deception that, to my knowledge, would be unprecedented in a liberal democracy, but also that the Democrats have been willing participants in a drama that regularly makes them look weak and ineffectual and results in their being stripped of their power and thrown out of office.

The bleeding across the divide of some of our corruptive tendencies is real, but it is a distraction from the real drama of our times.

So also is a third fallacy I've encountered frequently over the past decade: the idea that all the ills we see now in our power system have been around throughout the history of the nation, or at least for generations.

At some level, that is true. But just as we need to look at the asymmetry rather than the symmetry to understand what's important in this crisis, so also do we need to look at the discontinuities rather than the continuities.

While it is true that we can find the elements of plutocracy, racism, militarism, propaganda, divisiveness, etc. marbled throughout our history, what's important for us to understand now is how something new has coalesced in the American power system that has dangerously shifted the balance of power between constructive and destructive elements.

Many things are true of our moment in history. I do not claim that this "two-sided dynamic" captures everything worth our knowing. My claim, rather, is that this dynamic points us to the heart of this crisis, one of the most dangerous in our nation's history.

Even if our political system were as healthy as it has ever been, we—as Americans, and as part of humankind on this planet—would be facing enormous challenges, with the brightness or dimness of our future in doubt.

But with this dynamic working to give the worst elements in our national system the power to determine our nation's destiny, the most urgent task facing us is to address this particular part of the large, elaborately complex picture of the myriad forces at work in our civilization.

[NOTE: When I speak of the nightmares toward which we may be heading, I do not mean to say that the worst-case scenario is the most probable outcome. What I would claim, rather, is that the likelihood of such disastrous outcomes is large enough that prudence and responsibility require us to exert ourselves with all our strength to prevent them.]

The Extraordinary Pattern of Destructiveness in Today's Republican Party

Today's Republican Party has exhibited diverse patterns of destructive conduct. These raise the question: What is it that expresses itself in all these ways?

It's time, as a necessary step in seeing more clearly *what we are up against*, to put some flesh on the assertion that an extraordinarily destructive force has taken over the right.

We tend to see the world in bits and pieces. But, by virtue of the amazingly dense web of causes and effects, our world is one in which—to exaggerate only slightly—everything is connected to everything else. It has been my life's work to "see things whole," i.e. to attempt to discern the patterns in the complex world in which we live. And since my early twenties (which is some forty-five years ago), I have been particularly interested in those patterns that reveal the forces that we—as Americans and as humankind—need to contain if we are to have a better world.

Here are some of the patterns that emerge from a decade-long study of the force that has taken over the once-respectable Republican Party.

In the conduct of the Republican Party, for more than a decade, the picture that emerges is of:

A force that's insatiable in its lust for power and wealth.

Even though we have the greatest income inequality that we've had in living memory, this force works continually to widen that gap still further. All their budgetary proposals take from average Americans to give more to those who already have the most. As they have protected those who have tripled their share of our national income, they have cut food stamps to the most vulnerable Americans at a time when jobs are scarce and even the middle class is struggling.

In the realm of political power, this force has given us a Supreme Court that's handed down that disgraceful decision in *Citizens United*, making it still easier for the nation's widening inequalities of wealth to be translated into inequalities of political power. With our government up for auction, "All men are created equal" gets swamped by the Almighty Dollar. The Republicans have been working to turn our government from one "by the people" into one dominated by those giant so-called "persons" that make up the corporate world.

A force that makes a fight over everything.

When Barack Obama came to the presidency with the intent to restore cooperation to our political system, he reached out by proposing Republican ideas as solutions to important national problems. But the Republicans have turned politics into a form of warfare, so insistent upon conflict that they have fought even against their own ideas.

What Republicans had once proposed as cap and trade, they denounced as socialism. The idea of an individual mandate for health insurance—an idea originally put forward by Republicans in the Senate—they declared to be unconstitutional. And once it was picked up by the Democrats, a sensible idea Republicans had originally conceived and embraced became mischaracterized as "death panels."

A force that is consistently dishonest.

It lied us into the Iraq war. It lied about torture. It lied about where the Democratic president was born. Lied about their (lack of interest) in getting Americans back to work in the deepest recession since the Great Depression. Lied about their caring about the deficit. About Benghazi. About the IRS "scandal." A list that could go on for pages.

These are not a random set of patterns. Historically, there is a name that we in Western civilization have traditionally given to something that:

- Preys upon the vulnerable.

  Think food stamps, voter ID, torture, voter suppression.

- Divides people against each other.

  In the deepest recession in generations, this force proved unwilling to address the issue of jobs, on which Americans were agreed, and focused us instead on abortion on which, as the Republicans well know, our divisions have proved deep and irreconcilable.

- Tramples on hard-won structures of justice and good order.

  After giving us a president who usurped powers denied by the Constitution, this force then manifested itself in an opposition party that violated tradition in its use of the filibuster to grab power, that cast aside long-standing political norms on how the debt-ceiling is handled, that subverted the foundations of our democracy by delegitimizing the president and disenfranchising voters.

- Sacrifices the greater good for selfish advantage (well beyond the usual, flawed norm of democratic politics).

  As the disruption of the climate becomes ever more visibly a threat to the future of our children and even of the health of life on earth, has chosen greed over integrity. Rather than heed the warnings of 97 percent of scientists who know the most about the earth's climate system, this force has embraced the spirit of the Koch Brothers, disabling our nation from dealing responsibly with what may be the most urgent challenge humankind has ever faced.

- Deceives and manipulates in order to exploit those that support it.

  It persuades millions of Americans to be one-issue voters—on abortion, or on the gun issue—distracting them with matters that in no way impede the ability of this force to rob Americans of their birthright as citizens in a democratic society. It pretends to be conservative, while violating our traditions as no conservative would. It pretends to be patriotic while willingly damaging the nation for partisan advantage.

It is necessary to put the pieces together and see the phenomenon whole.

Each of these categories of action represents a pattern: in each case, dozens or even hundreds of facts could be adduced to reveal what in the law is called a consistent pattern of conduct.

But then there is the important next step: to see the pattern that is formed by this set of patterns. What do all these reprehensible tendencies have in common?

Even more important, for getting to the heart of the challenge we Americans face, there is the question: **What is it that expresses itself in all these ways?**

To which might be added the question: **Why is this question not at the center of our national discourse, or even, really, asked at all?**

America's Compromised Immune System

America's founders built into our system of government the means to protect our nation from such a force as this. But in today's America, that "immune system" has failed to recognize what an extraordinarily—and in many ways unprecedentedly— destructive force has arisen in our power system.

In the body, our immune system recognizes what is foreign and then works to disable it from doing us harm.

In a healthy democratic polity, the same applies. That so much of the conduct of the Republican Party has been unprecedented suggests that something foreign to the body politic has arisen—either something alien, or something breaking out of its customary bounds. That should trigger an alarm that mobilizes elements from the rest of the system to protect the integrity and health of the whole.

The Founders of our American system attempted to set up an "immune system" that would work to defend the integrity of the nation from an attack by a "foreign" element of this sort. The framers of our Constitution were well aware that a corrupting and destructive power could arise to subvert the governmental structure of liberty and self-government that they'd established. So they set up a system with the means to mobilize the rest of the body politic to contain and remove a destructive threat of that kind (including measures like impeachment among the "checks and balances," an independent judiciary, and a free press).

But instead, much of America has dealt with the extraordinary as if it were normal.

When, in 2012, two prominent and essentially centrist political analysts—Norman Ornstein of the American Enterprise Institute and Thomas Mann of the Brookings Institution—wrote about the Republican Party as an "outlier" in American politics, it was regarded by many as a kind of breakthrough. Ornstein and Mann presented their idea in a book, *It's Worse than You Think*, and more briefly in a *Washington Post* column, where this passage appears:

> "We have been studying Washington politics and Congress for more than 40 years, and never have we seen them this dysfunctional. In our past writings, we have criticized both parties when we believed it was warranted. Today, however, we have no choice but to acknowledge that the core of the problem lies with the Republican Party.
>
> "The GOP has become an insurgent outlier in American politics. It is ideologically extreme; scornful of compromise; unmoved by conventional understanding of facts, evidence and science; and dismissive of the legitimacy of its political opposition."

It was—in political terms—an important statement, but it is also disturbing that it needed to be said at all, let alone that it would be big news that they said it. Disturbing also that our national discourse has nonetheless continued to grant this Republican Party the status of acceptability, even respectability, as if it were a normal political party, when it has clearly become something quite abnormal.

But even so, the word "outlier" hardly does justice to the unprecedented and monstrous nature of what the Republican Party has become. It's actually a good deal worse than the authors of *It's Worse than You Think* think.

But the intellectual proclivities in Liberal America apparently prevent people from seeing clearly the nature of what we are up against: something far more dangerous and dark than "outlier" begins to suggest.

Many don't see this force because they take in the picture only piece by piece, day by day, issue by issue, news item by news item. If there were something coherent and systemic operating—some "It" that lies behind the many manifestations—it would not become visible through this casual piecemeal picture.

Others, reaching for some organizing generalization, see the problem on the right in terms of how "far right" the Republican Party has moved, how it has become more "extreme," and dominated by "ultra-conservatives." But this misses the mark as well: there is nothing truly conservative about today's Republican Party, and the real nature of the battle is not really at the level of right-vs.-left.

If "Mr. Conservative" of an earlier era were alive today—Senator Barry Goldwater, whose most famous quotation was a kind of defense of "extremism"—he would feel little kinship with this party: he was a man of integrity, while this party has none.

At a greater level of integration, many thoughtful members of Liberal America hold to the idea that what this crisis is about is "plutocracy," or "money in politics," or "corporate takeover" of our government.

Surely, this points to an important dimension of the problem. But there's a good deal more to the picture than this diagnosis can cover.

This force has also given us torture, and a level of dishonesty extraordinary even by the usual standards of politics. This force consistently chooses conflict over cooperation, and exhibits an unprecedented indifference to the public good.

America had an age of plutocracy before—in the late 19th century—and for all its faults and injustices, it was not so pervasively destructive as what now animates the Republican Party.

(See Chapter 2 for discussion of what an unusually "pure case" today's Republican Party presents, and what an unusual opportunity that provides for understanding how destructive forces operate in civilized societies.)

Something bigger and deeper is involved. It is of vital importance that we see that "something," even if that requires a non-trivial expansion of our worldview.

It is said in baseball that "you can't hit what you can't see." As we have here something that has itself been relentlessly on the attack, hitting at almost everything within reach, it is essential for our future that we become able to hit back effectively. And to do that, we must be able to see what we are up against.

A Time to Build Bridges, and a Time to Wage Battle

My long history as one who builds bridges to the other side shows that my present call to battle is not dictated by habitual bellicosity. Different kinds of challenges require us to have in our toolbox different tools for different situations.

A recent experience at a local Virginia radio station—on which I've discussed politics and other matters for more than 20 years—raised the question of where I'm coming from in painting such a negative picture of today's Republican Party.

One of the station's staff members, a Republican, came into the studio after a program in which I had denounced the fraud of the "voter fraud" issue: Republican governments in states around the nation have enacted "Voter ID" laws whose ostensible purpose is to prevent certain kinds of voter fraud; but every study shows such kinds of fraud to be so rare as to be almost non-existent. It could hardly be clearer that the real purpose is to effectively disenfranchise certain categories of voters that tend to vote against Republicans.

This fellow at the station challenged me: would I object if it was Democrats and not Republicans enacting and benefitting from these ID laws? I replied along the lines of the old song, "If you don't know me by now"—in other words, I 'd have thought he'd know, after all these years, that my basic commitment is to the principles and values I believe in, and that partisanship does not govern my positions.

He replied that I am "the most partisan person" he knows, and to prove his characterization of me he cited my repeatedly strong criticisms, in recent years, of the Republican Party.

How I responded at that point I think worth sharing with the more liberal audience I hope to reach with this book. My engaging in "partisan" politics in recent times (as the Democratic nominee for Congress from my overwhelmingly Republican rural district in Virginia) was an episode of but a couple years duration, I said. But what has endured for nearly half a century—and indeed what led to my unexpected jump into politics—is my work to understand and combat the destructive forces operating in civilized societies. It was in that role, I insisted, that I've been raising the alarm about what today's Republican Party has become.

(Not only was he not swayed by this rejoinder, but he gave no evidence of its even having registered as an idea. I imagine it served his needs better to dismiss me as a partisan than to confront even the possibility that honest intellectual inquiry might undercut his political assumptions. But I also imagined it possible that his mental map includes no place for someone whose calling and dedication are what I claimed mine to be.)

But I expect that it is not just committed Republicans who will feel uneasy about my harsh characterization of today's Republican Party. (And I say this from my decades of experience of communicating with mostly liberal audiences about issues like these.) Many liberals, upon encountering such a portrait as I just painted above, might wonder if I'm someone who, as a matter of character, gravitates toward conflict—someone inclined to demonize opponents and contribute to political polarization.

My history shows that's not who I am. In "My History as Man of Peace,"* I offer a brief account of how, during the 1980s and 1990s, I consistently sought to build bridges, find common ground, and seek a higher wisdom that combines the half-truths held on both sides of our political and moral divides.

But something has changed since then, and it is not I.

In a world where we confront many different kinds of challenges, we need more than one tool in our toolbox, more than one way of dealing with our world. There is a time for bridge-building, and there is a time for waging battle.

Wisdom lies not in consistency of approach no matter what, but in the judgment to know when to make peace and when to press the battle.

That which has now arisen on the right has only grown stronger—and thus able to wreak more destruction—from the misguided liberal insistence on being "even-handed" in a situation whose essence is asymmetry, and on maintaining a "peace" when there is no peace and no peace is possible until the force that is attacking so relentlessly is defeated.

Liberalism has injured the nation by too often emulating the spirit of Neville Chamberlain when we are up against something that should be confronted in the spirit of Winston Churchill.

Which brings us to the last piece of my assurance that I am not writing here as a partisan: this analysis of our crisis is a critique not only of the "other" in some "Us-vs.-Them" dynamic, but also of the "Us."

The pathology that jeopardizes the integrity of the United States as a civilized society is not located only on the right, but indeed pervades the entire body politic. (Indeed, as will be discussed in Chapter Eight, even though this crisis is manifest in the political realm, the real roots of this crisis are inseparable from the state of the American culture as a whole.)

Not Our Finest Hour: Why Is Liberal America Falling So Far Short?

Americans regard as heroes those who, in previous battles, have seen the evil, called it out, and pressed the battle. Why is it that, in the present battle, Liberal America has failed to do likewise?

I said earlier that it is not the ugliness on the right but the failings of Liberal America that I am most eager to engage here. It is to set the stage for that engagement that I've presented the portrait of the destructive force on the right. Time now to look more closely at how Liberal America has failed in the face of this crisis to live up to American ideals.

America has previously confronted battles in some ways akin to the battle in our times. How those Americans, whom we regard as heroes, responded in those earlier battles defined our ideals as a nation.

Compare how Liberal America is dealing with this destructive force with what Americans, through their greatest leaders, have done in their finest hours: the nation's founding; the Civil War; and the World War against fascism.

In all three crises, the leaders we regard as heroes 1) understood the evil they were up against, 2) called it out, and 3) fought for values they held sacred.

The Declaration of Independence spends most of its words decrying King George III's "repeated injuries and usurpations" which they saw as working toward "the establishment of an absolute Tyranny over these States." The document ended by declaring such a tyrant "unfit to be the ruler of a free people." A just government, our Founders declared, requires "the consent of the governed." They argued this on the basis of the "self-evident" truth "that all men are created equal, [and] that they are endowed by their Creator with certain unalienable Rights…."

The signatories to that document understood that declaring these rights would require them to fight, which is why they conclude the document by mutually pledging "to each other our Lives, our Fortunes and our sacred Honor."

We see the same willingness to fight for sacred values in *Abraham Lincoln*. Lincoln rose to the presidency on his opposition to slavery. He framed that opposition in terms of the same values on which our

Founders had declared independence: that "all men are created equal," and that "no man is good enough to govern another man, without that other's consent."

Lincoln saw the conflict over slavery in fundamentally moral terms: "Slavery is founded in the selfishness of man's nature—opposition to it, in his love of justice. These principles are an eternal antagonism." "If slavery is not wrong," Lincoln said, "nothing is wrong."

Lincoln did not want war. But to keep slavery from expanding—and to preserve the Union—he was ready, if necessary, to fight.

If Abraham Lincoln is ranked by historians as our greatest president, *Franklin Delano Roosevelt* is ranked second. FDR presided over two great national crises: the Great Depression and World War II. Running for a second term, FDR called out "the forces of selfishness and of lust for power." In his State of the Union speech after America's entry into the Second World War, FDR characterized the conflict in terms that Lincoln and the Founders would have recognized: "We are fighting, as our fathers have fought, to uphold the doctrine that all men are equal in the sight of God." The other side, he said, is fighting to destroy "this deep belief and create a world... of tyranny and cruelty and serfdom."

President Roosevelt shrank from neither battle: "I welcome their hatred" he said of anti-democratic forces at home. And against the forces of cruel fascism abroad, he brought the power of the United States to bear as quickly as public opinion and events would allow.

See the evil. Call it out. Press the battle. That's what America's heroes have done.

But that approach has been missing, or woefully weak, with President Obama [See "Calling Out the Republicans: Obama Hasn't So We Must" in the "More Depth" collection] and in Liberal America more generally, even though the same basic values are at stake today as in those earlier crises.

The formal apparatus for "the consent of the governed" remains. But never in U.S. history have so many been so deceived about the true nature of the political force they are supporting. Government based on misinformed consent can hardly be just.

The idea of equality remains, but the Republican Party has labored—the *Citizens United* decision being their most obvious success—to widen inequality of power in our supposedly democratic process. In countless ways, the political force that has arisen on the right has moved this nation toward tyranny and cruelty and serfdom.

Why has Liberal America in these times shown so little of the spirit of America's heroic forebears?

The Force Is Not With Us: We Identify with Our Fantasy Heroes. Why Don't We Emulate Them?

Why do we fight evil forces in our vicarious fantasies but not in the real world? Maybe it's because, while we willingly suspend disbelief in our fantasy lives, much of Liberal America doesn't believe there's any such thing as an "evil force" in reality.

We can get a clue to the answer to that question by examining the contrast between what we happily enact vicariously in our fantasy lives and what—though facing essentially the same situation as our fantasy heroes—we fail to do in our contemporary American reality.

Again and again, our popular stories and mythology take us vicariously and gratifyingly through the process of confronting a destructive force. Consider three of the most salient cultural narratives of our time: the films *Avatar, Star Wars,* and *Lord of the Rings.*

When we watch these films, our identification with our heroes puts us through our paces—evoking the pain and outrage of seeing injustice done and sacred things destroyed, and instilling in our hearts the will to fight the necessary battle to prevail over evil and set things right.

So we all *know* how to respond to a force like the one that faces us now in America. We know, because we make heroes of Sully in *Avatar,* of Luke in *Star Wars,* and of Frodo in *The Lord of the Rings.* What they do is what we know that someone in that situation *should* do.

- The film *Avatar,* for example, seen by many millions of us, shows us a rapacious and brutal force. It is a kind of military/industrial complex, ruthless in its willingness to violate the sacred web of life in order to enrich itself. We follow our protagonist, Sully, in switching our allegiance to an entirely different culture of human-like creatures imbued with reverence for the living world that sustains them.

We participate in their pain and rage at the despoliation of that world. At the film's inevitable climax, we identify passionately with the determination of our hero and his companions to fight and win the battle between these two approaches to life. It's a battle we understand as one of good against evil, fought to protect what is sacred from still further plunder.

- The *Star Wars* films have permeated American culture. From the beginning of the series, we were presented with a stark contrast between our underdog individualistic heroes, immersed in the stuff of life, and the dominating, life-denying Empire ruled from the "Death Star." We feel outrage when the Death Star brutally murders an entire living planet, causing (as the wise Obe Wan Kenobi discerns) "a disturbance in the Force." In *Star Wars*, as in *Avatar*, we eagerly follow the movement toward that inevitable climax, the all-out battle between the forces of good and evil. And we are thrilled when Luke - trusting "the Force" - threads his bomb into the core of the Death Star, using the explosive force of the Death Star's own power source to destroy it.
- In *The Lord of the Rings* saga, the simple courage and integrity of Frodo Baggins helps save the world from another representation of the force of evil. We are gratified as our stalwart heroes prevail in the climactic battle against Sauron and the forces of Mordor, forces for which there is no value beyond the power for which they lust. And it is with relief and deep satisfaction that - once the battle has been won, and with the cauldrons of war-making and dominance no longer threatening to burn up our world—we return to the realm of the Hobbits, a world green with life and well-ordered by the web of decent human relationships.

In those imagined worlds, we are capable of perceiving the evil force before our eyes, and responding emotionally with the requisite outrage at the despoliation of the sacred and with determination to protect it by fighting and winning the necessary battle.

But in the real world, in our times, we in Liberal America have acted not at all like our heroes, even though **we are in the same basic position as they: facing an evil force that threatens our most sacred values.**

- In the imagined world of *Avatar*, the destruction is wrought in the quest for the mineral "unobtanium," which nicely captures an essential truth about the spirit that has captured today's Republican Party: it is a spirit for which any sense of "enough" is simply unobtainable when it comes to amassing wealth. Nowhere is this more dramatically demonstrated than with the urgent issue of climate change, where the Republican Party has made it party dogma to deny what 97 percent of climate scientists say is a serious, potentially catastrophic threat that must be addressed, and has consistently blocked our nation's ability to respond to the challenge. Like the brutal and greedy system in *Avatar*—a system willing to destroy the living system of that planet for its own greater enrichment—the Republican Party willingly collaborates with the world's richest corporations, seeking to protect their short-term profits even at the cost of undermining the integrity of the earth's biosphere on which we, our children, and our grandchildren depend for our survival.

  An evil force is right before our eyes. But Liberal America has failed to rise up powerfully, like Sully, to lead the battle to protect sacred values.

- Like the Empire in the *Star Wars* films, today's Republican Party manifests an ugly (and often sadistic) lust for power. It gave us a presidency that launched a war of choice to extend the hegemony of "the world's one remaining superpower (and that brought the shame of torture to the highest levels of American government). Even though it was already legally wielding the greatest power on earth, that presidency arrogated still more powers to itself, with unprecedented usurpations of powers contrary to the Constitution, threatening the traditional American systems of checks and balances. Then, when cast from power, this Party gave us an opposition that, in an unprecedented strategy for regaining power for itself, made its top priority to make the president from the other party fail. This, despite the nation's being beset by several national crises, including the economy teetering on the edge of an abyss, and despite the inescapable reality that if the president failed the nation too would fail, and tens of millions of Americans would suffer.

The spirit of the Death Star is visible before us. But Liberal America has not acted like Luke.

- As with the depiction of the forces of evil in *The Lord of the Rings*, likewise in America in our times we can see operating a force that seduces and corrupts ordinary people. We can see a kind of "ring" operating through our political and economic systems, bringing out the worst in those under its sway. With their ambitions inflamed, people decent in their private lives act to further indecent policies. As in *The Lord of the Rings*, an insidious force tricks a great many of our fellow citizens into thinking they are serving the good while unwittingly they are serving the opposite. In this way, abetting a force inimical to their own real interests and deepest values, they help turn the democratic political process into a form of warfare and national policy into an instrument of injustice.

  To combat this insidious, deceptive force, how many in Liberal America have been willing, like Frodo, to leave our comfortable Hobbit-like niches and rise to the urgent challenge of our dangerous moment?

Yes, we are in basically the same situation as our heroes, but our side in this battle is not imitating their heroic defense of the good we love in our world. Indeed, the battle has been nearly one-sided.

Which returns us to the question of why the weakness. But this time, with a clue:

While the answer has many parts, a central part of it lies in the realm of beliefs—i.e. in the worldview of liberal/intellectual America.

In the fantasy worlds of the movies, we willingly suspend our disbelief in such ancient notions as "the battle between good and evil."

But when we look at the real world around us, our belief system tells us there is no such thing as an "evil force." That's a primitive notion, our sophisticated rational worldview tells us.

The old dictum from the baseball world was cited earlier: You can't hit what you can't see. To which I would now add: **you can't see what you don't believe can exist.**

Beliefs that Make Liberal America Weak: Barriers to the Source of Moral and Spiritual Passions

When people believe "value" is less than real and that the notion of "spiritual forces" is an antiquated fantasy, how could they bring passionate intensity to a battle that is fundamentally moral and spiritual? But it can be shown—in secular terms, applying reason to the evidence—that those beliefs are false.

The issue in America today is this: will constructive or destructive, life-serving or life-degrading forces prevail in shaping this nation's future? Or, to put the question in the terms of olden times, which side will prevail in America in the "battle between good and evil."

One cannot say that the battle to decide this question has been going well. And at one level it is not hard to see why: the side of the destructive force is relentlessly pressing the battle while those who must oppose that force shrink from the battle.

Why this mismatch between the people on the right, inflamed with an insistence on pressing the battle—an insistence that manifests itself, for example, in the Republicans voting to repeal Obamacare more than 50 times in the House of Representatives—while their counterparts in Liberal America show little appetite for the battle?

Let me begin an answer to that question by noting that, while this battle in America today is being fought in the political arena, the heart of it goes deeper than politics. It is at the moral and spiritual level.

And in a battle of this sort, the intensity of the combatants depends on their access to that place in the core of our humanity from which come our moral and spiritual passions. There is where the dangerous imbalance arises: the drama of our times is all too well captured by the line from Yeats: "the best lack all conviction, while the worst / Are filled with a passionate intensity."

The force that has taken over the right has acted as if it recognized fully that power in our democracy can be gained through the "passionate intensity" of people who believe themselves to be engaged in the battle of good against evil. This force has worked assiduously to set aflame millions of people on the right with the determination to defend their sacred values.

Unfortunately, their passionate intensity has been evoked and directed by lies. The picture of the world they have been sold is almost completely false, and the threats against which they have been mobilized to fight are bogus.

But it is among those who have been seduced by the "worst" of America's spirits that this "passionate intensity" is to be found.

The last time America faced a crisis of a kindred sort—in the decade leading up to the Civil War—the counterpart of Liberal America eventually rose to the occasion. It was moral and spiritual passion that animated leaders in the rise of the Union against the over-reaching dominance of the Slave Power—leaders like Harriet Beecher Stowe and Abraham Lincoln.

But so far, this time around, nothing has lit a fire in Liberal America like that lit by *Uncle Tom's Cabin.* And Liberal America has not yet raised up a leader like Abraham Lincoln, with moral and spiritual passion deeply integrated into his humanity—passions that fortified his resolve that there was only so far he would bend to keep the peace, but no further.

This change—this weakening—is, I believe, the consequence of an intellectual evolution. Recent generations have witnessed a change in worldview, among a large portion of liberal-minded people, from one in which the categories of traditional religion still exerted a dominant influence to one where that influence had declined and was replaced by ideas arrived at through reason applied to evidence.

Let me declare immediately that I am committed to that rational and empirical path of knowledge. What I will try to show in this book is that if one follows that path far enough, one arrives at a dif ferent worldview from the one that has crippled Liberal America in this crisis.

Years of discussing such matters as this with liberal audiences has shown me that much of Liberal America rejects the idea of there being any such thing as "the battle between good and evil."

To believe in any such "battle," it would be necessary first to believe in the reality of value. But many operate under the influence of ideas that, over the past century or more, have become embedded in the ethos of rational, intellectual culture. In this worldview, what is real is "objective," and since values are not to be found "out there" in our universe, they are not really real. Because values are "subjective," according to this view, they are but matters of opinion. ("What the Nazis did at Auschwitz isn't what I would have done," a college student of mine once said, "but what they did made sense within their value system, and so it was right for them.")

Imagine a subculture under assault from a force that, under the guise of being politically "conservative," is really waging a battle that is fundamentally moral and spiritual in nature. Imagine the subculture undergoing this attack is dominated by a worldview in which "value" is not considered really real (just a matter of opinion, lacking objective validity) and in which the idea of profound "spiritual" forces is considered an antiquated fantasy. How much passionate intensity would such a subculture be likely to bring to such a battle? (How likely would the people in that subculture be to rise to the occasion like our heroes Sully, Luke, and Frodo).

But, some will argue, that is the cost of intellectual integrity—the cost of pursuing truth by rational and empirical means. According to this view, although the false certainties provided by religion can inflame people, we have moved beyond such false certainties into a better-founded set of beliefs. The loss of that flame is the cost of seeing things as they truly are.

But I will argue that these beliefs are not only a source of weakness. They are also mistaken. Dangerously mistaken, for people in our situation.

In the remainder of this book, I will show how many of these old categories that were formerly provided on the basis of the authority of religious doctrine can be meaningfully acquired through the epistemology of applying reason to the evidence. And by "evidence," I mean not only of our times, but also the evidence of the evolution of life on earth, the evolution of social evolution from the dawn of civilization, and the patterns moving through the American civilization leading up to the drama in which we are participating today.

It is my belief—indeed, it is my personal experience—that the (secular) understanding thus reached can afford a deep connection with the source of those moral and spiritual passions by which the "best" might gain that passionate intensity to turn back the force that now endangers everything we hold dear.

Is Liberal America Capable of Making the Necessary Changes?

It isn't easy to change fundamental beliefs. If the rescue of the nation from this "evil force" requires many in Liberal America to take on that challenge of revising basic ideas about the world, how many will be willing to make the effort?

Time now for a second iteration of that central dynamic that underlies the American crisis of our times:

- The once-respectable Republican Party has become the instrument of something that warrants being called an "evil force."
- Liberal America has been rendered incapable of protecting the nation from this threat by a defect in its way of understanding, and therefore seeing, the world.

That formulation raises the question: What if the kindling of the necessary fire in Liberal America requires a significant change in the worldview that now predominates in the liberal side of the American culture?

If that's what's needed, how good would our chances be? Would the people of Liberal America be able—would they be willing—to do the work required to make the necessary changes?

Most people, it seems, abandon the practice of examining their fundamental ideas when they enter adulthood. As children, we tend to accept the worldview of those upon whom we depend and from whom we are learning the basics of what it means to be a human being and member of our culture. Then, in youth, as we individuate—at least in our middle-class, democratic, Anglo-Saxon-based culture—that worldview is subjected to scrutiny, and alternatives are brought forward for consideration. But when we settle into adulthood, even most of those with active minds are apt to put their basic beliefs up on a mental shelf to sit undisturbed.

While the passage of years, and then decades, may bring a slow evolution of outlook, these basic ideas tend to remain intact—at least, so long as the adult life is basically working all right for the person. For most people, it is only when that life hits a major crisis that significant adjustment of fundamental ideas becomes possible. Only when the existing framework of the life is no longer working comfortably does the door to the consideration of possible new frameworks swing open.

A major crisis of that kind now confronts us in America today, as a nation/society/civilization. The status quo is not working. In the absence of some significant shift, there is a strong chance that we are on course for a nightmarish future—maybe nightmares of a kind of which history affords so many examples (but from which most of us Americans have been thoroughly protected), and maybe nightmares of a kind for which there are no historical precedents.

Will this crisis spark in us the necessary motivation to look deeply into what in our present framework needs to change?

This crisis, it must be noted, is a collective one, not a personal one. That may be fortunate for us individually, but unfortunate for our nation's destiny. Although many of us are unhappy to see such ugliness and dysfunction displayed almost daily on our national stage, this grotesque drama does not now greatly impact our own individual lives. So, unlike someone whose personal life is on the rocks, we have the option of ignoring the gravity of the crisis, and evading the challenge of making fundamental changes in our ways.

We are not compelled to look. We can pretend it is not there.

Another factor compounds this challenge to galvanize Liberal America to make the necessary transformations: for us to perceive the gravity of this crisis requires us to look into the future toward which our present course is threatening to take us. For most of us, the immediate impact on ourselves of the current pathology is not enough to raise our alarm. We can be like the man in the joke who, while falling off a hundred-floor skyscraper, is asked as he passes the 50th floor how he is doing, and says, "So far, so good."

Which then leads to the question: In the face of this crisis—in which the stakes could not be higher, but from which many of us are not suffering directly—how many would be willing, in order to turn our collective future away from the nightmares, to do the work to make the necessary changes in ourselves? How many are motivated enough to address the sources of our weakness at a time when the nation needs for us to be strong enough to win an essential battle?

It is change at that level that this book will offer. And it is to those who are game to try out a new way of understanding the human world at a deep level that this work is addressed.

An Integrative Vision

The next part of this book will offer the intellectual basis for the necessary revision of the worldview that has been making Liberal America weak. It will describe, within a secular and rational framework, how forces that warrant being called "good" and "evil" arise and operate, perpetuate themselves, and contend against each other to shape the human world.

In the history of our civilization, several important concepts were introduced into our conceptual framework through the worldview of the Judeo-Christian religious tradition. It was religion that told us what was of value, and why; what is good and what is not, and why; how the world came to be a battlefield in which forces of good and evil contend with each other; how there is a dimension in our world where "spirit" (or "spirits") dwell.

Over the course of several centuries, as a more scientific (empirical and logical) approach to knowledge arose in the West, for an important segment of the population of the Western world (including of course the United States), the dominance of the religious framework began to recede.

As with all such transformations of consciousness, these changes did not all manifest themselves overnight.

[NOTE: An illustration of how such a "lag time" operates in the transformation of consciousness is provided by the founding of the American Republic. America's Founders in the late 18th century did not immediately realize (in both senses of the word) all the implications of their radical new liberal and democratic vision of human society—i.e. that vision according to which "All men are created equal," and government derives its just powers from "the consent of the governed." In the beginning, the system our founders created restricted the franchise to white men of property, and continued the institution of slavery. But over time, the implications of the new democratic premises imposed themselves, moving the nation toward completing the original "revolution" of thought and values. The franchise was gradually extended to groups originally excluded. Lincoln used "All men are created equal" to attack the moral foundations of slavery. The "Establishment clause" in the first amendment to the Constitution was seen to imply government neutrality not only between religions but between religion and non-religion, etc.

So it has been with the rise of the new more secular and rational ways of knowing.]

With the passage of the generations in America, the residual power of major religious categories (like "good and evil") persisted even among people whose orientation was becoming increasingly "secular." But it diminished over time—particularly, if my impression is correct, over the past half century. The longer the time since this segment of the culture left the religious framework, the less those people have understood the world in a way that provides a prominent place in their thinking for such things as good and evil.

But there is no need to let go of some of those important concepts. Just because it was religion that formerly provided the pathway for people to see "good" and "evil" as vital realities does not mean that other pathways can't be found. Leaving behind millennia of established ways of reaching important conclusions may leave a dangerous vacuum, but that vacuum may represent not a permanent loss but just a new challenge: how can kindred important conclusions be reached along the newly-adopted path?

A central purpose of Part II is to demonstrate that the secular, rational, empirical approach to knowledge can be used to establish the reality of old and indispensable ideas about our world.

As indicated before, this will include establishing the reality of "value," and of a dynamic in human affairs that warrants being called "the battle between good and evil." (I will also venture to describe a phenomenon that might reasonably be called "spirit" that operates in our world.) For the present political purposes—concerning the crisis in America today—I will be focusing on the reality of a phenomenon that warrants being called an "evil force." But my ambition here goes well beyond that.

Even if there were no immediate and urgent crisis facing us as a nation, I would feel impelled to share, before I go to my grave, this "integrative vision" of how the human world works. I do not make promises lightly—in nearly sixty-nine years, to the best of my recollection, I've never broken a promise—so it is with careful consideration that I hereby promise: the evolutionary perspective on the human story to be unfolded here shortly will at least make a good contribution toward answering these questions:

1. What is "the good," what makes "the good" real, and what makes "the good" good?
2. What is the nature of "evil," what is its source, and how does it operate in the world?
3. Why has human history contained so much torment and destructiveness?
4. What does the destructiveness in human history reveal—or not reveal—about basic human nature?
5. What do these ways of understanding the nature and workings of evil imply for the destiny of the human creature, for the species that stepped out of the niche in which it evolved biologically into the development—unprecedented in the history of life on this planet—of a non-biologically determined form of life (i.e. into civilization)?
6. How should we understand the central challenge that faces humankind (and that faces the system of life on earth from which our species arose)?

But before unfolding that "integrative vision, let me begin with providing—in Chapter Two—a picture of our quarry for the immediate purposes of addressing our national crisis, starting with a description/definition of the idea of an "evil force." It's a notion, I know from long experience, that a great many in Liberal America reject as a primitive idea to which nothing real in our world corresponds.

I will proceed now to the larger picture—beyond our immediate national crisis—to explore not only how such a phenomenon *does* exist, but also how it *can* exist.

Ideas about our crisis will be interwoven with that larger picture, but it will be in Part III that what's gone wrong in America, and how it can be set right, will again become the central focus.

> [NOTE: I invite readers to consider whether they want to skip Part II after reading the Interlude that is here next. (Or, if not to skip Part II entirely, then to skim through it by using the brief summaries that appear at the beginning of each segment.)
>
> Part II is for those who think there is no such a thing as an "evil force." It is also for those who interested in understanding the source and nature of evil and how it works in the human world.
>
> Those who are already on board with the idea that what we are up against can reasonably be called an "evil force," and those who want to maintain a focus on America's current political battle, should feel free to by-pass Part II and go directly to Part III. Part III is titled, "The Emperor's New Clothes Project": A Strategy for Fighting Evil in a Democracy," and it begins on page 215.
>
> I regard Part II as a big deal for understanding the human world. But I'd rather that a reader not interested in that level of analysis skip that part than that they enter it and never get to the other side.]

Interlude I:

To Light a Fire

All Necessary Risks

Feeling called to this mission compels me to take risks I'm uncomfortable taking, including what feels like the "obligatory chutzpah" of making some bold claims about this work and how people might use it to make a positive impact on our national crisis.

The other day, a friend asked me a question about the mission that drives me to write this book and that has driven me since the fall of 2004—to try to help turn around our present dangerous political dynamic. She is a person who understands something about being on a mission: for many years, she was aflame on a mission, in which she accomplished much, on behalf of battered women. She asked me if I was able to pursue this mission from a "spiritually centered" place.

After pondering a bit, I answered. "The picture seems mixed. With respect to what I am supposed to do, and what I've got to say, I feel great clarity. Is that some sort of centeredness? But at the same time, I am carrying a good deal of anxiety. And that doesn't feel 'centered.'"

It is from this combination that my anxiety comes.

1) I feel *called* to this mission—to share something important that I've seen. Whatever one makes of this idea of "calling," I experience it as meaning that it is not about me but about serving something much

bigger and more important than I am. And answering that call means I am obliged to take *all necessary risks* to accomplish my mission.

2) One big risk I feel obliged to take—in order to maximize the chance of my mission's success—is to make some claims that I think true, but whose boldness might be considered unseemly. Such chutzpah seems obligatory, because the most likely way this book—and my mission—will fail is by failing to get the kind of attention it needs.

3) But there's a very strong chance that my claims will go unsupported, and that I'll be left hanging out there having declared that what I have to say is a big deal, while the world shrugs its shoulders, uninterested.

Hence the anxiety—the fear that people will see me as a pretentious jerk with delusions of grandeur.

But the requirement to take "all necessary risks" means that such fears of embarrassment must be disregarded for the sake of the mission.

It's not the first such risk I've taken, but this one feels a good deal riskier than the previous ones, e.g. my jumping into the political arena, plunging heart and soul into a two-year campaign for Congress, even though I'd never run for office before and that role did not fall readily into my comfort zone.

So here's what I claim: 1) this book presents something that's true and important and not already being said elsewhere; and 2) that there is are scenarios—not probable, but plausible enough—in which the ideas in this book can be used to strike a meaningful blow in the battle in the American power system that must be fought and must be won.

About the importance of what I've seen, I have great confidence. I know what I've seen, and for ten years it has blown me away. About the impact that my showing it here in this book will have, I am far less sure.

Ten years have taught me a good deal about my target audience, and I do not write with the kind of faith in the reader that I had, say, forty years ago when I was writing my first book on the destructive forces that have arisen to warp the course of civilized societies.

Hence another risk I feel obliged to take: to challenge that target audience in ways that some may find less than endearing. There are obstacles that must be dealt with.

Continuing with the obligatory chutzpah, let me say that a case might be made that anyone who recognizes that power must be drained away from the force that has taken over the right has a moral obligation to at least check out whether my claims are valid.

1) Would it be OK, Oh Liberal America—given the precariousness of America's situation, and the terribly high stakes in the battle—if such claims from a plausible messenger were actually valid, but people didn't even bother to check them out?

2) If a person with my background and life story would not qualify as a plausible, possible carrier of a message of that sort, just what would a more plausible messenger look like?

> [NOTE: Two relevant portraits of me can be found: a biography on Wikipedia (at http://en.wikipedia.org/wiki/Andy_Schmookler) and an account by my wife (at http://www.nonesoblind.org/blog/?p=11999).]

So, dear reader, in the hopes of getting you on board I am risking putting you off and embarrassing myself. By "on board" would mean not only being willing to do the work that this book demands of the reader but also, if you are persuaded, being ready to invest your talents and passions in using what's here to help turn this dangerous dynamic in America around.

What compels me to take risks that feel almost reckless, is that my reason for writing this book is not just to be read, but to help make something better happen in our world.

An Uncle Tom's Cabin for Our Times?

> *The ambitious goal of this book is to do for this era what Uncle Tom's Cabin did for an earlier era: light a fire to oppose an evil. Why might an "integrative vision" accomplish now what a sentimental novel did then? Maybe, because whereas the readers of Uncle Tom's Cabin needed to* ***feel*** *more deeply what they already knew to be true, what Liberal America needs is to* ***see*** *a truth not yet recognized.*

"Make something better happen." For more than a decade, my immodest ambition has been for the ideas just presented in the first chapter to serve as the *Uncle Tom's Cabin* for this era. By that I mean that I have hoped that my message would do for the latent power of Liberal America what Stowe's novel, *Uncle Tom's Cabin*, did for the North in the first half of the 1850s.

The idea that slavery was a moral wrong had been getting an increasing foothold in the North in the decades before Harriet Beecher Stowe's best-selling book was published. But in the political realm, the force that opposed slavery (and the Slave Power) was still being out-fought by the pro-slavery forces from the South abetted by many Northern politicians.

Then came Stowe's book, dramatizing—or melo-dramatizing—the pernicious character of the institution of slavery. The book caught fire, helping stiffen the backbone of Northerners, readying them to stand up to the Slave Power. This was during a decade in which that Slave Power (as many called it) was acting the bully in the American power system, becoming ever more persistent in its overreaching efforts not just to protect but to expand the dominion of the economic system based on human bondage.

It was because of that fire that Lincoln, upon meeting Stowe during the Civil War, is said to have declared: "So you are the little woman who wrote the book that started this great war!"

Here we are once again in a situation with some important parallels —with Liberal America today being much like the North in the early 1850s. Once again the side that, however imperfect, is tasked to defend Wholeness is being bullied, and is responding in a weak, ineffectual fashion. Once again, a destructive force is dividing the country into antagonistic elements, and thereby damaging the ability of our democracy to navigate its way through our challenges in a wise and constructive way.

And so I've hoped that my message would rouse Liberal America to fight the same spirit against which Harriet Beecher Stowe kindled the fire with her book, the same force that, a century and a half ago, used the Slave Power to damage, and nearly destroy, this nation.

Such things happen, but very rarely. And thus far my efforts—as a blogger and as a political candidate—have failed to light a fire as *Uncle Tom's Cabin* did.

> [NOTE: Not much of a fire, anyway. There was a time during my congressional campaign, which was fortunately caught on a video* ("A Sick and Broken Spirit") took off on the Internet, when that fire did quite palpably get lit.]

It might reasonably be argued that—even if the message that has driven me were as on target as I've believed—my aspiration was unrealistic and inappropriate. *Uncle Tom's Cabin* was a novel, which means it used narrative to bring its readers through a well-orchestrated set of experiences.

By contrast, my message —particularly in the form of this book — is directed to the intellectual level, presenting a coherent set of ideas to explain the meaning of the facts before us.

Would Liberal America not be better kindled by something written in the mode of Stowe's moving message? The experiential dimension of a story (whether on the page, or in a film) has an elemental power to grab people "where they live." Moreover, Harriet Beecher Stowe wrote in a sentimental and melodramatic fashion that was especially powerful, in that era, for generating an emotional impact. The death of Little Eva, the cruelties of Simon Legree, the nobility and Christ-like self-sacrifice of Uncle Tom– all these were indelible images and they were presented in that powerful mode that mimics our lives as we live them.

By contrast, the passions are not so readily evoked when people are engaged at the intellectual level. So how could a book like this play anything life an *Uncle Tom's Cabin* kind of a role?

While there's validity to that argument, there is also an important point to be made on the other side.

At the time that *Uncle Tom's Cabin* was published, Stowe's readers already *knew* a basic truth—that slavery was an immoral and unjust system—and what was needed was for them to *feel* the compassion, the outrage, the yearning for justice called for by the truth that they knew.

In America in our time, the situation is different.

Yes, we in Liberal America need to feel more of the outrage and more passion for fight that our situation calls for. (See* "Where's the Moral Outrage.") But I believe that what underlies the lack of outrage and passion in the Liberal America of our times is an inadequate understanding of *the truth of our situation.*

Our weakness I am asserting —is a function of the inability to see what's before our eyes, and that inability in turn is a function —I am asserting —of important errors at the level of fundamental ideas.

If *what we are up against* is an "evil force" which has made today's Republican Party its instrument, but people cannot see it because their ideas about the world leave no room for such a thing as an "evil force," then the necessary response from people may require their changing their ideas about the world.

So lighting a fire in the part of America that must stand up and fight against an evil force is a different task in today's crisis than it was in the crisis over slavery in Harriet Beecher Stowe's day.

Uncle Tom's Cabin led people feel deeply a truth they already knew.

What We're Up Against attempts to get people to see a truth that they apparently do not yet recognize. And for that task, particularly with people who think, a compelling argument about the workings of the human world might well be the right instrument.

I still hold out a hope therefore—small, but real —that something might be kindled by an intellectually coherent argument that shows that "the battle between good and evil" is a dynamic at the core of the challenge facing us.

But there is another problem. It may be that the necessary change in liberal/secular America must begin at the level of some of our fundamental ideas. But there are other problems in how, in these times, Liberal America deals with ideas. And these might make it harder for these ideas to light the necessary fire.

These two problems are organically connected. That connection—which might be stated as habit of seeing things piecemeal, not putting the pieces together to see things whole—will be explored further in Interlude III (p. 71) and Interlude IV (p. 86).

Part Two

Part Two

A Secular Understanding of "the Battle Between Good and Evil" in the Human World

Chapter Two:

What I Talk about When I Talk about Evil

What I Mean by an "Evil Force"

Think of evil as a coherent force that works through the human world to impart brokenness to whatever it touches. The good is likewise a force, working similarly, but in the opposite direction, to make things more whole.

The idea of an "evil force" is important for us in Liberal America to wrap our minds around for two reasons: 1) What we are up against in America today—what threatens the future of all we hold dear—is something that warrants being called—indeed, I believe is best understood as—an "evil force"; and 2) The more people in Liberal America are enabled to see this phenomenon, and to see it as an "evil force," the more capable we will be to respond to it appropriately, i.e. to fight and defeat it.

In this chapter, I will try to show how the first of these two assertions is true. (That second proposition is based on the supposition—which may or may not be warranted—that if people see what I see, they will feel inspired and impassioned, as I have, to press the battle against this destructive force.)

The first step toward believing in the reality of an "evil force" is simply to **see** it. Whether or not the existence of such a thing fits into one's present worldview, intellectual integrity requires that—if one perceives something—one adjust one's views to accommodate that reality.

And the first step toward seeing what I'm calling an "evil force" is having a description or definition of what I mean by evil. Also, what I mean by "good." Both are naturalistic phenomena, i.e. simply part of what operates in the world of cause and effect.

Here's what I propose:

1. We should think of "evil" as a force—meaning that it operates to move things within the system in a consistent and identifiable direction.

   The same can be said of the force of the good, though the directions are opposite.

2. The direction toward which these forces move things—the consistency of their impact—has to do with the quality of the order. In the case of evil, the force works to impart—to the things it touches—a pattern of "brokenness." Imparting "a pattern of brokenness" (more on brokenness shortly—see Chapter Four) means breaking down those orders that serve and enhance the quality of life in the system. The force of evil works, for example, to replace justice with injustice, integrity with duplicity, peace with strife, ecological health with ecological breakdown, etc.

   The force of the good moves things in the opposite direction: where the force of evil destroys the order that enhances life, the force of the good strengthens structures that serve life.

   Each of these forces—the good and the evil—works to expand its domain in the world.

3. The force of evil has coherence. A dense network of interconnected causes and effects makes it coherent at any given time, so that the different elements of brokenness moving through the system are causally interconnected. And that same interconnectedness allows the force to move through time in a coherent way. (More on this shortly, in this chapter's section, "The Spirit that Drove Us to Civil War is Back.")

Again, the same can be said of the force of the good.

4. The force of "evil" not only creates brokenness, but also exploits brokenness where it finds it in the human system. The forms of brokenness it exploits include the anarchy in the intersocietal system, unjust social organization, and a lack of integration (or reconciliation) among the elements of the psyche and character of human beings (individually and collectively).

   The good operates similarly, but in the opposite direction. As evil utilizes brokenness in the human system to expand its influence, the good utilizes "wholeness" (life-serving order) in the human system to increase the wholeness of the human world.

5. When evil manifests itself in the world through the concrete actions of human beings, it "wears a human face" expressive of those human qualities that have historically been associated with evil - qualities like cruelty, deceit, greed, selfishness, and a lust for power.

   With the good, the symmetry continues—i.e. same general structure of operation, but with the opposite sorts of human traits—kindness instead of cruelty, honesty instead of deceptiveness, etc.—being visible in its workings.

I have described above a phenomenon which I call an "evil force." It is useful to differentiate the two elements here: the phenomenon, on the one hand, and the name one gives it on the other.

I will show that the phenomenon is real, that it operates in the human world, and that it plays a central role in the human drama. As for what to call it, such a phenomenon possesses most of the essence of what has traditionally been called evil. For that reason, and because I believe the name helps evoke the appropriate set of feelings in us, I think it right to call it "evil."

But the important thing is to see the phenomenon—see it in all its vastness and darkness. Call it whatever you want.

What matters is that we see it clearly enough to fight and defeat it, as this is the nature of what we are up against in America today. This is what I mean when I say that one part of the two-part dynamic behind our national crisis is that "Today's Republican Party has become an instrument of an evil force."

More About Evil

This concept of evil as a force, operating through cause and effect, implies neither an image of a malevolent being nor a demonization of those people through whom that force works.

From experience, I know there are pitfalls in using the word "evil": people understandably imagine that the word as I'm using it has all the same meanings as when they've heard it used before. It may be useful to articulate here some differences between my use of the word and some other uses with which people are familiar.

When I say evil is a force—to be understood in secular terms as a part of the dynamic operating in the human system through cause and effect—my use contrasts with one traditional religious notion of evil in that it involves no malevolent supernatural powers. So no, I am not conjuring up something Satanic here.

Another issue that arises is whether the use of the word means "demonizing" one's opponents or enemies with a toxic label. But the phenomenon I am describing is not best perceived in terms of "evil people." Again, think of "evil" as a *force.*

This "evil force" works through people, but those people are not the locus or source of the phenomenon. Those people who serve the force of evil in the world might be considered channels through which the force works. Or as "carriers" of the pattern of brokenness. So one might also think of Evil is a disease—a disorder—that we fight.

Although we need to stop the carriers from spreading the brokenness, it is not ultimately those people—those "carriers"—whom we fight, but the destructive force.

When it comes to those human beings who serve the force of evil, I'm firmly of that Christian school of thought: "Hate the sin, but love the sinner." (Not always easy, but that's what I believe is right.) (For more on this, see "With Malice Toward None," p. 121)

Besides which, it is plain to see that—in America today—many of those who lend their support to the evil force that has arisen on the right are in most ways good people. (See * "When Bad Politics Are Supported by Good People" in the "More Depth" collection on the web.)

So this is not about the demonization of one's opponents. It's about the recognition of a vast, subtle, but coherent force transmitting its patterns of brokenness by the straightforward (if also complex) operation of cause and effect.

The Clarifying Power of the "Pure Case"

Usually, good and evil are so thoroughly mixed in our world that it is not useful to think of our political battles in those terms. But the Republican Party of our time is such an unusually pure case that these terms are both morally and politically appropriate. Such pure cases also serve to reveal more clearly the nature of evil.

Much of the time, in human affairs—particularly in the (relatively fortunate) history of the United States—this force I'm calling evil is hard to see. The forces of good and evil are so thoroughly intermingled—within nations, within political parties, within individual human beings—that usually it doesn't clarify much to identify any single entity as "evil."

But occasionally, something manifests itself in the world that does not contain the usual interwoven mixture of elements. Occasionally, history presents us with a rather "pure case." We are living in one of those times.

One of America's two major political parties is unusual—perhaps even unique in the history of liberal democracies—in the proportions of constructive and destructive elements that govern its conduct. In today's Republican Party, the balance between honest and dishonest, just and unjust, caring and cruel, altruistic and selfish, has shifted dramatically toward those ways that degrade a society.

Consider a couple of thought experiments:

Imagine a list of all developments in America in the past 15 years that the national representatives of the Republican Party (the Republican president, and/or Republicans in Congress) played some role in shaping. Then imagine a list of those developments in which Republicans' efforts contributed to a better outcome for America.

Isn't it clear that the first list is very long, and that there are hardly any entries on the second?

(Indeed, is it not clear that during the presidency of Barack Obama, the Republicans made the outcome worse on virtually every issue the nation has faced—on the stimulus, on health care reform, on cap and trade, on reviving the American economy and getting people back to work?)

Has there ever, in American history, been a political party that has behaved in so consistently destructive a fashion? I think not.

Another experiment: Imagine a list of all communications these Republicans have put into our national discourse during the past fifteen years—every idea and assertion that has been voiced by national Republicans or right-wing talk radio or Fox News in an effort to inform and/or influence the public. Imagine further a second list of those statements that have improved their listeners' grasp of reality or understanding of the truth of the matters under discussion.

Again, it seems that the first list is very long, and that there are precious few entries on the second. Whether the subject has been the war in Iraq, or climate change, or Acorn, or where the president was born, or Benghazi, or the priority to be given the national debt, isn't it clear that powers on the right have consistently led their listeners astray?

Has a major America political party ever been half so consistently dishonest as today's Republicans in their messaging to their country? Has a political party ever been such a fraud in terms of its claims to be patriotic, or conservative, or defenders of Christian values?

> [NOTE: I do not concur with the idea that the problem with the Republicans is specifically with the Tea Party. The Tea Party did not originate until 2010, and by that time all the darkness was already visible—with what Gingrich, Limbaugh, Rove, Bush and Cheney had done to their party and to American politics. Certainly, the Party is not all of one piece, and much of interest can be said of its internal dynamics. But here are the two points that seem salient to me. The Tea Party is largely the fruit of an extreme element—e.g. the Koch Brothers, with their roots in the John Birch Society worldview—with which the "establishment" Republicans made the dangerous choice to make common cause. And the Tea Party is also the expression of the—craziness in the sense of a serious disconnection from reality—that the

Republicans deliberately cultivated in their followers. So the Party now consists of those who knowingly have told the lies, now reaping the consequences of the coming to power of some of those who actually believe them. The sociopathic wing now must contend with the delusional wing.]

Pure cases open a window into the fundamental realities of the human world. They lay bare the underpinnings of the force of evil as it operates in human affairs.

The nightmarish episode of the Third Reich in Germany—its rise out of the Weimar Republic, and then its brutal and murderous tyranny and expansion—led many thinkers of that era to important insights into the dynamics of that destructive time, and into the sources and workings of a force of brokenness in the human world. (E.g. Erich Fromm's *Escape from Freedom*, Theodore Adorno et al.'s *The Authoritarian Personality*, Norbert Elias's *The Germans.*)

Now in our times, another pure case—far less inflamed , fortunately, by a murderous lust to annihilate, but nonetheless similarly consistent in its working to make worse everything it contacts—has provided yet another opportunity to examine the nature and workings of the force of destruction within a civilized society.

See the Evil: A Portrait of the Coherence of the Force

The force shows "cross-sectional" coherence in that, at any given time, its various manifestations show a fundamental kinship through their shared work of spreading the pattern of brokenness.

How can such a force arise, I imagine the reader wondering? Here in Part II, I will soon attempt to present, in a step-by-step fashion, an integrated and grounded answer to that question. But first here's a bit more of a portrait of this coherent force that I claim we're up against in America today.

In the previous chapter, I described "The Republican Party's Extraordinary Pattern of Destructiveness." Putting together the hundreds of pieces from the news of our times, I identified a set of patterns that included

- an insatiable lust for power and wealth,
- an impulse to prey upon the vulnerable,
- a preference for conflict over cooperation,
- a persistent dishonesty,
- a proclivity to divide groups of people against each other,
- and a willingness to sacrifice the greater good for selfish advantage.

I asked the question, too long unasked: "What is it that would express itself in all these ways?" Which leads to the question, what is it that all these things have in common? The pattern made by all these patterns is that in each case the pattern of brokenness expands its domain.

Here is demonstrated a part of that *coherence* of the force. It expresses itself in a variety of ways, but the pattern of brokenness bears evidence of a common thrust, a consistent impact. Something seems to be working toward the achievement of a "purpose" to increase the power of "brokenness" in the world.

The way all these patterns share this quality of brokenness demonstrates what might be termed the *cross-sectional* coherence of this force, i.e. how the force's manifestations at a given time show a basic kinship.

Let's turn now to how this force also demonstrates a *longitudinal* coherence: a capacity of the force to maintain its nature through time.

The Spirit that Drove Us to Civil War is Back

The striking parallels between the destructive forces in two eras reveals the "longitudinal" coherence of evil, i.e. how a destructive force can maintain coherence through time.

It's like facial recognition technology: if the features match up, you conclude, "It's the same guy."

So it is with the match between the force that drove us to Civil War more than a century and a half ago, and the force that has taken over the Republican Party in our times.

In both cases, we see an elite insisting on their "liberty," by which they mean the freedom to dominate.

With *Citizens United*, in our times, the corporatists have declared that their "freedom of speech" gives them the right to buy our elections, unrestrained by concerns about the right of the average citizen to an equal say in their government.

Back in the 1850s, slaveholders insisted that their "liberty" meant they had the right to take their human "property" anywhere in American territory, an insistence that swept aside the previously respected concerns of millions of their countrymen that there be regions of the country free of slavery. (Not to mention the denial of liberty to the human beings they claimed as "property.")

In both cases, use of the ***structures*** *of American democracy was combined with a contempt for the democratic* ***values*** *that inspired our founders.*

Nowadays, the Republicans have made a national effort to pass voter ID laws to address a non-existent problem of voter fraud—a campaign that is itself a fraud whose transparent intent is to disenfranchise America's most vulnerable citizens, who predictably vote mostly for the Republicans' opponents.

Back in the years leading up to the Civil War, the slaveholders banned the distribution of anti-slavery writings, and sometimes suppressed anti-slavery talk by violence.

In both cases, the elites driving the polarization of the country justified their dominance by distorting, in belittling ways, the humanity of those they sought to exploit.

Today's Republicans talk about the 47 percent, the half of the country they characterize as "takers," even though many of those 47 percent work multiple jobs just to make ends meet; and these Republicans vote to strip them of unemployment benefits, at a time of massive joblessness, in the mistaken belief that only desperation will get these lazy people to work.

Back in the time of the Slave Power, the slaveholding class declared they were doing their black slaves a favor to discipline them into an ethic of work; freeing them would be cruel, the masters claimed, because those blacks were inherently too lazy and incompetent to survive on their own.

In both cases, the idea of compromise became a dirty word, as the inflamed insistence on getting everything one's own way took hold of the inflamed side.

Today's Republicans do not seek compromise, and the dynamics of the party are such that anyone who works toward compromise is demonized and run out of office by challenge from the more inflamed, uncompromising wing of the party.

Back in the years leading up to the Civil War, the South's insistence on the unfettered expansion of their domain led to the overturning of the great Missouri Compromise, which had held the nation together for more than thirty years. It was this fracturing of the peace that prompted Abraham Lincoln to return to the political arena. And it was this uncompromising spirit that set the nation on course to a bloody civil war.

In both cases, the powerful elite in the grip of that destructive force refused to accept that in a democracy sometimes you win and sometimes you lose, and sometimes you have to accept being governed by a duly-elected president you don't like.

Today's Republicans have done everything they could to nullify the presidency of Barack Obama, whom the American people duly elected twice. Like no other opposition party in American history, they refused to accept the temporary minority status to which American voters have consigned them. The Republicans' top priority, since Obama first took office, has been to block the president from performing the function for which the people hired him.

Back on the eve of the Civil War, Southerners—who had disproportionately dominated the upper echelons of the national government from the time of its founding—considered the election of Abraham Lincoln an intolerable insult, and promptly made a unilateral decision to break apart the Union; they then raised an army to defend that decision, rather than accept the outcome of the democratic process and regroup for the next election.

As with facial recognition, the configuration of the features tells us, "This is the same ugly thing, come back again."

(A fuller presentation of how "the spirit that drove us to Civil War is back" can be found in a series of pieces in the "More Depth" collection. Those pieces deal in turn with these disturbing patterns common to both eras: "the Spirit of Domination," "the Spirit of the Lie," and "the Spirit of War." Also available there is a bibliography of 20 or so of the books that I have used in the study of the period leading up to the Civil War.)

In coming chapters, I will explain how it is that such patterns can endure and re-emerge in a cultural system over the course of generations. (And how it is that such large and enduring patterns, though "abstract," are not only "real" but are in some ways the most deeply "real" aspects of the human world.)

Suffice it to say for now that, in its re-emerged form, this pattern or force or spirit has retained its destructive nature. Back in the mid-19th century, it broke the nation apart and gave us a nightmarish Civil War. And in our times, it is damaging everything in American civilization that it can reach.

Why Now?

With other times and places—like the Civil War in the United States and the rise of Nazism in Germany—one can readily see how the system was fractured by profound conflicts and traumas, creating openings for a force of brokenness to rise to power. Our time is different. It seems that what has allowed evil to advance is some weakening of the cultural "immune system."

Earlier I declared "unprecedented" the destructive force that's come to center stage of American politics in our times. That assertion must be qualified by the idea, just presented, that the "evil force" we see operating in America today, making the Republican Party into its instrument, is in some meaningful sense "the same" force that took possession of the American South in the 1850s and drove us into Civil War.

In different ways, I believe, both ideas are true. The force is in important respects the same, but also the circumstances are different. Without attempting to sort out what's a repeat and what's unprecedented, I'd like to call attention to one important difference. It's a difference in the nature of what opened the door to the rise of an evil force powerful enough to wreak great damage on the American nation.

In the 1850s, the nation faced a huge and deep-seated issue—slavery. It was through this issue—terribly divisive as it was—that an evil force could work its way to great power in the American political arena. Slavery was a significant dimension of brokenness long embedded in the American body politic: it was a well-established way of life—for a dominant American elite, representing a major share of the national wealth—that was at fundamental odds with founding values of the American nation ("all men are created equal"). In addition, important conflicts of economic interest corresponded to a geographic boundary between two well-defined regions—thus providing a physical fault line on which the nation could be split apart.

Today's crisis is not like that. There is no remotely comparable major issue confronting the nation. Our contemporary rise of an evil force to a position of great power seems to have happened just on its own, with no substance at its heart. It seems, indeed, that rather than the brokenness growing out of a vital issue, as in the earlier era, in today's crisis it is the brokenness that comes first and then the force of brokenness that has arisen makes a battlefield out of every issue that arises.

What this suggests is that there has been some deterioration in the overall fabric of wholeness—goodness/morality/integrity—in the American civilization. It suggests that the American body politic suffers from a compromised immune system, a diminished capacity of the cultural order to resist a force of disorder.

An analogy presents itself: When the immune system of the human body is weakened by the AIDS virus, opportunistic diseases—like Karposi sarcoma—that are held in check by a healthy body can take hold and kill the person. Likewise in America today: the weakening of the resistance to evil has allowed the political equivalent of Karposi sarcoma (that "spirit that drove us to Civil War," lurking for generations in the recesses of the body politic) to move opportunistically to a central place in the American power system.

This force has found in the Republican Party a channel through which to wreak destruction on the American organism. But it could only wreak this destruction because the American body politic provided the opening.

As was said before, this crisis is the product not only of the force that's taken over the political right, but of the failure of the rest of the American body politic—Liberal America (and its political arm, the Democratic Party), the press, and the American people—to respond appropriately.

American civilization would seem to have been weakened by some sort of "cultural AIDS" that has opened the door to the pathology. It therefore behooves us to investigate what kind of "cultural AIDS" has weakened

America's cultural "immune system."

Let me add, then, one more to the list of six questions (p. 33) to be addressed in the coming chapters with its "integrative vision":

7. Why now? What is it that has happened in the American cultural system to account for the rise of this evil force in our times, in the absence of any objective blow to the system that would open the door to evil?

The opening for the rise of Nazism in Germany was created by the traumas of World War I (and the punitive Versailles peace) compounded by the devastation of the economic order caused by the hyperinflation. The fracturing of the United States by the Civil War was made possible by the intractable issue of slavery, and two conflicting visions of society corresponding with a clear geographical fault line.

So what's our excuse? (See Chapter Nine—"How the Balance of Power Between Good and Evil Can Shift Adversely"—for at least a serious stab at an answer.)

INTERLUDE II:

Love of Wholeness May Have to Come First, Before Fighting Brokenness

My own experience suggests that one will not be inspired to fight against what spreads brokenness until one has deeply experienced a love of wholeness.

What does it take for a person, in the face of evil, to be motivated to fight it? Clearly, it is not enough simply to be exposed to an evil force at work. Many do not see the evil. And many who see something they detest are nevertheless not moved to put themselves on the line to combat it.

My own experience suggests the possibility that—in contrast with that old anti-war slogan, "Make Love, Not War"—the emotional, moral, and spiritual foundations for a battle against evil are laid first by the experience of being blown open, heart and soul, by a love of what's sacred.

I've had two main experiences of feeling called to take on the forces of destructiveness in the human world. In both, the call to battle I experienced was preceded—by some months—by a transformative spiritual experience of a more positive, beautiful kind.

My present decade-long battle against this dark force that has arisen in the American power system began in early September of 2004. I was not happy to answer that call because, for the preceding half year, I'd been following another far more beautiful calling.

A profound experience of Wholeness had transformed me, and I was tremendously excited about articulating an insight that I'd had about Wholeness as the source of our deepest fulfillment. I articulated that insight in an essay, and in a talk* I delivered in several places around the country, titled "Our Pathways into Deep Meaning." And I was happily outlining what I had chosen to be my next book, *Mapping the Sacred.*

That book remains unwritten because the call to battle summoned me away from the contemplation of the good, the true, and the beautiful, and required me to focus instead on the evil, the false, and the ugly. What a trade!

But still, there was no doubt that I must join the battle because: *the sacred that I'd come to appreciate so much more deeply than before was in jeopardy.*

The next major piece* of writing, and the next big talk I gave, was the next year (2005), and it had the title "The Concept of Evil: Why It is Intellectually Valid and Politically and Spiritually Important." In that speech, I said something about how it came to be that I perceived the evil force at work in America today:

> Much of my adult life has been spent studying the play of destructive forces in the human system. (The word "evil" even occurs in the subtitle of one of my books.) But it was not until recently that my experience of these destructive forces plumbed me so deeply that the notion of evil" became a palpable reality.
>
> Part of what opened that door, I believe, was my having had, in the spring of 2004, a spiritual breakthrough regarding the very opposite of evil. This experience gave me a vision of a Wholeness and a deeper sense of reverence for the good, the true, and the beautiful. This experience seems, in retrospect, to have sensitized me to those forces that work to destroy such wonderful forms of good order.

It is only recently that I have noticed the parallel between this sequence of events in 2004, and how I came to my earlier life-changing calling in 1970.

What happened in 1970 was that, in August of that year, I experienced a bone-shaking, life-changing moment of insight that led to my writing my first book, *The Parable of the Tribes: The Problem of Power in Social Evolution* (first published by the University of California Press in

1984). It is a work that seeks to answer the question, Why has civilization developed in such destructive ways, and why has the course of history been so tormented?

It would not be too much to say that my whole adult life hinged on that moment.

But upon reflection, I see that this moment itself hinged on another important experience—this one less about brokenness than about wholeness. Here's an excerpt from something I wrote (it can be found in the "More Depth" collection on the web as "One Big Thing I Once Saw"), years after the experience, about that moment:

> Suddenly I had a vision of the earth as this Great Living Whole, a single body of which we are part. And that vision of this Whole then moved into a sense of how we are part of that body of the earth. At that time, I'd been reading a book by a fellow named Fritz Kahn called *The Human Body in Structure and Function*, and from it I had developed a sense of a sacred and beautiful, intricate and life-serving wholeness to the human body. What a beautiful miracle it is that something so whole and synergistic and adaptive and exquisitely crafted as the human body—as indeed Life in all its forms–could just emerge into existence in this mysterious cosmos.
>
> So for me, at that time, the image of the body was one that had a kind of divine aura about it. And so when I saw the Earth as this wonderful Whole—and this was, I believe, some years before Lovelock came out with his Gaia hypothesis (or at least before I got wind of it)—I was already getting into a kind of numinous space.
>
> And then the spiritual excitement crested as I envisioned people like me as certain kinds of cells in that body. By "people like me" I mean those who were suffering because of the sorry state we saw the world to be in.... Just as a human body has special cells that fight infection by mobilizing for combat against invading cells, so did we human cells—upon beholding the infection of a sick civilization on our planet—experience suffering so that we will be moved to cure the sickness.... One can embrace the suffering if one can see it as an intrinsic part of Doing God's Work, so to speak.
>
> And months later, immediately preceding the coming of that insight

into the force that had swept the civilized creature up into a tormented social evolutionary process, there was a moment of seeing something sacred about the living systems out of which we emerged and those within us.

In both of those instances of major missions to confront the forces of brokenness, it was the experience of the sacred that had first lit my fire. The call to battle arose out of that.

I wonder: is this how it always is? Love of wholeness first. Being moved to deal with brokenness second?

> [NOTE: My brother, in his work as a psychotherapist who specializes in working with people who have suffered profound trauma, has observed something akin. Trauma, he says, occurs when people have experiences they do not have the resources to handle. The trauma remains an unintegrated experience—a kind of brokenness, one might say—in the person's psychological structure. In his work in trying to help such people move toward greater wholeness, my brother has written, "I have found that those who can access internal and external spiritual resources often are the ones with the most success in being able to work with their trauma." People need "resources" to heal, and he says, "the deepest resources are at the Spiritual level"—like "faith" that can allow people to "move through impossible spaces," and other kinds of connectedness that allows them to tap into "strength beyond their limited selves."]

CHAPTER THREE:

VALUE AT THE HEART OF OUR HUMANITY

As I suggested in Chapter One, it would hardly be possible for an "evil force" to be an important reality, or for "the battle between good and evil" to be an important dynamic in the human drama, unless there were reality to "value" itself (i.e. unless some things are really better than others).

So let's explore that issue now.

NOT ONLY IS GOD NOT NECESSARY, BUT GOD IS ALSO NOT SUFFICIENT, TO DEFINE "THE GOOD"

The idea that, if there's no God, there can be no real "good" has a big logical hole in it.

For years, I conducted radio conversations with a mostly conservative audience in Virginia's Shenandoah Valley. Many of my interlocutors had an attitude—as expressed in the words of a bumper-sticker of the time—"God said it, I believe it, and that settles it."

They and many secular liberals would agree on one thing: without the authority of God, there can be no sound basis for moral judgment.

But that judgment has a major flaw.

Would the fact that God said we should do something be sufficient to establish that it would be morally good for us to do it? When I asked that question, my fundamentalist callers seemed genuinely puzzled that I could even ask such a thing.

"What if God—what if the Creator of the Universe—were some sort of monster?" I would venture further. For people who have spent their entire lives putting the idea—the absolutely unquestioned idea—of an all-good God at the center of their worldview, it might be difficult to imagine a God who was not good. But a God who is not good is not logically impossible. Indeed, an Evil Creator has been part of some religions in history. We should at least be able to imagine what some people have deeply believed.

"Are you saying," I asked, "that whatever some All-Powerful Being that created the universe commanded us to do—even to torture babies and treat our neighbors cruelly—would be good by definition?"

It seemed hard for my callers to grasp the question: "But God is good," they contend, "so if He tells us 'This is good,' we know it's so."

In the statement, "Our God is good," we can see the logical hole in the argument. If these believers judge their God to be good, they must be using some other criterion than God's word to define what is good. And if it's conceivable that a God might not be good, then we need that other criterion.

The belief in God thus does nothing to solve the problem of the Good. True believers and secular rationalists alike face the same challenge: to come up with a basis for judging what is good.

Fortunately there is such a basis.

Value at the Heart of Our Humanity

Values don't need to be "out there" to be real. Indeed, value can only be meaningful as a function of the experience of beings to whom things matter. At its root, that quality of experience—with positive and negative value—is built into us by the same evolutionary process that creates our anatomy, as a design for life rather than death.

Ideas have consequences. And not just among those who create, or study, or work with them. The great John Maynard Keynes said that,

"Practical men, who believe themselves to be quite exempt from any intellectual influence, are usually the slaves of some defunct economist." In the same way, I expect that a lot of liberal, educated Americans—who spend no time exploring issues of epistemology or moral philosophy—are in the grip of some of the ostensibly "rational" philosophy that arose in Western civilization with the advancement of science and declared that values are not really real.

In his twin essays, "Science as a Vocation" and "Politics as a Vocation," the great early twentieth-century social thinker Max Weber declared that science is incapable of saying what we should do but can only advise about the probable consequences of one course of action or another.

Weber apparently would not have felt able to declare, as a statement of truth, that there was anything really wrong about a political force, such as that we see on the political right in America today. I say that this force is systematically damaging those structures in our society that serve the good. But Weber would say that judgments regarding "the good" lie outside of what can be known scientifically, with reason making sense of evidence.

Similarly, the logical positivists declared statements of value to be "meaningless." They cannot be objectively verified; they are statements of the speaker's subjective opinion, perhaps emotionally based, and they have no real truth value.

This is an unnecessarily cramped view of truth, and of what can be discerned from looking at the evidence and thinking rationally about what it shows.

Here's what I think science shows about value: *value is emergent with the evolution of life.*

In the beginning, science tells us, there was the Big Bang and billions of years passed before even the most primitive beginnings of life appeared (at least in our corner of the universe). For those billions of years, one cannot speak of "value." Value is about things mattering, and that means things mattering to someone. If there's no one for whom things matter, then there can be no value.

That way of looking at value suggests how wrong-headed it is to declare value not "real" because it is not "out there." Value can only exist inside the "in here" of creatures capable of *experience*, and whose experience is that things do matter.

But the emergence of such creatures was the inevitable outgrowth of the evolutionary processes that emerged "out there."

The first step in the differentiation of positive value from negative value is inherent in the process of natural selection central to the evolution of life. It is not, so far as can be seen scientifically, that there's any "designer" or "creator" who is expressing a preference. It is just an inevitable aspect of the evolutionary process—the operation of chance in a system where the laws of chemistry and physics are obeyed—that the system chooses life in preference to death. Those forms that can survive and replicate their kind are "chosen" over those that cannot. That is the essence of the process of "natural selection."

The "preference" of the selective process for life over death does not by itself create value. That's because—or at least so I imagine—the very primitive life forms that arose at first cannot be said to have, themselves, any preference for one thing (including life) over another (such as death). Whether or not I'm selling short those earliest forms of life, in time this selective process yields forms of life—- definitely including, but not only, us —- to whom things really do matter.

The "choice" of life over death leads directly to the next step in the emergence of value.

Each form of life is structured to do those things that, in the history of its kind, have been conducive to survival, and to avoid what has historically been associated with the failure to survive. Over time the evolutionary process's "preference" for life over death brings forth creatures whose motivational structures are powered by the positive or negative valence of their experience.

Creatures get put together so that what has served life feels "good" and what has hindered and destroyed life feels "bad."

At last, out of a universe in which nothing has mattered to anything or anyone, something matters. With the development of life, with the emergence of creatures to whom things matter, value enters the universe.

That is how value is an emergent dimension of what (apparently) began as a cold, lifeless, indifferent universe.

- It matters to a baby whether it is cuddled or tortured.

- It matters whether the world is more governed by "do unto others as you would have others do unto you" or by "the strong do what they can while the weak suffer what they must" (in the words of the Athenians in Thucydides' *Peloponnesian Wars*).

- It matters whether the human world is like "Bedford Falls" in the movie *It's a Wonderful Life*—a world in which community, love, and families thrive—or like the alternate version of the town,"Pottersville," a society ruled by greed and the lust for power, where people are wounded and the town is pervaded by brutality and meanness.
- It matters—to put it in the most fundamental terms—whether creatures who experience value have their needs fulfilled or whether they live in misery.

To say that value is not real, because it's "merely" based in experience, makes as much sense as to say that pain is not real.

[NOTE: I'm using "pain" and not pleasure or happiness as the exemplar for the undeniable reality of subjective experience for good evolutionary reasons. Pain is, simply, more powerful and undeniable. Any fool can inflict unbearable pain, but comparable pleasure—on a second-by-second basis—is difficult to achieve. We are wired, as the social psychologists say, to have greater motivation to avoid loss than to achieve gain. Life can be lost in an instant, but all that it takes to sustain life must be developed over time. Pompeii took generations to construct, but only moments to destroy.]

Indeed, without creatures experiencing, nothing *could* matter, and thus nothing could be better than anything else. There could be no value.

Experience is, of course, inherently "subjective." But subjective does not mean idiosyncratic. To say that value is not real because it is a function of "subjective" experience makes (almost) as little sense as to say that there's no such thing as human anatomy. Human values are real and generalized for the species just like human anatomy. Indeed, at their root, human values are part of the same evolved blueprint—a design for life—that yields our anatomy.

What About Disagreements about Value?

The reality of value is not undercut by the diversity of value systems in the world. Some of that diversity reflects brokenness; some reflects the multiplicity of valid ways of creating life-serving cultures.

But what about the fact that people disagree about questions of value? Does that not prove that value is merely a matter of opinion?

Here are two parts of an answer.

First, not all opinions deserve the same standing. Just as a mangled or diseased body does not show "human anatomy" as well as a healthy one does, some of the notions of "value" that we find in the human world are manifestations of a disorder, not reflective of the system of values that is ingrained in humankind.

Recall the quotation from a student of mine: "What the Nazis did at Auschwitz isn't what I would have done, but from within their perspective it was right, and so it was right for them."

Whether it was according to their "values" or not, what the Nazis did was profoundly injurious to the human world generally. The force that drove the Nazis was one of the darkest embodiments of "brokenness" that history has ever witnessed.

We'll be exploring the sources of this brokenness, how it reflects—and is the fruit of—a profound disturbance in the order of life on earth. Let it suffice for now to point out that fascists had a toast, "Vive la mort!" (Long live death).

Whereas the evolutionary process that created us itself chooses life over death, and therefore crafts creatures like us to make the most fundamental choice of life over death, the dark spirit of those Nazis whose values the students would say "was right for them" had reversed that choice. What clearer sign of human brokenness could there be?

That's the first response to the question about the reality of disagreement about values. The second is more complex.

In a complex world, and in a species that devises very diverse cultures to deal with that complexity, it is inevitable that cultures (as well as individuals) will vary in their hierarchy of values.

What matters here is not that there be just one valid way to devise a life-serving culture, but that there is a foundational criterion for what is good: what is good is what enhances life, what meets the needs of and brings fulfillment to living creatures.

The values built into us may be more malleable in the hands of culture than our anatomy—the bound foot of the traditional Chinese woman notwithstanding—but their essence is still part of the reality of our kind.

(We are by nature creatures who walk upright. But different cultures teach different styles of this fundamental human practice.)

It should also be stressed that this case for the *reality* of value by no means argues for the *simplicity* of questions involving value. In the real world, it is constantly necessary for us in our decision-making to weigh one value (or set of values) against another. We continually have to make decisions despite our uncertainty about what the actual consequences of our alternative course of action would be. (Indeed, I have written an unpublished book—which can be found, presented chapter by chapter, starting at http://www.nonesoblind.org/blog/?p=1079, and which has the title, *Not So Straight-and-Narrow: Why Knowing What's Best to Do Is Not a No-Brainer.*)

But the complexity of actual moral decision-making has nothing to do with the point of this argument: *that value is real.*

Once that basic point is established—that things actually do matter, in the only way value could ever meaningfully exist, i.e. in the lived experience of creatures to whom there is a better and a worse—we have escaped from the debilitating and hollow worldview that dismisses values as "mere" opinion.

Once it has been granted that one thing CAN be better than another by a meaningful and inescapable standard, the denial of value is seen to be a kind of disconnection, of brokenness.

In order to regain its moral and spiritual passions, Liberal America does not have to to embrace the forms used by traditional religion to represent the issues of good and evil. That reconnection can be achieved, by moving further forward along the path of rational, empirically-based scientific knowledge.

IS NOTHING SACRED?
THE SACRED AS VALUE TO THE NTH DEGREE

The capacity for an especially powerful experience of meaning and value seems to be built into our nature as a species. "The sacred"

> *seems to be "real" in the same sense that "value" is, and cross-cultural evidence through history suggests that the experience of sacredness is a reality of crucial importance..*

I declared above that to say that value is not real, because it's based in experience, makes as much sense as to say pain is not real. Value, like pain, is something that inherently must be in the realm of experience. The issue is much the same with the question of whether anything is "sacred."

Once again, as with value, our understanding of "the sacred" should begin with *facts about human experience.* The experience of things as partaking of a dimension that feels "sacred" is simply a fact of human life—not necessarily in every human life, but in many, across cultures and through the millennia.

Words can mean, of course, whatever we agree for them to mean. But the definition I am proposing is not an arbitrary one. It is not arbitrary because it gives a name to something that is clearly both real and of utmost importance. "The sacred" can be meaningfully understood as that which we experience as having a particularly special, exalted kind of value.

It is a human reality that people have experiences that are so luminous, so powerful and rich, that such moments seem to provide a vision into a deeper dimension of reality. People have experiences that imbue elements of their lives with a level of meaning and value that transcend the ability of words to describe. (Often people speak in terms of "the sacred" when describing these experiences.)

It seems fitting to define "the sacred" as what people experience as having "value to the nth" degree.

> As with value, there are many whose definition of the sacred is couched not in terms of human experience but rather of the authoritative pronouncements of a Deity. But again, as with value, it is not clear why any such pronouncement, from any *conceivable* deity, should compel our agreement.

> We might, out of fear of consequences—e.g. to avoid the fate of Uzzah in the Bible who is struck dead because he touched the Ark of the Covenant (albeit he did so not out of disrespect, but in order

to save it from falling)—pay close attention to a powerful Deity's idea of what's sacred. But heeding the Almighty's dictates as to how He wants us to treat what He regards as sacred is not the same as our being inspired with the feelings—love, devotion, reverence—that the experience of the sacred generally inspires.

(Again, as with "value," individuals and different cultures will inevitably differ in their priorities, and in how they structure their lives. Those differences can lead, in turn, to different ways of conceiving of the sacred. Yet, despite such variations, the cross-cultural overlap in the experience of the sacred is massive—starting with sacredness of life, of family as the main nexus of human relationships, of place and home, of the natural cycles that sustain life, of justice and beauty and love, etc.)

About value I wrote that "To deny that values are real makes as much sense as to deny that pain is real." Similarly with the sacred: *to deny that "the sacred" is real makes as much sense as to deny that excruciating pain is real.*

A billion years ago, one would assume, there was no such thing as "excruciating pain." But pain, like value and the sacred as well, has been "emergent" in the development of creatures to whom thing matter.

What is less clear about "the sacred" than about "value" generally is why it would have emerged out of the evolutionary process. With "value," it is clearly an important "strategy" for evolution to infuse creatures with the motivation to do what past history of their species has shown to be a good bet to aid in their surviving to pass along their genes. Thus the domain of "value" includes not just humans, but many other species as well.

(Certainly my cat experiences the difference between better and worse. Things definitely matter to her. But just how many of earth's millions of species have anything like an "experience of value"—some sort of fulfillment or misery—that warrants being included in the calculus of "the good," I feel in no position to judge.)

But with the human sense of "the sacred," matters are less clear. Do other creatures have a dimension of experience that corresponds to what human beings report, of value to the nth degree, of entering what seems like a deeper dimension of reality? If so, what role does it play in their lives? And if not, can one provide an explanation of how and why the process of natural selection would craft only in this one species this capacity or proclivity for experiencing the sacred?

Is there something perhaps about the degree of flexibility entailed by being a "cultural animal" that makes this special kind of experience of survival value? Does that great range of indeterminacy make deep and searing moments particularly valuable as a way of providing some needed deep orientation toward what is important, and good, and worthy of protection?

That line of possible explanation gains credence in view of yet another *fact*. Not only is it the case that the human experience of "the sacred" is real, but also it is factual reality that such impactful experiences play an unusually important role in the human story.

In the lives both of individuals and of entire cultures, the experience of the sacred seems to come with an imperative power that moves people to orient themselves around those experiences. Individuals will guide their lives by such moments. (That has certainly been true for me.)

> [NOTE: Such a moment in the life of Albert Schweitzer is described in the introduction (p. 25), by Charles R. Joy, to the book *Goethe: Four Studies* by Albert Schweitzer. Schweitzer described this experience as "an ecstatic experience, a transfiguring mount of vision." He had been "struggling to find the elementary and universal conception of the ethical that I had not discovered in any philosophy." Then: "Late on the third day, at the very moment when, at sunset, we were making our way through a herd of hippopotamuses, there flashed upon my mind unforeseen and unsought, the phrase, 'Reverence for Life.' The iron door had yielded: the path in the thicket had become visible. Now I had found my way to the idea in which world- and life-affirmation and ethics are contained side-by-side!"
>
> This became a central pillar of Schweitzer's intellectual, moral, and spiritual life.]

And entire cultures—having enshrined such moments in sacred texts—will structure themselves around them.

Individuals vary, it seems, in whether and how much they are susceptible to such a deepening of the experience of meaning and value in their lives. But it does seem to be empirically true that such a special dimension of experience has been pretty universal cross-culturally and throughout history.

Every human culture has language. From which we can infer that the propensity to develop and learn language is part of our humanity.

Every human culture has music. From which we can infer that the propensity to create and respond to music is a part of human nature.

Every human culture—as far as I know—has organized itself around a vision of the sacred. From which we can infer that experiencing the sacred dimension is a core part of our humanity.

And from the power that people and cultures give the experience of a sacred dimension, we can infer that contacting that dimension connects us with the human core and with the wellspring of meaning and feeling that comes from that core.

That is why it can be concluded that any worldview that fails to provide that connection—fails to provide access to an awareness of the sacred—is one that forfeits an important form of human power.

Are we to believe nothing is sacred? It seems to me unlikely that in any healthy culture, that would be a predominant belief.

Does Liberal America, in our time, convey a sense of the sacred? FDR did, which demonstrates that there is nothing inherent in the liberal approach that precludes it. But I don't hear it among the main spokespeople of Liberal America today. And that is almost certainly deeply connected with why in this time of profound national crisis, Liberal America has been so blind and so weak.

For the sacred, like value itself, is part of the deep core of our humanity. And a loss of connection with that level, that dimension, cuts us off from those moral and spiritual passions by which people of good will can defeat a mighty and evil force.

With that foundation now established, let us proceed with showing how something like an "evil force" has grown out of the evolutionary processes (biological and cultural) that have led our species to our present extraordinary—yet troubled—position in the whole system of life on earth.

Interlude III:

Ideas and Shirking the Work of Liberty

It is almost a platitude, pronounced by parents and political philosophers alike, that with greater liberty must come greater responsibility. But platitudes often contain important truth. In these times, Liberal America seems to be ignoring an instance of that truth.

A Time of Intellectual Sloth?

There are indications that much of Liberal America is not willing to grapple with ideas. When our political weakness is due to our ideas, that unwillingness is dangerous for America's future.

I've asserted that the rescuing of America may have to begin with its secular/liberal component making changes in some of its most fundamental ideas. Such changes are never easily made, but the intellectual culture in America today may be especially difficult to engage at that level. That difficulty may be organically connected with those defects in worldview that are making Liberal America weak in this crisis.

"Americans aren't that interested in ideas anymore," my friend said. I had asked him if he'd come across any books lately that had important, new, big ideas. (Most of the big ideas I've learned are from books I encountered years ago, and I was trying to find out what I might be missing.)

My friend thought that some kinds of thinking that were more highly valued when we were growing up a half century ago no longer command interest. "People learn by watching things on videos—more immediate and concrete—not by reading ideas that make sense about big pieces of the world."

I don't know if that's true, but I have reasons for suspecting it might be. Others besides that friend have expressed the same suspicion. (For example, Azar Nafisi speaks in her recent book, *The Republic of Imagination*, of "the growing lack of respect for ideas" in America.)

And my own recent experiences of trying "to light a fire in Liberal America"—with a series of articles I called "Press the Battle" [http://pressthebattle.org/]—offer support for that proposition.

Several of the good people who wanted my effort to succeed told me that, by offering a series of essays of roughly 1000 words, I was asking too much of my readers. "People don't want to read anything so long, especially if it's densely argued," I was told. What I needed to do, they said, was package my ideas in a briefer, punchier, more attention-grabbing form.

Though we worked at it, we never did find a quick way to express the message that didn't exclude essential parts of it. Not everything can be put on a bumper-sticker. And nothing simple and punchy is going to persuade people that any of their fundamental ideas need to be reconsidered.

For my purpose, even the 1000 words each was a significant concession to the medium's requirement for brevity. Breaking the picture into pieces was a way to adapt a larger argument to the demands of the blogging world. Although each article stood on its own, what I really wanted people to do was to follow the series and see how the articles, together, presented a coherent picture of the crisis in America. (Then to act on what they saw.)

And then there were the responses (in the form of comments) that my articles elicited. These seemed to support my friend's notion that the "American mind" had become less willing to do heavy intellectual lifting. Not only did the comments show a lack of engagement with the larger picture that the pieces together presented, but the responses almost always ignored the larger assertions within each piece and focused instead on the most immediate and concrete points. It was not clear if the readers had even noticed the larger ideas.

Of course, there's probably never been a time when the mass of people were eager to spend a great deal of effort on thinking things through. But cultures evolve, and the hypothesis seems at least plausible that our culture has become intellectually lazier than it was a half century ago.

A decline in the American appetite for grappling with fundamental ideas would be a dangerous development—particularly if it is also true that the weakness in Liberal America is due to defects in some of the basic ideas by which much of Liberal/intellectual America understands the human world.

It is dangerous to be unwilling to do the tough work of the mind, when too many of us are operating with mental maps that are incapable of registering important realities in our high-stakes battle.

The Broken Image

In the American intellectual world, big and comprehensive ideas seem to be out of fashion. If winning the present battle requires Liberal America to rethink some big answers to important questions, the emphasis on fragmented rather than integrated knowledge presents an obstacle.

Intellectual sloth may not be the only problem here. Our intellectual culture may have become particularly unreceptive to *big ideas* about the human world.

Here's one piece of evidence. In the America of the 1950s and 1960s, at least two major comprehensive systems of thought—the Marxian and the Freudian—were powerful elements of the intellectual culture. Now neither of them has more than a shadow if its former standing—if they were publicly traded, they'd be penny stocks (and, in my view, Freud's "stock" is especially "oversold")—and so far as I know nothing else has taken their place.

It is true that both those systems of thought had important defects. (And both solidified into orthodoxies.) So it is understandable that thinkers today might be skeptical about any big, comparably comprehensive picture.

But the intellectual world in America today seems to go beyond skepticism about such big ideas: Would it not be accurate to say that for the most part, in intellectual circles in America today, people are not even looking for comprehensive answers? That they cannot even imagine a comprehensive picture that gives meaningful answers to the big questions?

The process of breaking the world into discrete pieces (specialties and subspecialties), decried decades ago by Floyd W. Matson in his book *The Broken Image*, has proceeded apace.

This fragmentation of knowledge presents yet another barrier to the hope I expressed (in Interlude I) that these ideas—my "integrative vision"—might do for today's crisis what *Uncle Tom's Cabin* did for the earlier version of this battle.

For it is not just that we need to rethink some ideas, but that we need to rethink some *fundamental ideas*—or at least so I have asserted—if we are to meet the challenge of these times. It is, after all, with respect to the big answers to the important questions of meaning and value, of good and evil, that liberal/secular America seems to have been found dangerously ill-equipped.

Free Thinking Doesn't Come Free

> *Established cultural traditions used to provide people essential answers to big, important questions. Our present crisis shows that those who liberate themselves from reliance on such traditional answers must take on the job of finding good answers for themselves. It's not clear how many are up for the exertions that requires.*

Almost all of humanity, through almost all of history, in cultures across the planet, have had answers to the important questions of meaning and value provided ready-made by their (mostly religious) traditions. That's been one of the most important functions of cultures: providing a deep and comprehensive understanding of the meaning of life, individually and collectively, now and from the beginning, and onward in time.

By accepting the received wisdom of the culture, the great mass of people were equipped with a comprehensive understanding (whatever its merits or defects) that answered such important questions.

But in the modern societies of the West, a substantial portion of the population—disproportionately including those with the most education, and perhaps most intelligence—has abandoned the religious traditions of our civilization.

Are we to believe that we in the modern world have no need for the kind of basic answers to fundamental questions that formed the core of human cultures throughout our history?

One might have thought so—until now. One might have thought that the cost might be only that people would live more superficial lives without any meaningful answers to the kinds of questions that religions have long answered. Maybe people's understanding of things will be fragmented and scattered in the absence of a "comprehensive understanding." But so what? People can live their decent lives, fulfill a productive role in society, raise their families, get some enjoyment out of their existence, and move on out as new generations come up.

But, in light of our times, the inadequacy of such an argument has been exposed.

Here in our times we face an evil force that is devastating everything that's best about our country, and that threatens even the integrity of the biosphere, while the mass of Americans—even those who are repelled by this thing that's arisen on the right—look out at the world where this ugly thing is clenching the face of America like an ugly toad, but apparently without really seeing it, without really grasping the "sacred" values at stake. And rather few are moved to rouse themselves to oppose it in defense of all that's good.

[NOTE Later in this book, in Chapter Nine, I will describe how our very success as a society in creating an affluent, comfortable society may have undermined the kinds of moral discipline that kept "evil forces"—always lurking in a civilization—in check. Perhaps the apparently growing disinclination of our society generally to think things through rigorously is a form of that loss of discipline. Perhaps this disinclination is a form of softness and sloth that is analogous to what was described centuries ago by the Arab historiographer Ibn Kaldhun. Kahldun suggested that successful regimes grow ripe to be conquered by the time power passes into the more pampered, less disciplined hands of the grandchildren of those regimes' tougher founders. While those weakened regimes were conquered by some new wave of marauding nomads, our power system is being overrun by an ascendant evil force.]

With liberty comes responsibility. Our founders' understanding of that connection is shown by their concept of "republican virtue." They understood that the shift they were making—from the traditional mode of governance based on a top-down authoritarian system, to one based on the expressed will of the people—a government not only *of* the people, but also *for* and *by* them—would only work if the people were willing to undertake the work involved in responsible citizenship. And that meant more than reading the papers and voting on Election Day.

Likewise with the freedom involved in liberating ourselves from the orthodox worldviews handed down through our long-standing religious traditions.

With the freedom we claim when we leave behind the heritage of our culture's religious tradition and claim the right to be our own judges of truth about the most fundamental matters, there comes the responsibility to do the work of coming up with a worldview that provides good answers to the big questions.

Some might argue that even if such a worldview is necessary, that doesn't prove it is possible. Perhaps in this post-Marxist, post-Freudian, post-modern era, the lack of any comprehensive understanding that provides good answers to important questions, they might say, is inevitable.

Intellectual responsibility certainly justifies the skepticism, but it also requires that a plausible claim to the contrary be checked out. Intellectual integrity requires that one looks through Galileo's telescope to see whether the moons that one's assumptions dictate cannot be there, are there.

In the pages that follow here, I will attempt to provide a secular path to those good answers, including a comprehensive view of the meaning of the human story. While it doesn't answer *every* important question, it does offer good answers to an important core of questions—or so I claim.

I wish this message—this picture—could be wrapped up in a quick-and-easy, punchy and attention-grabbing package, as my advisors pressed me to supply. But ideas that constitute a worldview—and in particular, ideas that might persuade people to abandon one worldview for another—are not like that. (In particular, a worldview arrived at not by received doctrine but through evidence and reason.)

For a thinking person, at least, the ideas that comprise a world view require clarification and elaboration. Ideas at the level of "worldview" are by their nature "big," which means also *abstract.*

Just as we got the famous picture of this "blue marble" we live on from the astronauts, from a vantage point far removed from the earth of our daily lives—and thereby, it is said, changed the way many of us looked at our planet (literally, a "worldview")—so also it requires a more all-encompassing and abstract perspective on the human world to answer those questions I listed on page 33.

This abstract perspective may—and should—bring in more concrete events and phenomena—things like the torture memo, the talk of "death panels," the dysfunctional performance of an obstructionist-dominated Congress, the battle over slavery, the rise of the first cities and empires, the record of colonial systems, the fungus that came to North America on the Chinese chestnut, the asteroid that hit the earth 65 millions years ago, etc. etc. But the main ideas will necessarily have a high level of abstraction.

And, I fear, the abstraction of such a big picture may not be to the taste of many of the readers I would dearly love to reach.

Big ideas entail not only a level of abstraction, but they also tend toward comprehensiveness. A useful, comprehensive view of the world—in which nearly "everything is connected to everything else"—requires that a lot of pieces be put together in order to show things whole. A comprehensive understanding of things, therefore, will require of readers that they hold these many pieces in their minds and follow the ways in which they interconnect to provide an integrated picture. That takes concentrated attention, and therefore some real work.

I worry how many readers today are up for such effort.

One last thing: if a new set of ideas is going to replace (and/or supplement) an old set of ideas, it will have to be persuasive. Admittedly, people arrive at many of their beliefs by means other than reason. And maybe it's true that people cannot be reasoned out of beliefs in which reason played no role. But the readers I am writing for do care about reason, and about what the evidence shows. And for those readers, it is my intention not only to make my case, but to make that case compelling. To make it irresistible. As much as possible to build it so that it leaves no way out.

This seems the best available way to move the mental furniture that, I believe, our nation needs for Liberal/intellectual America to move.

That intention is challenging for me. But a sustained, rigorous argument also demands exertion from the reader.

But that demand is not irrelevant to the larger task at hand. For in making that demand, I may well be going up against an important contributor to the weakness of liberal/secular culture in America.

More on that last point in "Interlude IV: Not Putting the Pieces Together."

Chapter Four:

Wholeness and Brokenness, the Patterns Fostered by Good and Evil

Life and Death, Good and Evil: Parallel Sets of Dichotomies

Underlying the battle between good and evil is a foundation of dichotomies that start with life vs. death, and work their way up to contrasting structures of wholeness and brokenness.

The evolutionary view of value presents a set of dichotomies that open a path to understanding the reality of that dichotomous drama at the core of this investigation: "the battle between good and evil."

The first dichotomy—which is at the heart of "natural selection"—is that between life and death. ("Life," here, meaning not only the survival of the immediate organism but also the perpetuation of that form of life through time.)

As we just saw in Chapter 3, out of that dichotomy emerges another: a dichotomy in the experience of creatures that have been crafted to experience as *good* (fulfilling, pleasurable) those things that have proven—during the evolutionary process that created them—to be life-serving, and as *not-good* (painful, unpleasant) those things that have been associated with a greater likelihood of death.

Yet another dichotomy can be found in the structures (or patterns) that correspond to the life-serving vs. the life-destroying. This dichotomy is between two contrasting sorts of *structure.*

Life is matter and energy that has been intricately structured in certain ways. And the system of life depends upon the transmission of those structures through time. At the biological level of life, that transmission of patterns is accomplished through DNA, which represents a blueprint for recapitulating what has worked (i.e. been good for survival) in the past.

At the level of human life, there is the additional form of transmission through culture: through the generations, cultures transmit highly complex information about how to structure human life.

We are still a few steps removed from looking at the reality of the "forces of good and evil"—where they came from, how they operate in cultural systems, etc. Good and evil as I define them are both forces, and they both work to spread patterns.

But the essential difference between good and evil involves a dichotomy in the kinds of patterns they impart onto what they contact: good spreads life-serving and creature-fulfilling (and therefore good) patterns, while evil spreads life-degrading and misery-inducing (and therefore not-good) patterns.

These two opposite kinds of patterns can be characterized in terms of opposite structures: the force of the good spreads structures that are "whole," while the force of evil spreads structures that are "broken."

Let us now develop these two concepts more fully.

WHOLENESS AND BROKENNESS AS IMPORTANT PATTERNS IN THE HUMAN SYSTEM

Biological evolution creates profound kinds of wholeness—from the cell to the biosphere. That wholeness has always been vulnerable to injury from outside the living system, and in the past 10,000 years, because evolution unfolds without a plan, a different kind of "brokenness" has emerged from within the living system. With humankind's escape from the niche in which it evolved, this disruption of the old order allowed a force of "evil" to enter the world.

By favoring life over death, the evolutionary process molds certain kinds of order. It is a reasonable approximation of the truth to say that favoring life over death means favoring order over disorder.

Surely there is a degree of order in the cosmos from the level of the quark up through the level of clusters of galaxies. But with the emergence of life, the level of ordering increases by orders of magnitude. From the organization of the atoms and molecules that make up cells, to the way many cells can together constitute a living organism, up through species, communities, ecosystems, and the biosphere, it is the essence of the living system that it crafts orders of mind-blowing intricacy.

(Just imagine a time-lapse film of the earth from its original lifeless condition, through the course by which, over the past 3.5 billion years, this incredible order of life has unfolded upon this ball of matter suspended in space and orbiting this star.)

The life-serving order that the evolutionary process favors can be said to have the property of "Wholeness." "Wholeness" can be defined, for starters, in terms of "things fitting together well." It's about interconnectedness, about things rightly ordered. Right ordering at all the levels of the living system from smaller than the cell to the global flows of matter and energy.

While patterns of "Wholeness" are life-serving, "Brokenness," by contrast, is the opposite. Brokenness involves the absence or destruction of those patterns or structures that serve life and thus serve the fulfillment of living creatures.

Wholeness vs. Brokenness is another way of talking about the same set of realities as life-serving vs. life-degrading or good vs. evil. (With something as subtle and complex as "the battle between good and evil" it is useful to look at the same thing across various dimensions.) It is through the movement and transmission of certain kinds of patterns that we can discern the reality of the forces of good and evil.

Two components of "wholeness" in the systems of life can be called "synergy" and "viability."

Synergy. The evolution of life appears to have operated in a completely opportunistic fashion, without a plan or purposefulness in its unfolding. Where there's a niche that can be occupied by a predator, or a parasite, or pathogen, the opportunistic evolutionary process is likely to fill it.

Nonetheless, the tendency of evolution is to create synergistic patterns of interaction among the elements of a living system. In a synergistic interaction, each part functions in a way that tends to enhance the welfare of the other parts as well as its own. Even the relationship between predator and prey evolves over time to serve not only the predator, but the prey as well.

[NOTE: A recent article in *Science News*—"Lopped Off: Removal of top predators trickles through the food web," Science News, November 5, 2011, pp. 26-29—shows how eliminating predators hurts the system as a whole.]

What works, survives. What doesn't work, gets weeded out. Hence even the antagonistic relationships tend, over time, to operate within a larger context in which the system as a whole can be perpetuated.

2) *Viability.* A system has the second component—"viability"—to the extent that it is able to maintain, without diminution, whatever it is upon which the system's continued existence depends. A viable system does not eat itself out of house and home, does not foul its own nest, does not contain unsustainable practices.

The tendency of life to foster systemic wholeness—whether that system be a cell or the biosphere—is inseparable from the evolutionary preference (through the selective process) for life over death.

It's no innovation of mine to connect an idea of "wholeness" to the nature of the systems toward which life strives. The word "health" is etymologically rooted in the idea of "wholeness." A body can be healthy, or whole, and so can an ecosystem, even up to the global system of life. Life consists of an elaborate order of wholeness, and in medicine many of those things that cause a breakdown of health are called "disorders."

Clearly, however, there's nothing perfect about the order that has emerged here on earth. Suffering has been part of life as long as there have been creatures that feel. The course of life's development has been marked by waves of extinctions. And then there's the history of civilized humankind, with all the brokenness it displays.

How are we to understand these major aspects of disorder? How does "brokenness" enter into the system of life, which I've said is characterized by the establishment of patterns of "Wholeness"? And how does this brokenness relate to the issue of "evil" as a force that consistently transmits a pattern of brokenness into the human world?

Three Very Different Sources of Disorder

"Evil" is but one of three sources of the brokenness to which life is vulnerable, and it is the most recent in origin.

Three main sources of disorder can be identified. Only the third of these is connected with the force I'm calling "evil."

First, disorder—or brokenness—can enter the system of life from outside the realm of life, i.e. from those workings of the cosmos that preceded life and still lie beyond its control. Life has established a powerful presence on this planet. But life emerged out of a "cold" and (apparently) lifeless universe. That vast non-living world, with its own great forces at work, has by no means disappeared.

For example, a massive object streaming from the cold, lifeless realms of outer space might slam into our planet, devastating major parts of the wholeness of the living system. This seems to be what happened some 65 million years ago, rendering the dinosaurs and much else extinct.

Nor does the system of life control the movement of the earth's tectonic plates. Thus some millions of years ago, the two continents of the Americas, floating on the earth's outer surface, drifted into contact—at the isthmus of Panama—bringing together two previously-separated communities of animal life. These two communities had not evolved any life-serving order between them, and thus their sudden combination produced disorder, and a resulting wave of extinctions.

Likewise with earthquakes and tsunamis that occasionally wreak devastation on particular areas on into our times.

Such forces from outside the living system may be said to impart brokenness to the biological order, but they have nothing to do with what I am calling "evil." Unlike some who imagined that the catastrophic earthquake that devastated Lisbon in the 18th century was a punitive act of God, I accept the scientific worldview according to which these are, impersonal things that just happen. These kinds of forces involve no systematic "working" to impart brokenness, no exploitation of brokenness in the human world, no malevolent face that accompanies its expression.

Brokenness of this sort, as we will see, is unlike the force that has arisen from within the human system to spread brokenness onto whatever it touches.

A second source of brokenness—one mentioned above and one that should also be differentiated from that force of brokenness called "evil"—is the result of the wholly opportunistic nature of the evolutionary process. Because the workings of evolution are not, so far as one can see, directed by any benevolent force, biological evolution does not create a world where the lion will lie down with the lamb, except to make dinner of it.

Hence, rather than the wholeness of some utopian vision, the purely opportunistic process of evolution gives us predators and parasites living at the expense of other organisms. One creature's meat is inevitably another creature.

Nonetheless, as was said above, the process of biological evolution works over time to create a synergistic order to contain the conflictual elements in the system within an overarching wholeness. The wolf may be cruel, but when it kills the lamb, the death of the lamb is not an injury to lambkind. It is part of the pattern of survival not only for wolves but for the sheep as well. If there were no wolves, the sheep would overgraze the land, and before long the foundation on which the lives of the sheep rests would be undermined.

A pattern of wholeness has evolved over time to serve the perpetuation of the whole.

The American chestnut was virtually obliterated from the North American forests, in which they played so important a role, when the Chinese chestnut was suddenly introduced onto the American continent. The Chinese chestnut carried with it a fungus. While the American variety of chestnut was devastated by the sudden arrival of that fungus, the Chinese version of the chestnut and the fungus had evolved over millions of years a relationship that allowed them to co-exist.

As the ecologist Gregory Bateson once wrote: "No creature wins against its environment for long."

So given enough time, the parasitism of the fungus, like the predation of the wolf, gets contained in a larger wholeness.

The system of life is constantly evolving, with the tendency to protect the life of the whole and its parts.

It is true at one level that nature is "red in tooth and claw," and that suffering is inflicted in the natural order. But the "red in tooth and claw" level is embedded in a larger wholeness that differentiates it from the kind of brokenness that warrants being called evil.

Where "evil" enters the picture is through another, related property of the evolutionary process. The apparent fact that evolution proceeds without a plan has had the effect of opening the door for something to emerge out of the living system that is altogether new and that carries problematic long-term implications.

Over the past 10,000 years, humankind has demonstrated the peril that can result from that lack of forethought in life's evolution.

A creature with the intelligence and adaptability to create culture, and then eventually to utilize that capacity for culture to escape from the niche in which it evolved biologically and create an altogether new way of life—indeed, a new form of life—will inevitably unleash forces that it could not have anticipated and that it could not then control.

Showing how this is so will be the task of Chapter Five."

INTERLUDE IV:

Not Putting the Pieces Together

Two phenomena in Liberal America share a common root: the inability to see the "evil force" that's before our eyes, and the lack of interest in comprehensive ideas. Both connect with the mental habit of seeing the world just in pieces, rather than seeing things whole.

Interlude II ended with the idea that in trying to move my hoped-for readerships in Liberal America with a book like this—one that not only employs ideas, but ideas that are abstract, and that integrate many pieces into a comprehensive picture—"I may well be going up against a part of liberal/secular culture in America that has contributed to our weakness."

Here's an important dimension of that.

Two problems have been described: the failure of much of Liberal America to see the "evil force" that's right in front of our eyes; and the lack not only of comprehensive ideas, but even of a quest for such comprehensive understanding. These are not two different problems, but two different aspects of the same phenomenon.

Both phenomena represent a lack of wholeness of vision.

In the first chapter, in the section titled "The Republican Party's Extraordinary Pattern of Destructiveness," I listed various aspects of that party's conduct in recent years and then asked "What is it that expresses itself in all these ways?"

It is a question that is crucial to seeing our reality. But it is also one, as I said then, that is too little asked. Indeed, hardly asked at all.

The failure to ask it is not only a failure to see things whole. It is also a reflection of a mental habit in Liberal America not to think in terms of seeing things whole. This neglect of the dimension of interconnectedness is itself a kind of brokenness.

This is part of the same "broken image"—the lack of interest in comprehensive ideas—in which the world is beheld in (much of) the secular/liberal/intellectual world.

Our world is one of dense interconnectedness and vast forces. To be content with understanding our world just in myriad discrete pieces condemns us to being cut off from some of the most fundamental meanings of our existence.

And to be thus cut off is part of the same brokenness that has kept Liberal America from tapping into those deep moral and spiritual passions that could enable us to confront and defeat the evil force that's so gravely damaging all that's best—and sacred—in our nation.

CHAPTER FIVE:

HOW THE RISE OF CIVILIZATION MAKES INEVITABLE A "BATTLE BETWEEN GOOD AND EVIL"

HOW BROKENNESS EMERGED IN THE HUMAN SYSTEM

If we look at each emerging civilized society in isolation, it appears that the breakthrough into civilization gave humankind the freedom to invent its own way of life. But when we look at a multiplicity of such societies—compelled to act under the circumstance of an unprecedented kind of anarchy—we see how that apparent freedom actually brings a new kind of bondage.

For three and a half billion years, life evolved in such a way that each creature followed its own inborn law, but that law had been shaped by a process that tended to create a certain kind of Wholeness. From the single cell to the planetary biosphere, a process generated by chance in combination with natural selection crafted systems that work for the perpetuation of life.

Even the conflictual elements in the biological system get incorporated into an order that serves the whole.

(That was the theme of the discussion of "synergy" and "viability" in Chapter Four.)

Then came the unprecedented, problematic breakthrough.

That breakthrough was not the emergence of human intelligence, although that made it possible. Nor was it the emergence of culture, though that too made this disruption possible. Human intelligence and culture had long been present without greatly altering the basic structure of human life and our species' place in the ecological order.

The portentous breakthrough—the real point of discontinuity—occurred when human cultural development crossed the threshold into "civilization." By "civilization," I mean those forms of human culture that represented a breakout from the niche in which we had evolved, i.e. from hunting and gathering into the domestication of plants and animals and all the other changes those innovations made possible.

It took many, many generations for the revolutionary implications of the breakthrough in food production—re-organizing the ecosystem to serve human needs better, rather than living off what nature spontaneously provides—to manifest. Nonetheless, this breakthrough marked a decisive break in the history of life on earth: it made human societies the first living entities whose size and structure and *modus operandi* were not given in their biologically evolved blueprint. Human beings became the first creatures to invent their own way of life.

> [NOTE: Rather than saying that the creature "breaks through into civilization," it would probably be more accurate to say that it "stumbles into civilization," as none of the actors making this momentous shift likely had any idea that the tiny changes made in their lifetime—planting a few seeds here, putting a few animals in a pen there—represented anything momentous in the history of life on earth.]

Here we come upon a profoundly tragic irony: the freedom to invent one's own way of life sounds to us modern dwellers in liberal societies like an unmitigated blessing. But, paradoxically, that apparent freedom ushered in a new and harsh form of bondage.

I'm talking about something more than the comparatively benign way that a creature places itself in a potentially uncomfortable position by transforming the nature and structure of its life from what it had been during the prior eons of biological evolution. But let's begin with these relatively small potatoes.

Such is the evolutionary process that **for every other creature, expressing its inborn nature is generally an optimal strategy for getting**

its needs met. (That's why those needs evolved: they motivate those behaviors that, in the niche in which the creature's ancestors evolved, were most likely to lead to a successful outcome.)

But for the creature that has escaped from the niche in which its ancestors evolved, and has invented its own way of life, there will almost certainly be some mismatch between doing what comes naturally and doing what the new environment will reward.

Thus with some regularity we hear about such mismatches, e.g. how shift workers throw off their bodily rhythms because their times of activity no longer correspond to the diurnal cycle of day and night, how our living in situations of chronic stress for which our inborn flight/fight response is not adaptive creates health problems (raising our blood pressure, etc.).

Much could be said along the lines of, "Our bodies evolved to live *that* way, but our civilized life requires us to live *this* way." Indeed, awareness of that kind of problem is reasonably well established in the general culture.

But that problem, though important, is the least of our worries. An intelligent creature, we might reasonably assume, would make reasonable cost/benefit analyses in making its choices. If, that is, it were truly free to choose its destiny.

Here we come to the tragedy that has befallen humankind. The ability to invent its own way of life only appears to grant the creative creature a new kind of freedom. At another, more fundamental level, that freedom gets turned into a new kind necessity creating a new kind of pain and brokenness.

Let me show in two steps how an inevitable reign of power brought brokenness into the human system.

A New Kind of Anarchy and the Struggle for Power

The unprecedented breakthrough into civilization inevitably entailed a new kind of anarchy. And that anarchy inevitably condemned the innovative creature to an unstoppable struggle for power, a war of all against all.

If one form of wholeness in the natural (i.e. biologically evolved) order is that every creature is rewarded (statistically speaking) for behaving naturally, a second form of wholeness is that the interactions among the various actors in the system are "regulated" to provide for the synergy and viability of the system as a whole.

By "regulated," I don't mean in a top-down way, as a federal agency regulates its domain. Rather, the wholeness of the overall interactive pattern just gets built into the system. As was said above: Each creature follows its own "law," but that law itself has been written by an evolutionary process that secures the orderliness of the overarching system of life.

The rise of civilization marks a serious discontinuity in the history of life on earth because it represents an escape from that order.

An escape from the constraints of the old order into a trap of new kind of disorder.

If we look at one such society by itself, what we see is a "freedom to invent its own way of life." But if we look at a multiplicity of such societies, we find that a grave and inescapable problem has arisen.

These societies will have to interact with each other, as from the outset these societies emerged in clusters. (In all the places where civilization arose independently rather than being transplanted from elsewhere (e.g. Mesopotamia, the Nile Valley, the Indus Valley, the Yellow River valley, Mesoamerica, and Peru), it developed through clusters of independent societies budding up within relatively circumscribed areas of land. [Cf. Julian Steward, *Theory of Culture Change.*])

But here's the problem: *There is nothing to regulate the interactions among this new kind of living entities, these civilized societies.*

These societies—unlike primate bands and hunting-gathering societies, and unlike ant or bee societies—have had no "law" inscribed in them by the process of biological evolution. These new forms of human society have been invented through the cultural processes of these intelligent creatures. So there is nothing in the *biological order* to make sure that their interactions serve any life-enhancing purpose.

Nor is there any *order of human creation* to regulate their interactions. How could there be? The system is too fragmented to be governed.

These societies, of this new kind, are just springing up, and nothing is in place to make sure that the various actors act in a way that is compatible with the needs of the whole system. Indeed, all these millennia later, this problem of order in the system of civilized societies remains unsolved.

Life, whose specialty has been the creation of order, has thus stumbled into a dangerously anarchic situation.

We have a new living entity—the civilized society—coming up in clusters, inevitably compelled to interact in a kind of anarchy unprecedented in the history of life.

The English philosopher Thomas Hobbes rightly described the inevitable consequences of anarchy: a war of all against all.

We have witnessed, in our times, what are the terrible fruits of such anarchy—the breakdown of Lebanon in the 1980s, and that in Somalia since the early 1990s—and it is clear what ensues. Anarchy is violent and bloody and traumatic. It empowers warlords and victimizes almost everyone else.

All of us living in contemporary America may give thanks that we have not been living in a Lebanon or Somalia kind of anarchy. But we are the victims of anarchy nonetheless, for we are heirs to a history—in the interactive system of civilized societies—in which this anarchy has been a central factor in the drama of civilization, and it has left a huge mark on us as a species.

That mark would be traumatic enough—the brokenness that this anarchy has brought into the human world would be devastating enough—if the chronic problem of "war of all against all" were all there is to be said about the tragic irony of the breakthrough into civilization.

But the most destructive element in the picture is yet to come.

THE INEVITABLE SPREAD OF THE WAYS OF POWER: THE PARABLE OF THE TRIBES

Anarchy among civilized societies made a struggle for power inevitable. That struggle for power, combined with the open-ended possibilities for cultural innovation, meant the intersocietal competition would generate a process of selection for those cultural ways that maximize power. Thus the overall direction of the evolution of civilization was determined by an unchosen circumstance—an inevitable anarchy—rather than being something humankind chose.

As a result of this intersocietal anarchy, and of the chronic struggle for power that inevitably ensues from it, the rise of civilization inevitably generates a second evolutionary process.

And this second evolutionary process, overlaid on top of the first and *in important ways not in harmony with it*, inevitably imparts to the systems of the civilized creature *an impetus of brokenness.*

Let me describe how that is so.

This second evolutionary principle operates in a manner analogous to that of biological evolution. In Darwin's brilliant and elegant insight, two ingredients are sufficient to drive the evolutionary process: one is the existence of a variety of types, while the other is a non-random selective process among the types.

In biological evolution, the variety is provided by the process of genetic mutation. And then "natural selection" automatically sifts through the available forms and perpetuates those that are able to survive and pass along their genetic heritage, while eliminating those that fail to do so.

In this new evolutionary process, the variety is provided by cultural innovation. That sounds benign. New things come along, and the "best" get kept, right? Like the process that generates the wonders of Chinese cuisine.

But the problem comes in with the selective process.

The anarchy of the intersocietal system, it was said above, inevitably leads to the Hobbesean "war of all against all." And this struggle for power means the spread of the ways of the winners and the elimination of the ways of the losers.

Meanwhile, the breakthrough into civilization has meant open-ended possibilities for cultural innovation. No longer constrained by the limits—e.g. in the size and structure of societies—of the hunting/gathering bands whose structure traced back to before we were human, these new societies could develop new ways of operating almost limitlessly: new forms in political organization, in technology, in economic structure, in the mentality of its people, etc.

When some societies are successful in the intersocietal competition, and others are eliminated, it is not just specific societies that triumph but certain ways of organizing human socio-cultural life. Other cultural possibilities get eliminated. Not by human choice, but as a function of the unchosen, unregulated, over-arching system.

The triumphant forms of civilized society that are most successful in the struggle for power are not necessarily those that are best for people. What survives and spreads are the ways of power. They are, by definition, whatever it takes to succeed in that intersocietal power struggle.

And that struggle, it should be recalled, is an interactive pattern not fashioned by any overarching order that assures the wholeness—the synergy and viability—of the creature's system as a whole.

Over the centuries and millennia, the selection for the ways of power will determine which of the wide range of possibilities for civilized societies will be chosen by the system to shape the human future:

- the war-like may eliminate the peaceful;
- the ambitious overtake the content;
- the iron-makers those with copper or no metallurgy at all;
- the horsemen over the unmounted;
- those with effective central control over those with more casual power structures and local autonomy;
- those driven by a harsh work ethic over those oriented toward the enjoyment of life; etc.
- those able and willing to exploit nature fully over those who treat the wholeness of nature with respect.

The selection for the ways of power has a comprehensive impact on the shaping of civilized societies, because the power of a society is a function of virtually every dimension of that society's culture: political, technological, economic, a socio-cultural, psychological…

And moreover, the narrowing of cultural possibilities for human beings is more dramatic than one might first imagine, because *the ways of power spread in the system like a contaminant.*

All it takes is one society bent on predation and expansion at the expense of its neighbors, and the ways of power will spread throughout the system. Here, from in my previously discussed book *The Parable of the Tribes: The Problem of Power in Social Evolution*, is a description of how power acts as a contaminant in the system that emerged with civilization:

> "Imagine a group of tribes living within reach of one another. If all choose the way of peace, then all may live in peace. But what if all but one choose peace, and that one is ambitious for expansion and conquest? What can happen to the others when confronted by an ambitious and potent neighbor? Perhaps one

> tribe is attacked and defeated, its people destroyed and its lands seized for the use of the victors. Another is defeated, but this one is not exterminated; rather, it is subjugated and transformed to serve the conqueror. A third seeking to avoid such disaster flees from the area into some inaccessible (and undesirable) place, and its former homeland becomes part of the growing empire of the power-seeking tribe. Let us suppose that others observing these developments decide to defend themselves in order to preserve themselves and their autonomy. But the irony is that successful defense against a power-maximizing aggressor requires a society to become more like the society that threatens it. Power can be stopped only by power, and if the threatening society has discovered ways to magnify its power through innovations in organization or technology (or whatever), the defensive society will have to transform itself into something more like its foe in order to resist the external force.
>
> "I have just outlined four possible outcomes for the threatened tribes: destruction, absorption and transformation, withdrawal, and imitation. In every one of these outcomes the ways of power are spread throughout the system. This is the theory I call "the parable of the tribes."

Given the emergence of civilization, this selection for power is inevitable. It is an outgrowth of the inevitably unregulated interactions among these living entities of an altogether new kind.

This is why the course of social evolution, from hunting-gathering bands all the way up to the emergence of empires, traced profoundly similar paths in all those places, previously mentioned, where civilization first emerged in its pristine form in the Old World and the New.

The creature that breaks through into civilization will inevitably, without its so choosing, have its world and its way of life determined not by its own choice but by the properties of the (anarchic) system that it has unwittingly and unintentionally brought into existence.

The breakthrough to civilization—which appeared to be a grant of freedom to choose among countless cultural possibilities—inevitably channels humankind and its societies in a particular, unchosen direction.

[NOTE: This quick articulation of the idea I'm calling "the parable of the tribes" as a way of explaining much of the overall evolution of civilization, and in particular why it has unfolded in as destructive and tormented a way as it has, is developed throughout *The Parable of the Tribes*. Also, the first chapter* of that book—laying out the main idea—can be found in the "More Depth" collection of articles on the web at whatweareupagainst.org]

Two Implications of the Inevitable Selection for the Ways of Power

The overall direction in which civilization has evolved—toward power maximization—was inevitable, and not a reflection of the inherent nature of our species. Any other creature on this or any other planet that crossed the threshold into civilization would get swept up into that same agonizing social evolutionary process.

This was inevitable. If a creature broke through into civilization, it would inevitably if unwittingly be plunged into anarchy in the overarching system. So long as such anarchy continued in the intersocietal system, there would be a struggle for power among the societies. So long as there was a struggle for power, combined with the open-ended possibilities for cultural innovation, it was inevitable that the human societies that survived and spread would be those best able to generate the power necessary to prevail in the struggle. Thus, it was inevitable that the direction of the evolution of that creature's civilization would be toward the ways of power.

It's a pretty grim picture.

At the same time, however, this inevitability has an important and profoundly hopeful implication: the course of the evolution of civilization, and therefore also fundamental aspects of the course of human history, is thus more fundamentally a reflection of the dynamics of the system than of the nature of the creature caught up in those inescapable dynamics.

Any creature whose creativity enabled it to cross that threshold—into creating an entirely new, more productive way of harnessing the productivity of its natural environment—would have found itself inadvertently plunging into the same kind of social evolutionary process, ruled by power.

Any creature capable of escaping the niche in which it evolved biologically is, by definition, a cultural animal. And it is in the nature of a cultural animal that it can be molded by its surrounding culture into a very wide range of forms. So any creature caught up in a social evolutionary process like that described by the parable of the tribes has an inherent flexibility that enables a society to shape it to fit the society's requirements. *Thus, societies that are themselves shaped by the demands of power can turn the civilized creature into something far removed from the natural unfolding of its inborn nature.*

If humankind eventually blows it, and disappears from this earth, and then in millions of years the descendants of, say, raccoons have developed the intelligence and then the culture to break through into civilization, they too will inevitably be condemned to the painful and in many ways ugly course that human history has taken these past 10,000 years. Likewise, if another life form—on some other planet someplace else in the cosmos—crosses that crucial threshold out of its biologically evolved niche, it too would have to contend with "the parable of the tribes" and all its tormenting implications.

Human History, Therefore, Must Not be Interpreted as Human Nature Writ Large

If the nightmarish quality of the history of civilization has been inevitable, that offers an important ray of hope. We are likely much better creatures by nature than we imagine, and that our culture has told us we are. And if we can control the destructive forces we unwittingly unleashed, we can create a far better civilization.

Whatever we might determine to be the natural tendencies of human beings, they cannot be inferred from what civilization has molded us to be. ANY creature, caught up in such social evolutionary forces, would inevitably show in its history a face far uglier—crazier, more broken, more wounded—than its natural being. Wounded first by the inevitable struggle for power, and wounded second by having to adapt to societies shaped by the demands of power, often in important ways indifferent (or even hostile) to the needs of the human creature.

This logic not only explains the human tragedy, but it also provides an important ray of hope.

Would it not be a source of great hope to know that the nightmare of our history is not an indictment of human nature? That the ugliness and brutality that feature so prominently in the story of our kind can be explained without reference to what we are inclined to be by nature?

Is it not hopeful that, as we might be far better creatures than our history suggests, we might well be equipped to create a civilization on this planet far more beautiful, more just, more loving—more whole—than we have created so far? *Might* be able to, that is, if only we can bring under control the forces of brokenness that we've unleashed. For these are what we've been up against for millennia, and *what we're up against still.*

So there's good news. But the task is still before us to deal with the dilemma into which our ancestors stumbled millennia ago.

We can approach that task, however, with compassion for our wounded species, and with greater clarity about the challenge we must meet. For all these millennia of human history, we as a species have found ourselves in what was bound to be an impossible situation. But what was inevitable for the civilized creature from the outset need not remain inevitable—not if we understand the nature of the dynamic that we must bring under control.

In that context, let us turn to the second implication of "the parable of the tribes": how the impetus of brokenness that inevitably accompanied the emergence of civilization has reverberated through the millennia, transmitting a pattern of brokenness from level to level in the human world.

Deep Throat famously said, "Follow the money." Let us now "Follow the pattern."

"Evil" was defined earlier as a force that imparts a pattern of brokenness to everything it contacts. The next chapter will make clearer how the brokenness that entered the human world with the emergence of civilization became a force of that kind. I will clarify how that force perpetuates itself through the transmission of the pattern of brokenness.

That will also help clarify the nature of what we are up against in America today.

Interlude V:

We Are Naturally Drawn to Wholeness

Without attempting to make any definitive statements about the good or evil in human nature, I can offer several kinds of evidence that suggest that our natural affinity is for Wholeness, not brokenness.

In the history of our civilization, our religious traditions have delivered upon our species some harshly damning verdicts. "Original sin" is one such condemnatory judgment. Calvinist notions of human "depravity" is yet another.

This, I say, is a bum rap.

History, I hope I demonstrated in Chapter Five, is not human nature writ large. That is a major implication of the idea just presented, "the parable of the tribes." It is inevitable that any creature—anywhere in the cosmos—who breaks out of its biologically-evolved niche to develop civilization will have its societies shaped by a selection for the ways of power. Out of the many possible directions for such a creature's cultural development, this social evolutionary force mandates that only a particular power-serving direction is open for the creature's evolving civilization.

With the creature's flexibility, as a cultural animal, thus exploited, it will be twisted in wounding ways, still further distorting the picture it presents from a true portrait of its nature.

So, if our monstrous history does not prove an inherent monstrousness in humankind, how should we conceive human nature to be? How should we think of the elements of good and evil in it?

After more than 40 years of wrestling with this question—besides in *The Parable of the Tribes*, it is also a central issue explored in my 1999 book, *Debating the Good Society*—I do not feel able to proclaim any definitive judgment. (The picture of other primates and of prehistoric hunters and gatherers seems to have been darkened by more recent studies, compared to what I encountered when I researched these areas in the 1970s.)

But here are several pieces of evidence that support the proposition that, in the contest between the forces of wholeness and those of brokenness, we are naturally inclined toward wholeness.

Exhibit A: in the choice between life and death—and it is this basic choice made by natural selection that undergirds the dichotomies between wholeness and brokenness, good and evil—we humans overwhelmingly side with life. We instinctively exert ourselves with all our strength when our own life is in danger. We consider death a "mercy" only in the exceptional circumstances when the conditions of life are so terribly degraded (e.g. by profound and incurable suffering) that it has become of negative value.

When someone develops an infatuation with death, as Hitler did, and when the Spanish fascists toasted "Vive La Morte," we recognize that this is a symptom of something damaged in the human spirit. Is not "L'chaim" (to life) the toast that the overwhelming majority of people would prefer?

And why would we not prefer life to death, shaped as we are by a process that continually chooses what survives over what does not?

Exhibit B, in the form of a thought experiment: Imagine presenting people two portraits of a world to live in. One is characterized by justice and peace, love and beauty, honesty and health, and a thriving natural world. The other is the opposite—injustice and war, hate and ugliness, deception and sickness, and a degraded natural world. What proportion of people would choose the brokenness of the latter? Vanishingly few, I would wager.

And I would bet further that this preference would not be just self-interested, a choice made because people recognize that it is more fulfilling to live in a whole world than a broken one. If one tweaked the question and asked people how they would like for the world to be in a century's time—when they themselves would presumably not be around to experience the advantages of the better or the disadvantages of the worse—I would again wager that the overwhelming majority of people would choose for the people who come after them to live in a world where wholeness—peace and love and justice etc.—flourished, rather than their opposites.

Would you not predict likewise? And if that's so, does that not bespeak a natural human preference for wholeness?

Exhibit C is about the "pathways" that lead to fulfillment. And it comes from my own experience. (The science I believe in regards our personal experience as an important—and in some important ways irreplaceable—form of evidence.)

In the previously mentioned essay,* "Our Pathways into the Experience of Deep Meaning," I describe the three episodes in my life that brought me the most spiritual awakening and fulfillment.

When I wrote that essay, in 2004, I was still in the midst of one of those experiences. This one I described as "living with deeper *integrity*." And I had just come to a realization that this experience had something important in common with those other two previous times of spiritual awakening.

One of these previous experiences came about primarily by my having opened up to a deep experience of open-hearted *love* which sustained me through great fear. Another time the pathway into the experience involved recognizing the *sacred beauty* of earth's living systems and of the natural creature at the core of each of us.

It struck me that of these "pathways" were all forms of "Wholeness." (Wholeness being defined, as in Chapter Four, as things fitting together rightly, in harmony, in an ideal unity.)

There was something else in my experience that struck me with great force: this idea of "Wholeness" seemed a reality, not "just an abstraction," in view of how these "different forms of Wholeness" showed themselves to be aspects of the same thing. Let me share here what I experienced.

> As I moved into a place of deeper integrity, I noticed a significant shift in my entire spiritual condition. My engagement with people became more open-hearted; my sense of beauty intensified (I began hearing music, for example, like Beethoven's 7th Symphony, at a deeper level); my connection with my wife as a lover became fuller; my capacity for insight into the vast web of interconnections of cause and effect in our incredibly complex world became newly ignited.

> I became, in other words, spiritually much more alive. And I was struck by the fact that it seemed that going down any one of these pathways of Wholeness would make all the other paths more open to me.
>
> It seemed, indeed, as though all the paths fed each other. The more I opened my eyes to beauty, the more I opened my heart to love; the more I came from the core of my being, the more I devoted myself to the path of righteousness, the more I opened my mind to encompassing insight, the more I saw the beauty of it all. I was reminded of something I'd noticed when I was much younger– that when I fell in love, the flowers seemed markedly more beautiful.
>
> Reflecting on these different episodes of spiritual deepening in my life, I was struck with this thought: even though they had emerged from entirely different directions, they all seemed to lead toward very nearly the same place! The pattern of my experience suggested an "all roads lead to Rome" image of the spiritual terrain….
>
> It seems that the further one goes down any one of these pathways—beauty, or love, or integrity, or insight, etc.– the more they disclose themselves as aspects of the same thing.
>
> And that "same thing" seems to be Wholeness….

I don't know what this—the convergence of the pathways of Wholeness, and the deep fulfillment that comes from aligning oneself with Wholeness—says about the reality beyond ourselves. (This picture does seem to have some more than superficial kinship with much that is embedded in some of the world's religions.) But my experience—and I see no reason not to consider myself, in this respect, as representative of humankind—does say something important about the reality within us.

It strongly suggests to me that, at the deepest level, our natural allegiance and affinity is to Wholeness. And that alignment with that Wholeness offers us our deepest fulfillment.

Our experiences in the world can of course break us in ways that lead us to offer a toast to death, to seek abusive relationships, to be filled with rage, to be incapable of honesty, etc. But the existence of diseases does not undermine our bodies' inborn tendency to strive toward health.

CHAPTER SIX:

THE TRANSMISSION —THROUGH TIME— OF PATTERNS IN THE HUMAN WORLD

We live our lives in the immediate and the concrete. One thing after another. That's where our awareness most readily settles.

Even the newspapers, though looking at a bigger picture than our personal lives, are snapshots more concrete and close to our accustomed scale of life than what is presented in the history books. Of course, more people read the newspaper than the history books. And of the history books, it is the biographies—the pictures presented at the scale of the individual human life—that get the biggest readership. Certainly not the "theories of history," which attempt to describe the overall principles—at a still higher level of abstraction—that govern the movements of societies through time.

It would be convenient if all the understanding we need could be obtained by looking only at the numerous and various concrete phenomena we perceive and experience. It would be convenient because they are what we are best able to see, and most inclined to attend to. Putting the pieces together into a larger picture comes less naturally, and poses more of an intellectual challenge.

But our world is not made up of discrete, disconnected pieces. And it cannot be understood on those terms. (See more on this in Chapter Ten, "The Reality of the Abstract.")

Just as the DNA of a single individual can tell a story about whole peoples. Just as the recent finding from a 29,000 year-old bone from a boy in northeastern Asia reveals that European peoples mixed their genes with Asiatic peoples long before previously thought. So too do the various immediate things that we see contain within them clues about larger patterns and forces at work in the human world.

(The need to follow those clues is especially pressing in these stark times.)

The level of the concrete is real. But so are the forces and patterns that move through the system in which the concrete is embedded and, as they move, shape the concrete world before our eyes.

The Persistence of Culture

Just as our DNA transmits patterns through the generations, so also do the patterns of cultures persist powerfully through time.

The whole of the living system operates through the transmission of patterns. For all living things, DNA provides a blueprint of which the organism is an expression. Evolution shows that change takes place over time, but perhaps more remarkable is the extent to which the pattern is preserved in the transmission. Humans still have rudimentary tails, and the skeleton of the whale still shows the metacarpals of terrestrial mammals, retaining in vestigial form the template from which our hands also are constructed.

For one of earth's species—the human—a second layer of patterns has been added to the first: the patterns of culture.

Again, cultures evolve, but perhaps more remarkable is the extent to which cultures maintain their main patterns. Generations of individuals come and go, each socialized into the culture in a manner that allows (or compels) the individuals not only to function within the cultural system, but also to become transmitters of the established cultural pattern into the future.

Here's a dramatic, albeit relatively trivial, illustration of this perpetuation process:

In the north of New Mexico, it was discovered in our times that there were people who still lit candles every Friday evening at sundown, but had no idea why they did it. It was something that their parents had done, and so they preserved the tradition. It turns out that these people are the descendants of Jews from Spain via Mexico who were compelled to conceal their Jewish observance and to maintain the pretense of being Christian. Now, centuries later, their descendants—good Catholics by now, I would guess– are still lighting candles on Friday evenings.

More important examples of the transmission of a cultural pattern can be found in the discernible limits encountered in the efforts of revolutionaries to reject the old ways, to make a clean break, to create the altogether new.

It has been observed, for example, that the rulers that emerged out of the Russian Revolution—Stalin in particular—functioned in many ways like the Czars of the old regime they had overthrown. Something similar occurred with the Chinese revolution. Led by Mao Tse-Teng, that revolution attempted to extirpate much of Chinese tradition. But analysts of Communist China back during Mao's reign noted how profoundly Confucian, in many ways, was his way of ruling. And now, with the Maoist system dismantled in many ways by Mao's heirs, the classical Confucian works are best sellers in China.

> Here's another example from the cultural history of China: For many centuries, China was the dominant civilization in the area of the world in which it operated. This experience of power and status generated in the Chinese culture—in the minds of its people— the sense of Chinese civilization as the Center of the World, the Middle Kingdom, superior to all other cultures. What is amazing, in terms of the persistence of culture, is how that feeling survived in China even through many generations of disintegration, and humiliation, and subordination to foreign powers. The idea remained intact, ready to reassert itself.

This is not to deny change. But only to emphasize "the persistence of culture." Culture can persist because patterns are powerful forces—even though they are "abstracted" from "the immediate and concrete" right before our eyes.

The power of patterns is important for understanding just about everything in the living world and, more specifically, in the human world. Patterns are especially important for understanding the forces of "good" and "evil" in the human world—each of these being defined earlier as something "coherent" that operates "through time" and works at "spreading a pattern."

Let us focus in particular on the force of evil.

The Transmission of the Patterns of Brokenness

Having a second evolutionary process ("the parable of the tribes) overlaid on the first (biological evolution)—with the two not being altogether in harmony—creates a kind of brokenness. So also do the traumatic consequences of the inevitable struggle for power.

Patterns have to do with structure. In particular, we're interested in the patterns that form the structure of civilized human life. Forces are the mechanisms by which these structures get formed and transmitted through time.

We humans are transmitters of two important kinds of patterns. With our DNA, we transmit our genetic heritage. And, as said above, we are the species on which a second layer has been added: we transmit our cultural heritage.

But as "the parable of the tribes" showed (in the previous chapter), at a crucial point in our cultural evolution, that second layer brought with it a kind of disorder.

It is not that culture per se brought this disorder—not the emergence of language, nor the use of tools, nor the control of fire. The archaeological record reveals that our ancestors developed all those aspects of culture long, long before culture became problematic with the emergence, along with civilization, of a new evolutionary dynamic.

It was only when culture started to fundamentally alter the basic structure of how humans live (about 10,000 years ago) that the human system absorbed a great impetus of brokenness: the selection for the ways of power.

Two evolutionary processes then—where previously there had been only one—brought a loss of unity. On the one hand, we have creatures (humans) who have emerged through the order created by the almost four billion year process of the evolution of life—an order that includes what we by nature are, i.e. our basic humanity and our deepest needs. But on the other hand, these same creatures are now shaped by the demands made by cultures that are themselves shaped (in very important ways) by the demands of power.

Many are the ways that the brokenness of this superimposition of one evolutionary process upon another has made human history the ugly thing so much of it is.

We live with echoes of the brokenness of this double-evolutionary drama, which has been the source of much that is disturbed and disturbing in the history of human civilization. Let me now provide a quick sketch of how this pattern of brokenness has been transmitted in shape-shifting ways in the human world, since the dawn of this unfinished drama of civilization in the history of life on earth.

Much of the brokenness, as has been said earlier, begins in the unprecedented kind of anarchy—the lack of good order—that inevitably characterized the system made up of a multiplicity of this new kind of living entity (civilized societies).

Then there's the struggle for power that anarchy makes inevitable, i.e. the rise of warfare more destructive and far more consequential for the nature of human society than had been the case for hunter-gatherers before civilization. The fragmentation of the intersocietal system made the brokenness of chronic war inevitable.

> Consider how savage a place the world is shown to be in the Bible, with whole cities massacred to the last child. Yahweh was seen, at the outset, as a tribal war god. Many biblical stories provide a glimpse into the terrifying space into which civilization took our kind.

The rise of such warfare in itself would be enough to transmit the pattern of brokenness onto the human beings who are trapped in this disordered system. Wherever we look on this planet, we find peoples who are the heirs—if not the direct victims—to wars, tyrannies, oppression, and torment. Is there a piece of land on this earth that wasn't stolen by force from its prior inhabitants?

For thousands of years, now, our kind has been contending with an intersocietal anarchy that has condemned the human members of civilized societies to traumatic experiences. "Trauma" implies a kind of brokenness: an experience is traumatic if it is so painful and disruptive that the traumatized creature cannot integrate it into its overall psychic structure. The whole of humankind, one might say, suffers, in some sense, from PTSD, some of it handed down through the generations.

History has been a very rough ride. Rough, and with no one in a position to do much to change the overall dreadful dynamic (a dynamic described by the Athenians into whose mouths Thucydides put these words): **"The strong do what they can, and the weak suffer what they must."**

Our kind has suffered much brokenness in history as a result of that dynamic. Across the world—in one way or another, to one degree or another—our kind suffers still.

How Brokenness Leaves its Pattern on the Human Psyche

The wounding of human beings can create fuel to increase a society's power.

To the extent that the surviving civilized societies have been shaped to survive a war of all against all, they are not reliably shaped to fulfill the needs of their human members. Indeed, the societies best able to survive in such an environment are those most able to exploit the inherent flexibility of the cultural animal to maximize the societies' power.

Such exploitation inevitably means the frustration of some human needs. An important tool of that process is a cultural message—presented as the voice of "morality"—that condemns as "bad" those parts of human nature that the society, in its pursuit of competitive power, seeks to frustrate.

In the tragically disordered system of civilized societies, in other words, the selective process in the civilized system fosters societies that socialize their young to be at war with themselves.

History reveals us human creatures embedded in cultures that harshly condemn our nature (original sin, depravity, mortification of the flesh). This pattern of an injurious internalization of a condemnatory spirit has been played out in many an abusive society, and in many an abusive family.

The wounding of human beings is not just a by-product, but has also been a strategy for societies' maximization of power. The ways civilized societies have been able to magnify their powers by wounding their members include:

- fostering rage, thereby providing a reservoir of fierceness that magnifies the society's might on the battlefield;
- stimulating a lust for power, a motivation to extend the society's dominance over others;
- instilling an inner slave driver, an intense "work ethic" that can magnify the productivity of the social machine;
- disconnecting thought from emotion, enabling the society to harness intelligence that operates in a purely functional way, detached from the evaluation of goals.

How such things have worked through history is described in greater detail in Chapter 5 of *The Parable of the Tribes*, "Power and the Psychological Evolution of Civilized Man."

Broken Creatures Act in Broken Ways

People who have been socialized in ways that create disharmony within themselves are apt to externalize that conflict back into the wider world. The racism of the Jim Crow South and the anti-Semitism of Nazi Germany illustrate how this cycling of patterns of brokenness works from level to level.

Those who have been broken by the forces imposed on them by the systems in which they are embedded are readied to channel that brokenness back into the surrounding world —- back into their own societies, and often back into the larger world.

Here are a couple of examples.

The broken regime of racial persecution in the American South— as Lillian Smith showed in her classic *Killers of the Dream*—made use of broken elements in the psyche of white Southerners. Many were brought up with harsh moral strictures that prevented the harmonious integration of natural sexual impulses. The forbidden impulses were then projected outward to be rediscovered—and punished—in the subjugated darker race.

In Nazi Germany—-as Alice Miller showed in *For Your Own Good*—the regime of brokenness behind the Nazis' ethnic annihilation harnessed the psychic brokenness created by generations of child-rearing practices that legitimized the systematic brutal treatment of children. What was driven underground in the child by parental power emerged with a fury against "inferior peoples" to be destroyed in the name of the noble Fatherland.

In each case, the pattern of brokenness gets spread from the culture to the individual and then back again. The harsh culture, making war against the natural needs and will of the growing human, spreads its pattern of division by preventing the human creature from reconciling—or, in the most dangerous cases, even acknowledging—the conflicting elements within it.

And such a broken psyche—with its conscious identification with the harsh morality that has been imposed upon it, and with its denial of (and estrangement from) the natural creature—feels impelled to find enemies against whom to enact its unresolved inner conflicts.

Hence, societies deformed by the intersocietal war of all against all can create in their members the need for war. (Recall that pattern in the conduct of today's Republican Party: "They make a fight over everything.") Those whose inner life involves a conflict so irreconcilable that it is kept below consciousness will feel most comfortable—or rather, least uncomfortable—in a world beset by *external* conflict. Better to fight some outside "devil" than face the war within that, trauma-driven as it is, is too painful to face.

Hence the central role that the lie plays in the force of brokenness. At its core, the lie of false righteousness is a lie to oneself—a basic split between a person's real inner experience, which is rejected for being intolerably painful, and the false representation of that experience, which is fabricated as an escape from that pain.

(These ideas are developed much more elaborately in my book, *Out of Weakness: Healing the Wounds That Drive Us to War.*)

Brokenness Begets Brokenness

In those times and places when an evil force runs rampant, we can see that it manifests itself in a variety of forms of brokenness. While these forms are very different from each other, their kinship is shown in how they all spread brokenness. And this kinship helps demonstrate the reality of that evil force that is their parent.

In a given cultural system, the various elements of brokenness tend to be related and to reinforce each other. Because they have, as it were, a common ancestor—all of them having been engendered by the same coherent force I'm calling "evil"—these various elements tend to be "cousins" of each other.

(That is why, in Chapter One, I made much of the question, "What is it that expresses itself in all these ways?")

It is no coincidence that the force that drove America into Civil War a century and a half ago showed itself in all these diverse broken ways:

- fighting for the right of some human beings to own and exploit other human beings;
- willing to cheat and commit fraud to secure its advantage (e.g. imposing the fraudulent Lecompton constitution onto "Bleeding Kansas" in the late 1850s);
- enforcing orthodoxy of belief on as much of the country as it could, contrary to the Bill of Rights (e.g. banning anti-slavery materials);
- refusing to abide by the legitimate outcome of an election process (Lincoln's election in 1860) conducted according to a constitutional system that had enabled the slaveholders to dominate the American power system up to that point;
- holding blatantly contradictory beliefs (about the slaves and their relationship with them);
- manifesting an extraordinary degree of hypocrisy and self-deception;

- not bothering to proceed by legal means to establish their disputed right to leave the Union;
- lying to itself, after the end of the war it had precipitated, about what they had been fighting for.

Likewise, of course, with that quintessential representative of extreme evil, the Nazi regime in Germany. It is no coincidence that the regime that gave us the Big Lie also gave us

- the theory of the Master Race;
- the largest war in human history;
- unspeakable brutality in its wielding of power, crowned by the atrocity of the Holocaust;

among so much else that degraded or destroyed so much that is whole in the human system.

In each case, the various manifestations are not the same thing. Lying is not the same thing as warmongering which is not the same thing as sadism. But they are all expressions of the same spirit, the same force of brokenness, the same coherent thing I'm calling "evil." All are transmutations of the pattern of brokenness.

Nor, in our times, is it a coincidence that when America became officially a nation that tortures, it was under an administration that also

- lied us into a war,
- widened the gap between rich and poor,
- trampled on the Constitution,
- made a mockery of the rule of law,
- damaged the nation's reputation among our traditional friends,
- botched the wars it chose to wage,
- and left the American economy in shambles.

Brokenness begets brokenness in its many forms.

The Coherence of the Force: How "Evil" Transmits Its Pattern of Brokenness in Shape-Shifting Ways

One can follow how brokenness gets transmitted: from the large arena of intersocietal conflict, which warps the spirit of societies and cultures, which in turn inflicts wounds upon the members of those societies. Then the brokenness reverberates back up into the higher levels. This shape-shifting transmission of brokenness can be seen in the history leading to the Nazi nightmare.

I began this chapter saying, "We live our lives in the immediate and the concrete." One important thing we miss if the concrete is all we see is that more abstract "thing"—that pattern of brokenness moving through our world in shape-shifting ways.

The connections among chronic war, unjust societies, harsh morality, a desire to kick the vulnerable, and people unable to integrate aspects of themselves are not readily visible. They do not look like aspects of the same thing. But they are. At least, in some very meaningful ways, and to a non-trivial extent, they are.

That prototypical historical nightmare—the rise and brutal reign of Nazism in Germany in the first half of the twentieth century—can again provide an illustration. Many outstanding thinkers have sought to make sense of the evil that arose at that time and place. And some of their insights can be brought together to show how the patterns of brokenness get transmitted from form to form and from level to level, demonstrating the coherence of that force I'm calling "evil."

The causal connections among these phenomena are of course more complex and multidimensional than can be shown with just a few brushstrokes. (The interplay of causes and effects in human civilizations and in human history is way too complex to say simply that, by itself, A caused B which, by itself, caused C, etc.) But delineating a few such connections does capture some important sinews of the causal structure.

We can begin with the level of the overarching system of "sovereign societies." It is at this level, according to "the parable of the tribes," and not at the level of some innate human depravity, that the main impetus toward brokenness entered the world of human civilization.

From the disordered intersocietal system, the brokenness ramifies to the other levels (social and psychological) of the human system.

The Nazis, with their brutal sense of themselves as the Master Race entitled to "do what they can" and to compel those weaker to "suffer what they must," represented a transmutation of the trauma of victimhood into the traumatizing of other victims. According to the profound German-Jewish social thinker, Norbert Elias, the militaristic, domineering, and sadistic behavior in that monstrous 20th century upsurgence of German power was itself, in part, the consequence of Germans' experience in previous centuries of their relative weakness—hence their victimization—in the international arena.

Elias writes:

> "Following the internal clashes between reigning Protestant regional princes and the Catholic imperial house, and the smouldering religious wars of the sixteenth century, in the seventeenth century Germany became a major arena of war where the rulers and armies of other Catholic and Protestant countries fought out their battles for supremacy. And the armies of regional magnates fought each other in German territories, too. They all needed quarters, and food from the fields. Insecurity grew. Bands roamed the land, burning and murdering. A great proportion of the German populace became impoverished. Experts reckon that during the Thirty Years War Germany lost a third of its population."

Describing the painful consequences for the Germans, over several centuries, from their weakness relative to neighboring nations that had achieved national unification sooner, Elias writes:

> "[T]he relative weakness of their own state, compared with other states, entails specific crises for the people involved. They suffer from physical danger, begin to doubt their own intrinsic worth, feel humiliated and degraded, and are prone to wishful thinking about the revenge they would like to take on the perpetrators of this situation."

This free play of power among societies generated within German society an orientation toward power and the compensatory urge to dominate others. Elias describes German culture—in the generations leading up to the rise of the Nazis—as one where "a tradition of conduct in which life is seen as a struggle of all against all has gained dominance, and where there are institutions directed towards bringing up people with an appropriate personality structure [for that struggle]..."

Thus, the brokenness in the overarching system gets transmitted—and transmuted—into the form of a society, within that system, characterized by a "harshness of human relationships which finds expression in the use of physical violence." (Elias is speaking here particularly of the German dueling culture.) And this harshness, he says, "spreads [within the society] like an infection."

Tracing the transmutation process further, from the level of the society to the level of the family, we find that certain kinds of harsh power relationships get transmitted. Wilhelm Reich, in his book *The Mass Psychology of Fascism*, writes that "the authoritarian family...is a factory where reactionary ideology and reactionary structures are produced." The "first cultural precept" of "every reactionary polity," he says, is the protection of this kind of family as a means for "safeguarding of the state, culture, and civilization."

For an understanding of how this authoritarian family transmits brokenness to the level of the developing human individual, we can turn to Alice Miller's fascinating book, *For Your Own Good.*

Miller writes about a "poisonous pedagogy" articulated in Germanic culture over several centuries. This frightening literature presents not something covert, done by just a few criminally abusive parents. It shows, rather, the proudly enunciated recommendations of well-respected cultural authorities—"experts"—regarding how children should be brought up.

Among the core beliefs identified by Miller are that "responding to a child's needs is wrong " and that "severity and coldness are a good preparation for life." "Suppress everything in the child," she quotes the highly respected nineteenth-century expert telling parents. Parental love, these Germanic child-rearing experts taught, should work to assure "that the child learn at an early age to renounce, control, and master himself, that he not blindly follow the promptings of the flesh . . ."

This "poisonous pedagogy" works to get parents to convey to the child that his very nature is evil, something that must be rejected and overcome. Simply because he is a child, he is treated as unworthy of respect.

Now what began as the brokenness of an uncontrolled struggle for power manifests as a war within the individual human being. Society's demands, internalized by the vulnerable and dependent young human being, make war upon the innate needs of the human creature.

In the face of this assault, if it is harsh enough, the child surrenders to the greater power. He identifies with the dominating will of the parent—Anna Freud called this "identification with the aggressor"—representing the power structure of the authoritarian society. He surrenders his will. Another expert claimed that there will be no "serious consequences" from the annihilation of the child's will. The child will "forget he ever had a will."

It seems to me likely that this annihilation of the will, embedded in the child-rearing practices of the Germanic culture in the generations leading to the Nazi nightmare, is connected with another insight to be found in the literature seeking to explain the rise of the Nazi power. Erich Fromm, one of several interpreters to make this point, emphasized in his 1941 book *Escape From Freedom*, that those who were drawn to the Nazi totalitarianism under the domination of the Fuehrer, were unable to cope with the freedom of a more democratic order. It makes sense that, if the will of the child has been "annihilated," the adult would not be in touch with that part of himself that, in conditions of freedom, can find its own way without being commanded by superiors what to do.

The brokenness thus transmitted down to the level of the individual human psyche generates an energy of brokenness that turns the direction of the transmission back around, sending the pattern of brokenness back up into the higher levels in the larger world.

Miller describes a woman, for example, who had been ill-treated in her family, but was not allowed to express her resentment. The energy of resentment, however, could find a more socially acceptable avenue of expression—toward a scapegoat. In a passage that might be a text-book example of the psychological mechanism of "displacement," Miller writes:

> "[S]he told me with what enthusiasm she had read about "the crimes of the Jews" in *Mein Kampf* and what a sense of relief it had given her to find out that it was permissible to hate someone so unequivocally. She had never been allowed to envy her siblings openly for being able to pursue their careers.

> But the Jewish banker to whom her uncle had to pay interest on a loan—he was an exploiter of her poor uncle, with whom she identified. She herself was actually being exploited by her parents and was envious of her siblings, but a well-behaved girl was not permitted to have these feelings."

(This story connects, of course, with another aspect of brokenness—endemic in German culture for centuries—that was available for the spirit that animated Nazism to exploit: German anti-Semitism. The historical background leading up to the Holocaust has been presented in various places, including *The Pity of It All: A Portrait of the German-Jewish Epoch, 1743-1933*, a rather elegiac picture, and the more outraged picture presented by Daniel Goldhagen's *Hitler's Willing Executioners: Ordinary Germans and the Holocaust.*)

The Roman poet Horace said, "If you drive nature out with a pitchfork, she will soon find a way back." That is how it is with the natural will of the human being. The will may bend to submission, the child may "forget" he has a will, but the will does not disappear.

Hermann Hoess, commandant of Auschwitz, recalled his own upbringing in late nineteenth century Germany:

> "It was constantly impressed upon me in forceful terms that I must obey promptly the wishes and commands of my parents, teachers, and priests, and indeed of all grown-up people, including servants, and that nothing must distract me from this duty. Whatever they said was always right. These basic principles by which I was brought up became second nature to me." [quoted in Alice Miller, p. 146]

Submission may have become "second nature" to Hermann Hoess, as he says, but look what happened to his first nature. Even as he fitted himself as a dutiful servant of a tyrannical regime—overseeing the horrors of Auschwitz—he conveyed to others the brutality of dehumanization that he had been compelled to absorb.

Here is nature, thwarted, coming back with a pitchfork of its own: the will, driven underground, reappears in a diabolical form.

Brokenness cycles through the system, changing forms as it moves from level to level, but forming a pattern that subtly infiltrates the human world.

"Among the leaders of the Third Reich," writes Alice Miller, "I have not been able to find a single one who did not have a strict and rigid upbringing."

A Contending of Forces

Although a culture's pattern tends to persist, it is also true that a culture is not just of a piece, but contains different sets of patterns. These patterns can contend against each other for dominance. Especially contentious is the struggle between the patterns of wholeness and of brokenness. It is this contention that constitutes "the battle between good and evil."

I hope that by now the image is becoming visible of a force that—through a vast network of causes and effects—imparts a pattern of brokenness.

And a similar picture could be painted of a force of Wholeness: there, too, we see many forms, and a system of feedback loops from level to level. Peace and love and nurturance and hope and justice and honesty and beauty and fulfillment all feed each other—just as, on the other side, war and hatred and abuse and fear and injustice and deception and ugliness and misery/frustration feed each other.

Every civilized culture contains both of these forces, but presumably not all to the same degree and—much more important for our present purposes—not always, in any given society, to the same degree over time.

The idea presented here (earlier in this chapter) of "the persistence of culture" needs to be modified. The "culture" that encompasses the whole of some human society, or wider human system, is not so *unitary* as that idea of persistence suggests. Forces within a cultural system contend against each other for influence.

In particular, within any given culture, the reverberating impetus of brokenness is continually contending against the persistent life-serving forces of wholeness in a battle to determine which of the two will shape the future of the system.

It is time now to move from the present focus on how these patterns get transmitted over time to looking at the battle between these two kinds of patterns.

It is time, that is, time to look—in Chapter Seven—more directly at “the battle between good and evil.”

INTERLUDE VI:

With Malice Toward None

Understanding how forces operate to shape people should lead us to have compassion, not hatred, for even those through whom evil works. We need to fight the force of evil, but the enlightened warrior in that battle has "malice toward none."

We human beings are caught up in forces that have been beyond our control. Indeed, at the fundamental level, we have been caught up in forces beyond our ken.

That is true at the level of humankind as a species. And ultimately it is true of each of us individually.

So while it is regrettably necessary sometimes to do battle against the carriers of brokenness, the enemy is not really those carriers, but the force of brokenness that has shaped them into channels for destructiveness.

"Hate the sin. Love the sinner," is the enlightened attitude, as I mentioned earlier.

As president, Abraham Lincoln never knew a day not dominated by war—he had a month or so of the nation careening toward war, followed by four years of the most savage of wars, then less than a week of dawning peace before he was assassinated. But a month before he was shot, while the war was still grinding on, he called for an attitude of "malice toward none, and charity for all."

This was of a piece with his having said, in 1854, that he did not bear ill-will toward those in the South, even though he also said of the

Southerners' "peculiar institution" that "if slavery is not wrong, then nothing is wrong." "They are just what we would be in their situation," Lincoln said.

"There but for the Grace of God..."

As a species, we have been put into an impossible situation. It's true that it was our own doing that brought us into this situation. But the only qualities in us that unleashed this force of brokenness (growing out of the anarchy that would inevitably accompany the breakthrough into civilization) was our creativity combined with our desire to survive. "We are just what any other creature would be in our situation."

We should therefore be compassionate toward ourselves as a species. And extend compassion also to those whom this broken world has rendered broken in ways that require us to oppose them in order to drive away the brokenness working through them.

But what about holding people responsible for their choices? What about "free will"?

Yes, we make choices. We all experience that. But where did the "we" come from who make those choices.

At the deepest level, we are ultimately all like the iron filings in Oscar Wilde's little fable, "Fable of the Magnet":

> Once upon a time there was a magnet, and in its close neighbourhood lived some steel filings. One day two or three little filings felt a sudden desire to go and visit the magnet, and they began to talk of what a pleasant thing it would be to do. Other filings nearby overheard their conversation, and they, too, became infected with the same desire. Still others joined them, till at last all the filings began to discuss the matter, and more and more their vague desire grew into an impulse. 'Why not go to-day' said some of them; but others were of opinion that it would be better to wait till to-morrow. Meanwhile, without their having noticed it, they had been involuntarily moving nearer to the magnet, which lay there quite still, apparently taking no heed of them. And so they went on discussing, all the time insensibly drawing nearer to their neighbor; and the more they talked, the more they felt the impulse growing stronger, till the more impatient ones declared that they would go that day, whatever the rest did. Some were heard to say that it was their duty to visit the magnet, and that they ought to have gone long ago. And,

while they talked, they moved always nearer and nearer, without realizing that they had moved. Then, at last, the impatient ones prevailed, and, with one irresistible impulse, the whole body cried out, 'There's no use waiting. We will go today. We will go now. We will go at once.' And then in one unanimous mass they swept along, and in another moment were clinging fast to the magnet on every side. Then the magnet smiled—for the steel filings had no doubt at all but that they were paying that visit of their own free will.

We make choices, but the place within us from which the choices come is in itself the fruit of the world. Is there any reason to believe that human beings are **in any way** outside the nexus of cause and effect that operates in the world generally?

Some have sought to derive an idea of "free will" out of a randomness in the universe. Lucretius, the Roman philosopher of two millennia ago, simply postulated that an occasional random swerve of atoms provided the basis for free will. More recently, some people have claimed that our free will can be salvaged through the indeterminacy found by quantum mechanics at the subatomic level.

But it is hardly evident how randomness at that microscopic level could provide a means for a large organism to gain "freedom" at the level of its decision-making.

The problem with free will goes deeper than the problem with, say, unicorns, or phlogiston, or any of the other things that science says do not exist. While a unicorn does not exist, one can readily imagine how such a creature *might* exist. But with the "free will" of the kind some people want to claim, there is no way it *could* exist in any way that makes sense.

Rather than go deeper into that philosophic ground now, let me refer you to "Free Will?" in the "More Depth" collection, in which I provide what seems to me virtually a mathematical proof that *ultimately* our choices—and what we are —is and must be the fruit of the world.

By "ultimately," I mean that the choices we make—though our choosing is of crucial importance, and an essential part of our humanity—are not "free" in any way that would justify our being less than compassionate even with the evil-doers among us.

Let me make a distinction between "responsibility" and "blame," where holding people responsible is aimed toward fostering better outcomes in the future, and blame brings a punitive spirit toward what has been wrong in the past.

We human beings are not *to blame* for the evils of the world. We've done what we could, under the circumstances. But we are *responsible* for these evils, as it is up to us to do what we can to clean up the mess we've made.

Likewise, we should hold people (including evil-doers) responsible for what they do. Holding one another responsible is one of the ways that we introduce a force into the mix of causes that can produce better effects, i.e. move people to make better choices. It is like introducing another magnet into the situation, pulling iron filings more in the desirable direction.

Paradoxically, it might be beneficial to treat one another *as if* we had a kind of freedom that, ultimately, we do not have: it is all a question of whether our way of treating each other makes the world better or worse.

But ultimately, there is no place for real ill-will toward our fellow human beings. The pain and suffering of the evil-doers does not, in itself, constitute a good.

We are at a time now in American history where some very repulsive human beings—people like Rush Limbaugh, Newt Gingrich, the Koch Brothers, Karl Rove, Dick Cheney—have been enabled by an adverse shift in the balance of the forces of wholeness and brokenness to play a huge and destructive role in our nation. They and their ilk must be fought and defeated.

And we are at a time when many millions of Americans have thrown their support behind such people, and more importantly behind the force that has empowered such people. These people also must be confronted in this battle.

But it is the brokenness that is the enemy.

When it comes to the human beings, the most enlightened course is that proposed by Lincoln: With malice toward none.

Chapter Seven

The Battle Between Good and Evil

Two Powerful Forces

A central dynamic—perhaps ***the*** *central dynamic—in human affairs is the struggle between two basic forces, one constructive and one destructive, derived from the two evolutionary processes that have shaped us and our civilization.*

The human drama is, of course, enormously complex, with multiple factors operating continually to weave the fabric of our history. But among the forces at work, two are quite central to the drama, and operate as antagonists in the shaping of our world.

James Joyce's Stephen Daedalus described history as "a nightmare from which I am trying to awake." But in addition to the nightmare, one can also see in history the fruits of human dreams.

On the one hand, we come from wholeness. We by nature cling to life. And "the pursuit of happiness" is not only the "inalienable right" America's founders declared it to be but is also the natural inclination of a healthy human. In that pursuit, our natural preference is for a world characterized by justice, not injustice; by beauty, not ugliness; by kindness, not cruelty; etc.

The life-serving element has always been strong in human civilization. In the various cultural structures created by civilized peoples—the social institutions, customs, religions, legal systems, political orders—we can see how people have worked hard and creatively to bring wholeness into their world.

This natural human orientation toward wholeness may be considered the basic source of "the good" in our world.

But, on the other hand, there's no denying the nightmarish element to which Joyce calls attention. For against "the good," there arose the second of the major antagonists in the human drama.

There are a good many reasons why a species would encounter difficulties as it tried to navigate its way through the *terra incognita* of inventing a civilization.

It is in the nature of a *terra incognita* that the turns one takes may lead to unexpected difficulties. The early grazers of sheep in North Africa millennia ago presumably had no idea they were spreading lifeless deserts where green had been.

It has not been the unforeseen consequence, however, but the *inescapable consequence* that has been the real problem for civilized humankind. In particular, the inevitable selection for the ways of power (explored here particularly in Chapter Five).

Civilization broke the system of life into two different evolutionary systems, a division that implants a pattern of brokenness at the heart of the human world. This pattern of brokenness then ramifies through the whole of the human world, from level to level, reverberating through time (as described in Chapter Six).

The unchecked play of power thus generates the brokenness of chronic war, of injustice, of systems structured to exploit their human members, not only to serve them, and of psychic structures in which the conflicts plaguing the larger system are internalized. The reign of power has made for broken people, twisted into channels for the forces of greed, or cruelty, or the lust for power, or the lie.

Here, then, is that second antagonist, opposing the force for the good. Here is the (primary) source for the force of evil.

The battle between these two forces—the battle between good and evil—represents a central dynamic of the human drama. Perhaps *the* central dynamic. Various human religious traditions have represented a similar dynamic—e.g. an opposition between God and Satan, or between gods of Creation and those of Destruction. But the account offered here is conceived in wholly secular terms.

Will Good or Evil —Life or Death—Win this Battle?

As human powers have grown, so also have the powers of good and evil. The human future therefore now contains the potential for either far greater Wholeness or catastrophic destruction.

Martin Luther called the Devil "the prince of this world." And indeed in many times and places in history, it would have seemed that this world is indeed ruled by the force of evil.

The world of Renaissance Italy, for example, in the time of Leonardo and Machiavelli, might have seemed such a time, with the unbridled struggle for power, the corruption, the rise to dominance of sociopaths who murdered rivals to become Pope or to dominate sections of territory. And of course there have been many other such nightmarish times and places: the brutal times depicted in the Old Testament, with the slaughter of whole cities; the world of Shakespeare's histories, with its insurrections and betrayals and revenge; the Spanish treatment of the natives in the New World; the English subjugation of Ireland; the Congo under the exploitive domination by the Belgians. Russians suppressing the Caucuses.

Indeed, perhaps one might say: much of the world most of the time.

And one might also add that, in terms of our time and place, most of us—my likely readers, and I—are among the most fortunate of humans in the history of civilization. When have so many people been able to live with such freedom, such security, such abundance, such inclusion in the democratic structures of power, allowed to live their lives in considerable peace? Just comparing the lives of people in the nations of Western Europe in our times with those of their forebears during the preceding two millennia of history, we might be warranted in believing that the battle between the forces of wholeness and those of brokenness has been going rather well in our times.

But the picture is more complicated than that. For even as there are signs that civilization is making some advancement against the forces of brokenness, so also have we in our times been compelled to contemplate the possibility of brokenness gaining some ultimate triumph.

Never before our times has humankind had the capacity to destroy itself and perhaps even the planet. That possibility loomed over our heads like a Sword of Damocles during the Cold War, as two nations armed with thousands of nuclear warheads confronted each other in a hostile and competitive spirit. Through a combination of human wisdom and care on the one hand, and good luck on the other, we survived that danger. (But we also know the cold war might have ended otherwise. A few wrong decisions during the Cuban Missile Crisis might have led to the destruction of civilization.) And that proverbial nuclear genie is out of the bottle, and who knows what other genies that specialize in mass destruction may yet be unleashed by the advance of human knowledge and technology?

Now we face another potential triumph of brokenness. This new potential catastrophe involves humankind's disruption of the earth's climate system, on which we and the rest of life on earth depend. The threat of nuclear holocaust was more like a binary set of possibilities—it will happen, or it won't happen (admittedly with some intermediate possibilities). With climate disruption, it now appears certain that disaster is beginning, and the question is but one of degree.

In the case of climate disruption, the threat did not arise originally out of evil, but from the problem of unintended consequences. But once this danger became visible—I first wrote about it almost 40 years ago—the force of brokenness stepped to center stage. Would humankind act responsibly to mitigate the magnitude of the damage to the earth's climatic system, or would human greed and selfishness and sloth, together with corporate powers structured to act sociopathically, sacrifice the viability of the whole for profit and ease in the present? (Regarding the sociopathic structuring of corporate powers, see pp. 173-9 in Chapter Nine.)

(Already, between disruption of the climate and various other human impacts on the environment, we are bringing about what has been called "the Sixth Extinction"—i.e. a wave of erasures of life-forms on this planet that, unlike the previous five over the past eons, caused by a part of the system of life, i.e. by humankind in its brokenness.)

So, the outcome of this millennia-old battle between good and evil remains in doubt. Both forces in the human system seem to be gaining strength as, on the one hand, we make progress in some important areas (e.g. the spread of democracy, displacing the age-old domination of the many by the few), while our power to destroy has likewise leapt forward.

Shifts in the Balance of Power Between Good and Evil

The elements of good and evil are always present in every culture. The issue is, which will govern. The nightmares of history come when the worst elements in the system, rather than being held in check by the best, gain the the power to dominate the whole.

"The battle between good and evil" is like other struggles in that its outcome depends on how the different sides of the battle use their opportunities. Or fail to.

The two forces may trace their origins to long-established sources—with **evil** (primarily) tracing to the problem of power that has been endemic in civilization from the outset, with the roots of the **good** reaching still further back to the very structure of life and to that part of the life's order that we as a species bear within us at our core—but the interplay between them is by no means fixed.

In a given civilized system—or cultural order, or nation or subset of a nation—the balance of power between the two elements can shift significantly depending on the circumstances.

My own investigations have focused on three main times and places where that balance of power has shifted adversely with disastrous (or, in the third and contemporary circumstance, potentially disastrous) consequences: 1) the American South in the decades leading up to the Civil War, 2) Germany in the decades following the First World War and leading up to the Second World War, and 3) the United States over the past generation with a destructive force gaining ever more power to shape the nature and destiny of the United States as a civilization.

The urgent impulse behind this book is the last of these three. But let's look for a moment at what happened in the other two.

Among the components of the significant change that occurred in the American South from, say, 1830 to 1860, was a change in the attitudes of the region's governing elite toward its "peculiar institution," slavery.

In the earlier time, the South maintained a strong element of the attitude toward slavery like Thomas Jefferson's. Jefferson was acutely sensitive to the tension between the enslavement of a race of fellow human beings and the idea that "All men are created equal, and endowed by their Creator with certain unalienable rights." Although it is reasonable to fault Jefferson, as is nowadays commonly done, for his failure to walk his talk, he nonetheless did at least have the integrity to acknowledge the profound brokenness of the institution on which his class had based its wealth and power. Wrote Jefferson:

> "The whole commerce between master and slave is a perpetual exercise of the most boisterous passions, the most unremitting despotism on the one part, and degrading submissions on the other. Our children see this, and learn to imitate it; for man is an imitative animal. This quality is the germ of all education in him. From his cradle to his grave he is learning to do what he sees others do. If a parent could find no motive either in his philanthropy or his self love, for restraining the intemperance of passion towards his slave, it should always be a sufficient one that his child is present. But generally it is not sufficient. The parent storms, the child looks on, catches the lineaments of wrath, puts on the same airs in the circle of smaller slaves, gives a loose to the worst of passions, and thus nursed, educated, and daily exercised in tyranny, cannot but be stamped by it with odious peculiarities. The man must be a prodigy who can retain his manners and morals undepraved by such circumstances."

Decades later, the attitude of Alexander Stephens, a U.S. Senator from Georgia about to become the Vice President of the Confederate States of America who, it should be noted, was very much a moderate in the context of the Southern politics of his time —reflected the transformation. Stephens acknowledged that the idea that all men are created equal was the idea on which the United States had been founded, but he declared that idea false. The Confederacy, by contrast, said Stephens,

> is founded upon exactly the opposite idea; its foundations are laid, its cornerstone rests, upon the great truth that the negro is not equal to the white man; that slavery, subordination to the superior race, is his natural and moral condition. This, our new Government, is the first, in the history of the world, based on this great physical, philosophical, and moral truth.

This of course stands for a whole range of transformations in the set of attitudes, beliefs, and political conduct in the political culture of the South, almost all of them, I assert, in the direction of greater brokenness.

It should also be said that these transformations were less a matter of wholly new elements entering into the culture than a shift in power among the various elements. The forces of racism and greed and lust for power were present in the earlier era, and the elements of regard for equality and liberty and a Christian regard for one's fellow human beings remained part of the Southern cultural system in the later era. But over the course of that antebellum era, one set of elements receded in power as the other set of elements became dominant.

It is in such ways that the battle between good and evil unfolds. Within cultural systems, and within even the character structure of individuals, the elements of good and evil are always there. **The question, ultimately, is which elements will govern the system and which will be held in check.** And that, in turn, depends upon which elements get strengthened and which get weakened as the system unfolds through time. And that, in turn, depends on such things as circumstance, the impact of experience, and the nature of the leadership that can bring out the best or the worst of the system's potentialities.

There will be more reflections in later chapters on the factors that led to the rise in power of the broken parts of the cultural system of the South to subordinate the "better angels" of its nature. (See e.g. "The Civil War as the Duel the South Required to Defend its 'Honor,'" in Chapter Nine.)

Another clear case of an "adverse shift" in the balance between good and evil within a cultural system is presented by the rise of Nazism in Germany. When Germany, under the Nazis, became the monstrous thing the world then beheld with incredulity, one reason for the astonishment was that Germany had been seen as such a "civilized" and "cultured" society. How did the Germanic civilization that had given the world such beauty as the music of Bach and the poetry of Goethe become something whose governing brutal regime shocked the world with its ugliness?

Once again, it was not a matter of evil creating completely new forms of brokenness, but rather of the evil bringing the broken elements to positions of dominance in the system.

The elements of German culture that the Nazis tapped into, and magnified, were long-standing—e.g. the militarism and the anti-Semitism. Some of these currents of brokenness had contributed to the bloodbath of World War I. But nothing foretold the grotesqueness of the evil of the Nazi era, which brought out the very worst forces in the German cultural system and gave them unfettered rule.

But in the interval between the world wars, the overall order of the German cultural system had been impacted by various blows that created opportunities for the forces of brokenness.

Among the factors that are commonly, and it would seem rightly, adduced are these: 1) the trauma of World War I, in which the Germans had lost millions and killed millions, only to end in defeat; 2) the imposition on Germany, by the victors, of a peace that not only the Germans but soon also a great many in the victorious nations saw as unjust and punitive; and 3) the extraordinary inflationary catastrophe that undercut the foundations of people's material security.

That such factors can advance the forces of evil demonstrates that trauma, fear, pain, and rage—all consequences of brokenness in the human system—also represent openings for the Spirit of Brokenness to advance further in the world.

The broken places—in human beings and in our collective systems—are there, ready to serve as a channel for an evil force to flow through to create still more woundedness in the world.

In the next chapter, let's look at some of the ways that the force of evil operates—the strategies it employs—to spread its pattern of brokenness in the human world, including in the American crisis of our time. And then in the chapter after that, we will examine further "How the Balance of Power Between Good and Evil Can Shift Adversely."

Interlude VII:

Love of the Sacred Might Need to Precede the Readiness to Fight Evil, Continued

Powerful messages in American history and culture demonstrate the strategy of connecting people with the sacred as a means of readying them emotionally for the battle against evil.

In Interlude II, I suggested—based largely on my own experience—that a person's readiness to fight against the force of brokenness may depend upon first making meaningful contact with the realm of wholeness. The idea is that we must first open our hearts and souls to the vital importance of some sacred values before we can be impassioned enough to make sacrifices to defend those values.

Upon reflection, I have thought of examples where this sequence has been effectively used to move an audience toward such readiness for battle.

It seems, for example, that Abraham Lincoln employed something of this strategy in his Gettysburg Address. He begins that speech by conjuring up the fundamental values for which the nation—for whose preservation his listeners are now embattled—was founded: a nation "conceived in Liberty, and dedicated to the proposition that all men are created equal." He then proceeds to talk about the battle and the battlefield that are the occasion for the speech, and about the larger war which they still must fight and win. Finally, he concludes this very brief speech by calling upon his audience to join him in resolving "that these dead shall not have died in vain—that this nation, under God, shall have a new birth of freedom—and that the government of the people, by the people, for the people, shall not perish from the earth." His words, following that course—connect with the sacred, gather inspiration for the battle to preserve and protect it—fortified his audience for the days of sacrifice that still lay ahead.

(While the United States is not as unique in embodying those values as it was then, it might be noted that we are still—or again—fighting for those same values.)

The film *Avatar* makes especially dramatic use of that sequence—sacred first, battle against evil second. Following our protagonist, we meet first the militaristic-industrial system, but like our hero we do not at first fully see its nature. Our allegiance is held in suspense. Then, still following our hero, we enter into the starkly contrasting realm. We discover there a species of human-like creatures embedded in a natural order in which beautiful and sacred forces are at work, sanctifying and guiding the life of those creatures. Once our allegiance with that sacred beauty has been secured, the narrative then exposes us to the sacrilegious nature of that first system with its rapacious greed and ruthless violence. After we see this system wreaking destruction on the sacred beauty we have come to cherish, we are ready to follow our impassioned hero into battle against that evil force.

For more than ten years, I have been focused on battling the evil force that has arisen in America. I regret that I am not as practiced at evoking the sacred as at depicting the evil. (My yearning to start focusing on the sacred is why it was so painful to switch from the *Mapping the Sacred* project to battling the evil I had suddenly perceived.) Perhaps there will be a later edition of this book that explores the sacred more.

But I did try, during my campaign for Congress, to bring our sacred values into focus in order to help inspire my potential supporters to join the battle.

On one occasion—a large Labor Day banquet in Buena Vista, Virginia, in 2011—I worked into my talk a passage from FDR's great 1940 campaign speech. With the refrain of "I see an America," FDR eloquently laid out a picture of the kind of America he as president was battling to achieve: "I see an America where factory workers are not discarded…I see an America whose rivers and valleys…are protected as the rightful heritage of all the people…I see an America of great cultural and educational opportunity for all its people…where those who have reached the evening of life shall live out their years in peace and security...." And more. This is what he was fighting for, and it is what we still—or again—need to fight for.

I used FDR in that case as Lincoln had used the Declaration of Independence: bringing forward texts and symbols already venerated in the political culture, to borrow their authority and deepen the response of the audience.

I conjured up FDR's vision of the sacred ideal for America as the banner behind which we should march off to electoral battle.

Here's another example. In a series of articles I posted during my campaign around Christmas, I sought to use narrative texts about Christmas--with Christmas here functioning less as a religious holiday than as a part of our national culture. I employed the values, conveyed by these narratives about the meaning of Christmas, to bring into clear relief the sacred values at stake in our present political battle. Values dear to the heart of Americans. And values magnified in their power and status by their connection with the nation's majority religion.

The series of articles* dealt in turn with four prominent cultural expressions of the spirit of Christmas: 1) Dickens' *A Christmas Carol*, 2) the film *It's a Wonderful Life*, 3) the opera *Amahl and the Night Visitors* (the televised broadcast of which was for many years an annual national event), and 4) the film *Miracle on 34th Street.*

I'll report here on what I said about one of these, *It's a Wonderful Life.*

One might say that this national Christmas favorite is an investigation of the question, "Has the life our hero George Bailey has lived—a life of sacrifice—been worthwhile?" And that question, in turn, hinges on a most fundamental moral and spiritual question: is it good to live an unselfish life?

While we begin with the hero in a state of despair, on the verge of suicide, all the action in the first more-than-half of the movie takes place (through flashbacks) in his hometown of Bedford Falls. At first, like our hero, we don't realize that this place will represent the values of wholeness in a stark moral contrast to come. This portrait of Bedford Falls is plugged solidly into the mythology of American values: a small town that embraces its members with a sense of community, where people support each other in their efforts to make something of themselves and raise healthy families. We see and embrace the sacred first.

But we and our hero fully appreciate just how much wholeness there is to Bedford Falls only when the angel—sent to help George Bailey through his crisis—takes him through an alternative vision of what his world could be if brokenness rather than wholeness prevailed. The angel shows him what Bedford Falls would have become had he never lived.

Not even the name of the town is the same: the town bears the name of the one evil person ("sick in the soul" is how George's father described him) we've seen before: Mr. Potter, the richest (and greediest) man in town.

Pottersville is a mean and dismal place, filled with vice and injury and privation. The rich human lives we have seen are here, in this alternate reality, filled with pain and bitterness. The lovely Donna Reed, the wonderful wife to George and mother to their children, just to give one (albeit somewhat implausible) example, is a reticent spinster in her Pottersville life, seemingly filled with fear of the world around her and, likely, of life itself.

George Bailey has lived a life of sacrifice—not because he wanted to, but because every time he was about to take the path toward the life focused on his own desires (for college, for travel), some crisis in the town required that he attend to it. He was always serving something bigger than himself.

Now, with the stark contrast between Bedford Falls and Pottersville having been presented, George learns that his sacrifices have purchased extraordinary human good for all the people he cares about.

And then, in the climactic scene, that willingness to give that George has displayed throughout his life is now reciprocated by virtually everyone in the town. The bread he had cast upon the waters is now returned to him. His little bank is saved. With his spirit renewed, George Bailey is restored to his family and his community.

The wholeness and decency of Bedford Falls is preserved.

It is, of course, entirely clear how this idea of the sanctity of self-sacrifice for the good of the whole fits into the meaning of Christmas, as a celebration of the birth of the one who accepted death on the cross for the sake of humankind.

Clear also is the pertinence of the values displayed in *It's a Wonderful Life* to the political crisis that led me to take on the role of politician. At a time when plutocratic forces are eroding our democracy, the issue of whether money or people will prevail is central. At a time when a destructive force is deliberately setting groups of people against each other, the values of mutual support and of caring community need their champions.

Indeed, one might say that a central question facing America in our times is: Will America evolve into Pottersville, or will we succeed in defending the values of Bedford Falls against the force that embodies so fully the sick and destructive spirit of Mr. Potter?

Chapter Eight:

A Gallery of Some of Evil's Strategies

Does talk of "the strategies of evil" imply a strategist? Does it imply that Evil is some Malevolent Being, like Satan, with a consciousness and a purpose?

Not as I intend it be understood. After all, is it not legitimate to speak of the "strategy" of a virus for penetrating a cell or for getting past the defenses of the immune system? It is the way in which the virus has been structured to work and to perpetuate its kind. One might also say, the way in which the virus achieves its "purpose." But if biologists speak this way, they are not imputing to the virus a consciousness that devises cleverly successful strategies, or that possesses deliberate purpose.

Likewise, we can speak of the strategies of this "coherent force" that "works" to impart a pattern of brokenness in the human world. We can have strategies without a strategist, just as we can have a "design"—the clockwork universe, and the intricate order of a living organism—without a watchmaker or a "designer."

Here are a few of the strategies by which, over the past generation, the "evil force" we now confront has moved the American system in the direction of brokenness.

POLARIZATION AND THE STRATEGY OF DIVIDE AND CONQUER

If groups of people in a democracy become unable to make common cause—either because they have driven each other into extreme positions, or because they have become too inflamed with animosity, or because their versions of reality do not overlap—they cancel each other out. By a strategy to foment such divisions and thus nullify the power of the will of the people, the force of brokenness can open the path for it to rule.

My understanding of the dynamics of polarization in America today has gone through three stages. The first accentuated the dynamics of human relationships that, despite people intending otherwise, can drive people from concord into discord. The second included the role of some of the actors in deliberately working to create division. And the third incorporates both of those into the larger picture of a "coherent force" working to foster brokenness in the human system.

I believe all three are valid, and completely consistent with the others.

Driving Each Other to Extremes

In the early 1990s, I became aware of how right and left, conservatives and liberals, were becoming "polarized." At that time, I saw the problem in symmetrical terms, as each side reacted to the excesses of the other by moving further off in an opposite direction.

Here is how I characterized the dynamic in an op/ed I wrote in the mid-90s:

> Polarization is something we can see happening constantly in human [systems and] relationships, on scales large and small. I have observed some relatively benign examples in my own life.
>
> When I drive with my mother—who can envision accidents occurring at every turn—she voices the need for caution to a degree I regard as extreme. In response, an impulse arises in me to drive less carefully than I usually do. In the presence of what I see as my mother's over-cautiousness, I have to work to maintain my more typical prudence. This dynamic leads to a division of labor concerning the polarity of caution and daring.

Something analogous happens between me and my 18-year-old son. To my mind, he procrastinates too much; I lean on him to take care of business more promptly and reliably. His tendency toward procrastination may have developed in reaction to my tighter relationship with my inner Taskmaster. But whatever its origin, when I am in his presence, I tend to become even more like myself than usual: my taking-care-of-business muscles get tighter than even I am comfortable with.

You have probably noticed how married couples can polarize in various ways—between the slob and the compulsive straightener, the spendthrift and the miser, the one who does all the feeling and the one who is always rational and controlled, etc.

At that time, I saw the right and the left playing similar roles in generating this polarization. Although it was my alarm at what Rush Limbaugh was doing to our national discourse that motivated me to get onto the radio to create constructive conversations across the divide, my understanding of the polarization developing in America focused, in this op/ed, on the symmetry of the dynamic at work:

> When people divide on an issue, unless they find a resolution, they tend to push each other further out toward the opposite ends of the spectrum. Each end represents a value that is legitimate, but that also must be balanced against another value. Polarization is one way the system preserves balance, but it is an unstable and conflictual balance. Far better if the actors in the system, instead of dividing into mirror-image opposites of one another, could achieve the healthier balance of integration.
>
> But such integration is difficult. It represents that high human achievement: wisdom. In the absence of wisdom, people are compelled to struggle in their folly. Each side, wedded to its half-truth, sees the other as the problem. But the problem is a property of the system: the polarization and conflict are symptoms of the failure to find a way to bring together those values that are in tension.

Brokenness here takes the form of conflict between half-truths that become ever further apart, whereas wisdom is the Wholeness that brings the pieces of the truth together in a sound and constructive, life-serving way. (It was as an effort to model how our national right-left polarization might be brought together that I wrote my book, published in 1999 by M.I.T. Press, with the subtitle, *A Quest to Bridge America's Moral Divide.*)

The brokenness of increasing division of understanding and perception can, of course, become the means by which other, still more damaging forms of brokenness can gain entry into the civilizational system and degrade it. Here, for example, is how David Potter, in his exceptionally fine history of that period, *The Impending Crisis*, characterized the increasing polarization of the United States in the 1850s, opening the way for the carnage to come:

> Thus in cultural and economic matters, as well as in terms of values, slavery had an effect which no other sectional factor exercised in isolating North and South from each other. As they became isolated, instead of reacting to each other as they were in actuality, each reacted to a distorted mental image of the other—the North to an image of a southern world of lascivious and sadistic slavedrivers; the South to the image of a northern world of cunning Yankee traders and of rabid abolitionists plotting slave insurrections. This process of substituting stereotypes for realities could be very damaging indeed to the spirit of union, for it caused both northerners and southerners to lose sight of how much alike they were and how many values they shared. It also had an effect of changing men's attitudes toward the disagreements which are always certain to arise in politics: ordinary, resolvable disputes were converted into questions of principle, involving rigid, unnegotiable dogma.... One might say that the issue structured and polarized many random, unoriented points of conflict on which sectional interest diverged. It transformed political action from a process of accommodation to a mode of combat. Once this divisive tendency set in, sectional rivalry increased the tensions of the slavery issue and the slavery issue embittered sectional rivalries in a reciprocating process which the majority of Americans found themselves unable to check even though they deplored it.

Throughout the 1850s, we see a spirit taking possession of part of the country that insisted on inflaming divisive passions until the country had fairly broken in two. Potter writes:

> Certainly the psychological ties of union were much attenuated at the end of 1859. [John Brown's raid on] Harpers Ferry had revealed a division between North and South so much deeper than generally suspected that a newspaper in Mobile questioned whether the American republic continued to be a single nation or whether it had become two nations appearing to be one.

Then came the election of 1860, ushering in a new president—Abraham Lincoln—elected without any electoral votes from the South. (Lincoln's election represented a break from the established pattern in which, for most of the years since the beginning of the Republic, the South had dominated the federal government.) The breaking up of the nation—by secession to form a new nation out of the southern part of what had been the Union—commenced even before Lincoln took office. Potter writes:

> Ten days after the election of Lincoln, the Augusta, Georgia "Daily Constitutionalist" published an editorial reflecting on what had happened to American nationalism: 'The most inveterate and sanguine Unionist [i.e. person favoring preservation of the Union, as opposed to the secessionists] in Georgia, if he is an observant man. must read, in the signs of the times, the hopelessness of the Union cause, and the feebleness of the Union sentiment in this State. The differences between North and South have been growing more marked for years, and the mutual repulsion more radical, until not a single sympathy is left between the dominant influences in each section.'

Divide and Conquer

It might be reasonably argued that the polarization in America in the 1850s didn't "just happen," but rather that there was an important role played in the process by deliberate human intention. The so-called "fire-eaters" in the South (an extreme, pro-slavery faction) were already eager to break up the Union at the beginning of that period.

But the fire-eaters were a minority viewpoint at that time and proved unable, in the early 1850s, to bring the rest of the South with them. Their power increased over the course of the decade, however. And, as William Freehling shows in his *Road to Disunion*, even with that greater power, they needed to execute an extremely effective strategy in the end-game leading up to secession in order to carry the day in the South. By that means, an intense, organized, and strategically adept minority was able to govern the course of the South in the secession crisis and set the nation on the course toward war.

> [NOTE: There is no real parallelism between the fire-eaters in the South and the Abolitionists in the North, in terms of their political power and their place in their regions. The Abolitionists were persecuted even by the Northerners. They were fringe, and political poison, while the fire-eaters were always a respectable, respected part of the Southern elite.]

But whatever the role of deliberate intention in generating the polarization during that era—and I feel unable to judge how much weight it deserves—in our own time the role of deliberate human intention in creating divisions between groups in America seems undeniable.

Fostering and exacerbating divisions among groups has been a tactic of "evil rulers" throughout history. So also in America in these times. People like Newt Gingrich and Rush Limbaugh employed deliberate rhetorical strategies to demonize "librels." Over the course of the years, their efforts—which American liberalism for the most part failed to call out or counter—led many millions of Americans to hold their fellow citizens on the other side with a mixture of hatred and contempt that was far from the norm in American political history.

(During the G.W. Bush presidency, I did a radio show in which I asked my conservative audience to what extent they saw liberals as their fellow citizens with whom they should work to come up with solutions to our nation's problems, and to what extent as "enemies who should be given no say in our national decisions." What most of the callers had to say set my hair on end.)

Clearly, "love thy neighbor" is the counsel of the good, while "hate whoever disagrees" is that of evil, just as harmony is better than discord and peace is better than war.

Fanning the flames of animosity is not the only way divisions among people can be created. People can be driven apart also by eliminating the basis for potentially constructive discussion. The force that has taken over the American right has practiced this tactic as well. It has done so by creating an "alternative universe" constructed of falsehoods for its followers to believe. In a piece, addressed mostly to the conservative majority in our district, that I published during my campaign for Congress, I addressed this lack of a shared set of "facts" among Americans in our times. In that context, I felt it appropriate to mention, but not emphasize, that the source of the problem lay on the right (e.g. Fox News) rather than being a matter of "both sides do it." Here's how, in an op/ed published in my conservative area under the title "Tower of Babel," I made the case for the importance in a healthy democracy of us citizens having some common understanding of the facts:

> Many have noticed that it has become unusually difficult, in recent years, for Americans to talk constructively across the political divide. One reason for this regrettable development has been a change in our nation's media culture.
>
> In the America I grew up in, we all got our news from similar, basically trustworthy sources. The people I recall were such excellent journalists as Chet Huntley and David Brinkley on NBC, and Walter Cronkite on CBS.
>
> Now, Americans have segmented themselves into audiences for different newscasts with different political slant.
>
> That would not be a big problem-except for one thing. The people following these different sources of 'news' are getting different sets of 'facts.'
>
> I relish conversation where we can get into the different values and principles that are emphasized in the different political worldviews. As I see it, both liberal and conservative principles are important for a healthy society. No camp has a monopoly on the moral truth. As I used to say on my radio shows in the Shenandoah Valley, "we should talk with each other as if we might actually learn from each other."
>
> But it's different when we enter into the conversation with different, and mutually contradictory, sets of facts. While it can be educational for everyone to talk about different values and principles, if either side of a discussion is mistakenly convinced of the truth of 'facts' that are actually false, good conversation becomes effectively impossible.
>
> On almost every issue our country faces, we encounter this barrier of contradictory sets of facts-e.g. on whether this piece of legislation has created or killed jobs, on which policies promoted by which party have contributed to the national debt or helped reduce it, on what the science says about the climate.

Studies have shown that this problem is not a matter of 'both sides do it.' It's been shown, for example, that people who get their information from Fox News are far more likely than others to hold beliefs that are false. (Liberal America definitely has some important faults in our times, but systematic deception about the facts is not one of them.)

While a whole book could be written to establish that this problem—the division of our country into different political camps with different facts—is the fruit of the forces that have come to dominate the American right, that's not my main point here.

Rather, I want to offer an interpretation of what the likely purpose is behind the erection of this barrier to our being able to communicate productively about the challenges we face as a people.

The biblical story of the Tower of Babel sheds light here. That story in the Bible demonstrates that one very effective way of preventing a community of people from achieving their common purposes is to make it impossible for those people to communicate meaningfully with each other.

We Americans have common purposes. The great majority of us want a government that looks out for the interests of average Americans, that protects the interest of the vast American middle class, that maintains the integrity of our democratic institutions, that operates on the basis of "the consent of the governed," of "one person, one vote," that respects "the rule of law."

If we can act together, we will achieve these common purposes. And if we can talk constructively with each other, we will be able to act together.

But if there are elements in our society that want a different kind of America, THEIR aims will be served by preventing us from acting together. And to achieve that, just as in the story of the Tower of Babel, all they need to do is prevent us from talking constructively together.

One way to prevent constructive discussion is to make sure that different groups have different sets of "facts." The purveying of false "facts" is one major component of a strategy of "divide and conquer" that these powerful elements are waging against us, the American people.

Our Founders gave us a system of government—of self-government—that is predicated on the notion that our citizens will be able to talk productively about our politics. For that system to work, we need to make sure that we can establish a common factual basis for discussion.

To establish a common set of facts, for Americans in our times, we need to work harder to make sure that, in the world of news reporting, the truth defeats the lie.

After a very fulfilling decade of doing radio conversations with a conservative audience from 1992-2002, I found the door to constructive conversation increasingly closed. Instead of discussing our values and principles, we would be blocked at the very start by the lack of overlap in our basic notion of what was and was not true. What kind of conversation can one have about a president whom some people "know" was born in Kenya, about a health care bill that some "know" would have "death panels" making decisions to pull the plug on granny?

It was, indeed, like the builders of the tower whose speech was confounded by the speaking of mutually incomprehensible tongues.

This "Tower of Babel" strategy might be regarded as a version of the ancient strategy of "divide and conquer," an idea that goes back to the classical world of the Greeks and then the Romans. But in the context of a democracy, where power is given by the voters, "divide and conquer" has a special application.

As usually implemented, a divide and conquer strategy involves breaking up concentrations of power into smaller units, so that each can be conquered individually when otherwise the conquered groups might have prevailed by banding together. That much still applies in the current American drama in which certain actors—and behind them, a coherent force of brokenness—wish to control the destiny of the nation. But the strategy for dominance here is not to pick off the competition one by one so much as to get the competing power—in this case, the power of the American people—to nullify itself.

America's founders wanted a nation to be ruled justly through the system they set up so that the ruling power had "the consent of the governed." But if the governed can be divided into polarized camps that are antagonistic to each other and have been rendered unable to deliberate together, then the two opposing groups essentially cancel each other out. The "will of the people" becomes a case of 1 + (-1) = 0.

Into the void of that zero, those people and systems—whose "divide and conquer" strategy has succeeded—can steer the nation as they choose.

Behind them—with their insatiable lusts for power and wealth, and their willingness to deceive and manipulate and exploit their fellow human beings—lies that coherent force of brokenness. It has worked to shape those people and systems, and to elevate them to positions of dominance. And it can use the power stolen from the people to break the nation still further.

Top-Down Enforcement of Orthodoxy as a Tool of the Lie

While the disorder that can arise from the liberal side is typically from the bottom up and fragmented, and due to laxity, the typical disorder from the right comes from the top-down, when a destructive force compels lock-step conformity on a course of evil. An example of this can explain how the force now animating the right in America has led intelligent people to believe blatant falsehoods.

According to "the parable of the tribes" (Chapter Five) it was through the problem of uncontrolled power that the major impetus for brokenness entered into the human system as an unintended by-product of the breakthrough into civilization. The breakthrough created an ungoverned situation, and thereafter humankind—the civilized creature—would be compelled to struggle with the brokenness of disorder.

The right and the left have different characteristic ways of creating disorder. By "left" here, I mean not communist or any other authoritarian form of "leftist" politics. Rather, I mean "liberal," i.e. that approach to politics and society that emphasizes the liberty of the individual in choosing how to live and therefore also the toleration of difference, and that seeks to use the power of the state to help those individuals thrive on their chosen path. Liberalism tends to eschew orthodoxy, to embrace diversity, and to prefer a social policy of "live and let live."

Not surprisingly, therefore, the characteristic error of liberalism is the error of excessive laxity: too little control, too little enforcement of standards, too much toleration of choices that lead to disordered lives and, if enough of such disorder adds up, to a disordered society.

It is a bottom-up approach to order (at the level of private life-choices, though not of corporate conduct) and, as such, when it errs it does so in the direction of too little power invested in the "up" and too much free rein at the "bottom."

This is not the place for going into such pitfalls of the liberal approach because, except for how they connect with liberalism's weakness and blindness in the present crisis, they are not central to the big dangers now facing America.

It is, rather, with the problems of power that come from the top-down approach characteristic of the right that we need to contend. For the pathology of the right in our time is in many ways an exemplification of the dangers that come from the hierarchical structures created by the more authoritarian approach to power and control.

It is said about Democrats and Unitarians that trying to get them to act as a coherent force is like "herding cats." That is not the problem with the right. At their best, conservative cultures gain a constructive kind of coherence that comes from the high value placed on such things as *loyalty, duty, discipline, and obedience* to a legitimate authority.

At their worst—i.e. when the power that is demanding loyalty and obedience is an evil power—these structures override the best that is in their followers. Where the liberals' error can create disorder from the micro level upward, the error of the right can create a destructive order enforced from the top downward onto those who are below.

We can see pathologies of the top-down kind in various authoritarian regimes of the modern world, which can get people to march together in lock-step, both literally and figuratively. These pathologies are illustrated also, in these times, in the virtual unanimity that the Republicans have enforced among their members in Congress—voting in lock-step in ways that have virtually never served the good of the nation. (See the discussion of the "pure case" in Chapter Two.)

The following is an illustration of how the force of brokenness can use top-down power to break people in ways that serve to extend its power further, and thus to wreak more brokenness upon the world in which it is operating.

This illustration begins with one of the mysteries of our present national crisis: how is it that people, who are intelligent in most aspects of their lives, can be led to believe incredible things? and how is it that people who show real goodness in most domains can be enlisted, in the political realm—i.e. in that arena where issues of power get decided—to give support to an evil force?

One important part of the answer involves the means by which people come to their beliefs.

My own original family culture led me to focus, in arriving at my beliefs, on what is shown by the evidence, considered by disciplined reason. (It also led me to expect that this was more generally the way of the world than it turns out to be, and made me slow to recognize that many people arrive at their beliefs in a very different way.)

One can observe that for many people—at least on some subjects—the most important criterion for what to believe is that it maintains one's good standing with one's community.

That need imposes more pressure in some communites than in others, as some communities are considerably more tolerant than others of a diversity of opinion.

The culture of today's political right is strikingly intolerant, by American standards, of political opinions that stray from that faction's orthodoxy. And in this intolerance, it shows its continuity with the historic nature of the political culture of the South (which, as I've argued, gave us much of the heart of the spirit that has taken over today's Republican Party).

This enforced conformity of political belief is why we've long seen a "Solid South"—solid first, from before the Civil War through the Civil Rights era, as a stronghold of the Democratic Party and then in recent times a solidly "red state" region.

But the domain of enforced orthodoxy is not all-encompassing. Only some issues fall within it. People can have whatever opinion they want on a whole myriad of matters both important and trivial.

It is specifically on those issues that bear upon the wielding of power in America, as identified by the top-down structures of the right, that the unorthodox position is treated as heresy.

From before the Civil War until a few decades ago, the paramount issues on which orthodoxy was enforced concerned race: first there was slavery, then there was Jim Crow segregation. No white Southerner could publicly oppose the prevailing opinion on those issues without suffering severe social (and possibly even physical) consequences. (And certainly no Southern politician could survive politically if he deviated from the orthodox position on white dominance.)

Now the enforced orthodoxy concerns anything that the power structure of the right has deemed "liberal." For most of the ordinary people in my neck of the woods, being seen as politically liberal would carry significant adverse consequences in terms of a person's relationship to his or her community. For many, likely most, it would mean alienation from the people they live among, the people they work with, the people they worship with.

- Imagine a member of the white, rural, overwhelmingly Republican-voting community in which I live in the Shenandoah Valley, declaring publicly his or her strong support for Obamacare.
- Imagine such a person stating publicly that climate change is real and requires action.
- Imagine such a person telling his neighbors that Barack Obama is far from being the monster/traitor/America-hater that they've been led to believe by the powers that dominate the right.

A person who took such positions, while not in any physical danger, would likely be regarded as a kind of heretic, with the strain on their community standing that implies in a community that is on the fringe of the Bible Belt.

As it was for more than a century on keeping the darker race down, so it is now with the rejection of "the other side" of the political divide. Though the dichotomy has changed, it is the same spirit that persists: in both cases, the orthodoxy that is enforced is focused upon an Us-vs.-Them division of the world. A pattern built upon division is a pattern of brokenness.

With a pattern this enduring, the culture has had time to so structure the socialization of children that every generation internalizes the psychological structures that make such conformity of belief possible. The culture has had a very long time to develop the means to inculcate this basic lesson: *on some matters, one will simply believe what the community says to believe.*

With this pattern of enforced conformity of belief within a specific domain, a kind of compartmentalization can develop in people's mental and emotional habits. Intelligent people learn to turn off their intelligence when dealing with the realm of community orthodoxy, and good people will disconnect from their usual kind of moral awareness and avert their gaze from the moral implications of what this orthodoxy requires. And none of this is likely to be conscious.

(See my article*, "It's a Mistake to Think of our Fellow Americans on the Right as 'Stupid' People: Here's a Better Way," where I wrote: "We might think of people as having different 'modules' of consciousness that kick in depending on what 'programs' they've learned to apply in each realm of their lives."

> [NOTE: This connects with the idea of "part selves" (e.g. in *Internal Family Systems* Therapy by Richard C. Schwartz) in which the human personality is usually (or always, according to Schwartz) made up to some degree of a plurality of selves that operate more or less independently. The formation of part selves, Schwartz says, is especially likely to happen in response to trauma. The connection of such divided structures with the idea of brokenness is clear.]

All of a piece. The integrated self is one of the sacred dimensions of wholeness in the human world. And the self that is fractured—especially if it is fractured into unreconciled parts—provides evil with one of its essential points of entry into the human world.

Thus socialized to have modules of consciousness in which certain vital capabilities are disabled, people will be responsive to the community pressures to hold the required beliefs.

One of the ways that power can trump our humanity, then, is to socialize people to turn off their intelligence so they will not resist beliefs that the community requires of people in order to maintain the structures of power.

Although in liberal circles as well there is some social pressure to believe what others believe, and some cost to having divergent opinions, the pressure to conform is nothing like what exists on the right.

There's been no "solid North" corresponding to the "solid South." In the South, if you disregard the voting of blacks (who of course for generations were prevented from voting), you have practically a one-party system.

This right-wing enforcement of conformity—well beyond what characterizes Liberal America—can also be found further up the hierarchy of the right's political power system: in the 2012 race for the Republican presidential nomination, Governor Huntsman felt compelled to recant his heresy in taking the climate science seriously; and meanwhile the Republicans in the House voted *unanimously* against almost everything President Obama proposed. Toeing the line is nearly mandatory.

The coercive power of sticking with the party line is manifest from the top of the right-wing system down to the level of the base.

This enforced conformity helps explain how is it that intelligent people can believe such blatant falsehoods as the right generally peddles. The community exerts an essentially coercive power over the individual with respect to those beliefs central to the political force with which the community is aligned.

The American nation may have been "conceived in liberty." But the development of American civilization contains other, very different elements as well. Some of these other elements created, as a subset of the American political culture, a system where true freedom of belief was effectively blocked by the power of the community over the individual.

But it is not really the "community" that is in charge. The community serves as the deputy to a power at the top of the hierarchy.

With the force of brokenness, we are almost always dealing with "the problem of power." To understand this specific problem of power, it is necessary to trace the pattern's ramifications beyond the relationship between community and individual. A more fundamental aspect of this dynamic of brokenness concerns *how the community itself has historically been shaped by the society's dominating power for its own purposes.*

Every society has some inequalities of power, but in the South—with an economy based on slavery, and with the early emergence of a powerful slaveholding class—the inequalities *during the formative years of the region's political culture* were far greater than in the North.

By the time any class achieved dominance to a comparable degree in the North—in the latter decades of the 19th century with the rise of industrial corporate capitalism and the era of the robber barons—the culture of the Northern states like New York, Pennsylvania, and Massachusetts, had already been forming for more than two centuries.

In the South, by contrast, even during the most formative period in the generations before the American Revolution, much of the South was powerfully dominated by a class that drew its power from the ownership of many slaves and vast tracts of land.

With great inequalities of power already present during the formative stages of Southern society, the dominant class was in a position to shape the nature of the emerging Southern community. More the top/down of elite rule than the bottom/up of democracy. As a result, over the generations, the ruling class was able to mold a kind of community culture that would tolerate no heresies on those beliefs that were important for maintaining (and extending) the elite's power.

Nowhere is this insistence on orthodoxy more dramatically displayed than in the treatment of the issue of slavery during the years leading up to the Civil War.

(The enforcement of orthodoxy, therefore, not only reflected a higher degree of dominance than was found in the North, but it also was focused on an institution whose essence was the complete domination and exploitation of some human beings by others—the combination of these two elements thus magnified the role in the culture of the Spirit of Domination.)

It is shocking for one who has grown up imagining that the liberties granted by the Bill of Rights have been the established norms of this "land of the free" to discover how little liberty was allowed in the South when it came to opinions regarding slavery.

In his excellent book, *Road to Disunion*, William H. Freehling describes the "Slaveholders' attempts to silence critics, whether by cries of disloyalty to slavery or by lynch mobs or by gag rules or by censoring the mails or by precluding Lincoln's appointees' campaigning…" (p. 533) Anti-slavery literature was effectively banned from the South. Opponents of slavery could be tarred and feathered and run out of town on a rail.

Freehling refers to "the Old South's colliding governing systems," i.e. the collision between the system that we learn about from the Declaration of Independence, based on the "unalienable rights" of equal men and the wielding of governmental power based on "the consent of the governed," and that other system based on that ancient principle, "The strong do what they can, and the weak suffer what they must."

On the issue of slavery, on which the dominant power rested, power trumped democracy. Again, Freeling: "Slaveholders particularly dreaded the impact of open debate on duplicitous slaves and suspect nonslaveholders."

The coercive community was molded to preclude "open debate." No free "market of ideas" on that central question.

The whole issue of slavery got bound up, by the pronouncements and manipulations of the powerful slaveholders, in values of Southern honor. Criticism of slavery was to be experienced as a slur against the heart of the culture—fighting words, for honorable men. (For more on the role of the idea of "honor," see pp. 166-168 below.)

People were taught what they were required to believe, and taught also to fight to protect those beliefs from any who would challenge them. Where the defense of falsehoods could become a matter of honor, the power of the truth in the political realm could be overwhelmed by other emotional forces conducive to battle.

By the time the Civil War began, the culture of enforced conformity of belief on matters central to the Slaveholders' power was well established. In the century following the Civil War, the same enforced conformity obtained with respect to the continued system of racial oppression called "Jim Crow."

No one who cared about being in harmony with his social world could afford to be seen as an "N-word lover."

Yesterday's "N-word lover" is today's "librel." (And so we can find many, in the "conservative" community of my area, who talk as if in absolutes against anything associated with liberalism—as if all taxes, all redistribution of wealth, all regulation of business, all environmental laws were bad.)

It is not just that the individual is controlled by the power wielded by the community. It is also the community that has been shaped through history by the wielders of great power.

In America in our times, a political culture that—in large measure—is built upon the culture created by the slaveholding class has substituted a different set of dogmas for the old ones.

[NOTE: It is not only the cultural descendants of the slaveholding class—might one consider people like Texas oil tycoons as extensions of that class?—who employ this structure of brokenness. They have been joined nowadays by (often Yankee) corporate powers (the cultural descendants of the old Robber Barons), who now gladly utilize the primordial brokenness in Southern culture to advance their power. This time, the spirit that previously animated the antebellum South has a powerful ally in the spirit of a kind of rapacious corporate capitalism. That corporate element is strong at the top of the Republican power system. In terms of the source of its power in the American electorate, however, it is "the spirit that drove us to Civil War" that is predominant.]

The descendants of those who were socialized to conform on matters of racial domination are now taught a new set of doctrines to which they are pressured to conform: that all government regulation of corporations amounts to tyranny, that climate change is a hoax perpetrated by pointy-headed intellectuals they call "scientists," that money is speech and corporations are people, that if you're worried about your "liberty" the best way to protect it is to prevent any regulation of guns, that any attempt to address inequalities of wealth is unAmerican class warfare, etc.

Thus do the patterns of brokenness, created by the reign of power, perpetuate themselves and extend the reign of power.

USING THE WOUNDS IT INFLICTS TO CREATE MORE WOUNDS

One response to trauma is to perpetuate trauma. An evil force can use that to expand its power.

A general principle is that brokenness begets brokenness (and wholeness begets wholeness). It is no surprise, therefore, that the damage inflicted on people by the force of brokenness can generate the fuel to drive the engine of further brokenness in the world. This idea, introduced here earlier (pp. 116-119), will be expanded here.

My cold-war era book *Out of Weakness: Healing the Wounds That Drive Us To War* looked at three major sets of wounds that engender the "excesses of the warrior spirit," i.e. that make the problem of war in civilized history still worse than intersocietal anarchy alone would make it.

The thesis of that book is that, while it is sane to defend our lives and homelands against those who would take them from us, the engines of destruction in human affairs are often fueled by a defensiveness of a different kind. Contrary to rationalist and materialist assumptions about human motivation, what we human beings seem most ferocious in defending are certain beliefs that we hold—-or, rather, that we want to hold, but inwardly and subconsciously experience to be false—about ourselves.

"We Are Not Weak, But Mighty"

People can make war to deny the frightening feelings left from their past traumatic experience of victimization.

As was said earlier (in Chapter Six): The inevitable struggle for power and the reign of the ways of power have rendered the historical experience of humankind traumatic. It is the very essence of trauma that it entails experience that people cannot integrate within themselves in a whole way (See my brother, on the meaning of trauma, on page 50 above.).

This historical experience—both for societies, and for young humans being socialized into cultures hostile to human needs—inflicts the traumatic learning that weakness and vulnerability are an intolerably dangerous condition, and that, if we lack the strength to impose our will, the world can treat our deepest longings as insignificant.

We would accept being weak in a safe world. But it is unacceptable to be weak in a world where the mighty rule by force.

One absorbs from bad treatment the intolerable feeling that one is bad. The narcissistic project is an insistence on the opposite and compensatory image of oneself as superior.

So it is visible in history how the engines of war get fueled by people's need to fight in order to deny feelings of weakness and worthlessness. People can gain some feeling of safety by compelling others to play the role of the weak and victimized.

Historical forces that disregard human needs and treat people as of no account can push people toward defensive grandiosity. The inevitability of the rule of power will inevitably lead some people, who have been wounded by power, to worship power. A species caught up in a destructive spiral out of its control will place *control* inordinately high among its values.

People will seek occasions where they can impose their will to compensate for the epidemic experience of impotence.

Thus are the engines of war stoked by the very injuries that war inflicts.

(For more on this, see Parts 1 and 2 of *Out of Weakness*: "Winning: The Worship of Strength" and "Winning: A World of Scarcity.")

[NOTE: A version of this has been enacted in America in our times. Less educated white men in America, according to the statistics, have been left behind in the American economy, actually losing ground over the past forty years. The corporate component of the right-wing force has played an important role in the disempowering of these men. With the help of the government in which they buy their influence, the corporate powers have succeeded in weakening the labor movement, and gaining the power to take for themselves an ever-greater proportion of the wealth gained through growth in the productivity of American workers.

Yet a great many of these men are giving their political power as voting citizens over to that same force on the political right that has been victimizing them. Joe Bageant's book *Deer Hunting with Jesus* provides a heart-rending portrait of how this works among the people the author grew up with in Winchester, Virginia.

In their own lives, these men experience weakness on an ongoing basis—in relation to their employers and their government. And then, with the aid of the propaganda fed them by the same powers, they can alleviate that feeling of weakness by identifying with the powerful in the American system, and with the might of the nation itself. (One might cite the collective narcissism that nowadays surrounds the idea of "American exceptionalism," and the increasing conflation of patriotism with the assertion of national superiority—"We're # 1!").

"You are not weak, but strong—so long as you identify with us who wield power we have gained at your expense."]

"We Have God's Truth, You Are Heretics"

The more the world is experienced as dangerous, the less tolerable is the sense of uncertainty. The scarier the world, therefore, the more people are apt to view discordant beliefs as threatening, and the more they will rend the world with dogmatic intolerance of other views.

As the traumas inflicted by the force of brokenness lead people to deny their true experience of vulnerability, so also do they drive people to deny their intolerable confusion and uncertainty.

In a safe world, uncertainties might be embraced as mystery. But the more those who peer out into the darkness have experienced the landscape as strewn with traps and land mines, the greater will be their need to feel certain that their maps are reliable. The sense of mystery that, in a more benign world, we might have apprehended with wonder and awe now creeps toward us with terror mounted upon its back.

By condemning civilized peoples to inescapable insecurity, civilization has therefore greatly intensified the temptation to cling to false certainties.

The experiments of social psychologists show that the greater the stress, the less tolerance for ambiguity. Over thousands of years of civilization, the larger human experiment has demonstrated the same relationship. The more one senses that a false step may mean disaster, the more impelled one feels to know with certainty that one is walking on the true path.

Dogma is the child of anxiety.

Those who think differently from those who need certainty, therefore, are thus experienced as a threat. Thus do the traumatized (broken) fuel the war system by insisting that their truth is God's truth, and anyone who disagrees should be fought as enemies of God.

(For more on this theme, see Part 4 of *Out of Weakness*: "God's Truth.")

"We Are Not Evil, You Are"

The harsher the demands of society on the human being, the more painful it is for the members of that society to acknowledge those parts of themselves that society forbids. This provides the impetus for people, distressed by their irreconcilable inner conflicts, to project onto some enemy what they have denied in themselves.

We have discussed here earlier how power-maximizing societies often impose harsh moralities. That dynamic opens yet another way in which the brokenness created by the rule of power drives people to create still more brokenness by fueling the fires of conflict.

The demands of power are at best only partially aligned with the needs of the human organism. Thus, the greater the pressure on societies to maximize their power the more fiercely will the society's demands make war upon the natural inclinations of the human animal.

Internalizing these demands, which are the fruits of the war outside, intensifies a war within the human psyche. The greater the gap between the internalized social demands and human nature, the more painful will be the intrapsychic conflict. The more our culture teaches us to regard our natural desires as evil, the less capable will we be, as growing human beings, to reconcile the warring parts within us. And the greater the need to turn away from that painful inner reality.

To deliver ourselves from the pain of that internal war, to experience ourselves as more whole and harmonious within, we will be tempted to deny our "evil" parts and identify with the power that has imposed its will upon us in the guise of "moral" authority. But since the sense of evil does not simply disappear, we will have a need to locate that evil somewhere outside the boundaries of one's self, projecting our forbidden desires out into the world, and reconfiguring the war inside us as a war out in the world.

(For more on this theme, see Part 3 of *Out of Weakness*: "Boundaries: The Dirty Business of Cleaning House.")

It is in defense of these beliefs that we humans have so often been ready to kill and to die. This helps explain why the warrior spirit has often been tinged with madness. For these beliefs about ourselves we defend so zealously we inwardly sense to be false.

The denial of the realities of our experience—as weak, uncertain, tainted with "evil"—thus lays down the template for the rule of the lie.

Trauma makes truth intolerable, incapable of being integrated. Once we lose the integrity of dealing with reality, the embrace of all kinds of falsehood becomes possible.

It is for good reason that traditional Western religion has regarded as central to Satan's identity that he is the Deceiver.

INTERLUDE VIII:

Why Isn't the Story Being Told?

WHO WILL RAISE THE ALARM?

> *Why, out of all the Democrats who have been in Congress during the Obama presidency, has there not been a single one to step up and call out—in the most powerful but truthful ways—this Republican Party for the atrocity that it has become?*

In January of 2011, I decided to run for Congress. My decision grew out of my having then given up on the idea that Barack Obama would or could do what I saw as Job One for leadership in our times: to help the American people perceive what an extraordinarily destructive and downright unpatriotic thing the Republican Party had become, and thus to persuade the good and decent people who support that Party to repudiate it until it changed its ways.

Had I won that election—against a 20-year Republican incumbent, in a strongly Republican district—it was my intention to use that larger platform of a congressman to do what I could to raise that alarm. (While I did not win the election, the campaign itself—in which I enjoyed the status of major party nominee—gave me a worthwhile platform for that purpose.)

I never got that congressional platform. But is it not remarkable that not one of the more than 250 Democrats who do serve in one or the other of the Houses of Congress has taken on that mission?

Certainly, there are Democrats who criticize the Republicans over this thing or that. Senators like Bernie Sanders and Elizabeth Warren have spoken out against various aspects of this force. But is there a single one who has come out to declare in a powerful way what an atrocity this Republican Party has become, and to lay out the irrefutable, compelling case that's right at hand?

Obama's failure to press the battle against those who have so relentlessly assaulted him is but the most dramatic and prominent embodiment of a more general failure. What might have been accomplished, for example, by just one Senator (out of the more than 50 Democrats in that body for the first six years of the Obama presidency), calling out the Republican Party for all the ways it has trampled on our long-established political traditions, norms, and ideals?

Such a condemnation is sorely needed, and should be made strongly and continuously enough to get attention. I wouldn't expect a major presidential contender to make such a condemnation as powerfully as the truth of our times would warrant, for not enough people are yet ready to recognize its truth. But as for many of the other Democrats in Congress, especially those in "safe seats," I can see no danger in painting the picture starkly.

It would be hard to make a case that is so harsh it could not be backed up with abundant evidence.

What, after all, would be too harsh to say about a political party that refuses to respond to the gravest warnings the scientific community has ever issued to humankind; that works to transfer wealth and power to those who already are the richest and mightiest at a time when the gulf between them and the average citizen has already grown wider than it has been in living memory; that gave us not only torture but the travesty of the fig-leaf torture memos, undermining the foundational idea of the rule of law; that's working to turn our democracy into a plutocracy?

How could the nation not benefit from calling out in the strongest terms a political party that is fundamentally dishonest in virtually all its communications:

- from the lies that took us into the botched war in Iraq
- to the birther lie used to delegitimize the president the American people elected

- to the lies about climate change
- lies about caring about the federal deficit
- and deceiving people into believing that America can best be kept free of the boot of tyranny by preventing the government from regulating citizen ownership of weapons of military grade, capable of firing multiple rounds within seconds?

And if the condemnation of this atrocious political party proved controversial, all the better—all the better to have more public attention focused on a strong case well made.

But as I said, it seems that not one of the Democrats serving in Congress has stepped up to make this strong case. Why is that? Is it blindness: Do they not see this unprecedented darkness? Is it cowardice: Do they fear that they could not survive politically by raising the alarm for our imperiled nation?

Whatever the reason, the story is not getting told.

The Abdication of the Press

Quite obvious questions about significant national problems have remained unasked by the major news media of this nation. Why such abdication of the proper role of a free press in a democracy?

And then there's the press in our times—the press, whose job in a democracy like ours is to tell the citizens what they need to know to be able to perform well their responsibilities as citizens.

Here we have one of the biggest stories in American history—only the struggle over slavery and the Civil War to which it led seems comparable—and the press is failing to tell it.

Some might argue that it is not the role of the press to issue condemnations of a major political party, even when it is taken over by something so destructive and dishonest. But how about just asking the obvious questions?

Consider: The great majority of the American people feel that the nation is heading in the "wrong direction," and this striking and worrisome popular judgment has persisted almost uninterruptedly for some years now. Is that not as clear an indication as there could be that in our nation something of great importance has gone wrong? Is it not an extraordinary thing for most of the American people to feel their country has lost its way?

And when the nation has a deep problem—as this one surely is—is it not the job of the press to get to the bottom of the matter? Would not a responsible press be asking: what is it that leads people to feel that things are heading wrongly, and what are the causes—what is responsible—for the direction things are going?

Obvious questions, these. Questions that should be getting the full journalistic investigatory treatment. Surely such questions warrant at least as much investigation as was given, back in the 1990s, to a stain on a blue dress. But where in the American press are these obvious lines of inquiry being pursued with full investigative vigor?

And consider: It's almost universally recognized that the American political system has become dysfunctional. The Congress, held by the American people in a level of esteem so low it is setting records, has been making the "do-nothing Congress" Truman ran against look like a hive of productive activity.

Clearly, it's a major national problem when the instruments our founders gave us for meeting our national challenges are failing to work. And is it not the job of the press to help the citizenry understand what it is that's gone wrong, investigating such questions as: Whose fault it it that our politics are so messed up? Are both sides equally "extreme"? Are both sides equally unwilling to compromise? Are both sides equally unwilling to address our national problems? If the dysfunctionality of our government is reaching unprecedented levels, is one side or the other acting in relevant ways that are likewise unprecedented?

Obvious questions. Important questions, the very kind a responsible press in a democracy would tackle. And questions unasked.

One of the biggest stories in American history has been unfolding right before our eyes, for more than a decade. And those who should be telling that story are not.

This crisis may be centered on that part of the American body politic that has been taken over by a pathological force and made into an instrument for its destructive purposes. But this crisis is also exposing that some sort of rot that has eaten away at the foundations of the American cultural/political/moral/spiritual system as a whole.

Chapter Nine:

Why Now? How the Balance of Power Between Good and Evil Can Shift Adversely

My thinking about evil in terms of the transmission of patterns of brokenness was precipitated in the fall of 2004 by my recognizing a pattern being used by that manipulative genius, Karl Rove, to seduce many traditionalist Americans. It was the same pattern that had been used a century and more before to seduce poor whites in the Jim Crow South.

Here's how I put it in an essay* I wrote the following year, "The Concept of Evil: Why It is Intellectually Valid and Politically and Spiritually Important":

> In the Jim Crow South, and now again in Karl Rove's America, the leaders inflame passions around peripheral issues to distract their supporters from what the leaders are really doing with their power. A century ago, the hot-button distraction was racial purity. Now, the leaders whip people up about issues of moral purity. In both cases, unjust leaders use deception to exacerbate divisions useful to magnifying their own power and wealth.

Dark patterns lurk in the system, like some dormant virus, ready to erupt when the culture's immune system weakens.

Time now to look into how it is that a culture's immune system—and especially our own in these times—can weaken, allowing the opportunistic force of evil to advance.

The Shifting Balance of Power

As in any battle, the tide can shift depending on changing circumstance and how well the sides fight.

"The battle between good and evil" is like other struggles. Its outcome depends on the opportunities presented to the different sides of the battle, and how well each side uses them.

In a given civilized system—in any cultural order, or nation, or subset of a nation—the balance of power between the two elements can shift significantly, depending on the circumstances.

In Chapter Seven's final section ("Shifts in the Balance of Power Between Good and Evil"), we already looked briefly at how the balance of power between good and evil shifted adversely in the American South, in the years leading up to the Civil War, and in Germany, in the decades following the First World War and leading up to the Second World War.

Here I will expand on the account of how the opening for a dark force expanded in the American South. And then we will turn to the third and most urgent case for us to consider the question of "Why Now?" to account for the advance of an evil force in America in our times.

The Civil War as the Duel the South Required to Defend its "Honor"

Central to the culture of the Old South was a code of honor. This code derived from a warrior culture formed in a dangerous world. Out of injuries grows an acute sensitivity to insult, and a need to avenge the blow to a precarious self-esteem. The moral critique of slavery from Abolitionists in the North provoked such a response among the honor-bound men of the South.

The growing conflict between North and South leading up to the Civil War was all about slavery. As the conflict grew in intensity, virtually every issue became swallowed up by the slavery issue. The Civil War was not about states' rights. Or rather, it was about states' rights, after a decade of strife over slavery, only in the very limited sense that the war itself was fought over the right of states to secede—by their own unilateral decision, and contrary to what the duly-elected President declared to be allowable under the Constitution—when they didn't like that their opponents over the issue of slavery had gained power.

About the meaning of slavery to the South, and more particularly to the slaveholding class that dominated the politics of the region, there are many deep and important points to be made. Here I will focus on one point that illustrates the workings of the force of brokenness that emerges out of the problem of power endemic to civilization.

To the semi-aristocratic class that dominated the South, the concept of "honor" was of central importance. (See Bertram Wyatt-Brown's *Southern Honor: Ethics and Behavior in the Old South.*) In many of its meanings and connotations, "Honor" is a fine thing. There are good reasons, for example, why it is a term of praise to say of someone that he (or she) is "honorable," or why we "honor" people who have achieved great things.

But there is also a darker side to the idea of "honor." It is telling that the code of honor, and how a man's honor must be defended, developed especially in those cultural environments afflicted by chronic strife and domination, attack and revenge. Such honor codes are found in societies in which the problem of power has made the role of the warrior especially central to the sense of manhood. The warrior's concept of honor is especially strong where the dynamics of interaction make the cleavage between "winners" and "losers" especially salient.

Such dynamics infuse the issues of domination/subordination, superiority/ inferiority, the manned/the unmanned with great intensity.

In a world afflicted by such brokenness, the form of "honor" that develops has within it the dark shadow of narcissistic wounds, a prickly and precarious sense of self-worth that is defended in excessive, and therefore destructive ways. (See "The Role of Narcissistic Injury in the Warrior's Code of Honor," in my book *Out of Weakness*, pp. 131-2.)

The culture of the American South was strongly shaped by such patterns of the warrior ethic that had emerged in Europe and then were perpetuated by the hierarchical society that developed in the American South, shaped by an aristocracy of plantation slaveholders.

In the South, the code of honor gave expression to a hypersensitivity to insult, i.e. to an assault, which honor requires be avenged, on one's asserted value and status.

Here, then, was an element of brokenness—embedded both in the culture, and in the psychology of the individuals—upon which the force of brokenness could seize, when the opportunity arose, to wreak destruction. In a few quick brushstrokes, here is how that happened.

In the North—starting in the 1830s—out of the religious revival of the Second Great Awakening, a moral and spiritual force gave rise to a growing anti-slavery movement. This movement infused into the American discourse a powerful moral condemnation of slavery, and through it of the slaveholding class in the South.

It is in the response to this condemnatory message that the brokenness involved in the structures of the sense of "honor" came into play, increasing the power of the force of brokenness in the South.

Ideally, a moral/political/psychological cultural system would encourage its human members to respond to such moral criticism with soul-searching and an openness to making moral improvements. In the South of that era, one finds hardly any of that. The response, rather, was not only defensive but also full of rage.

That rage reflects the latent role of narcissistic injury—the precariousness of the underlying self-worth—embedded in the ethic of "honor." Criticism is experienced as a recapitulation of the original assaults on the sense of self-worth of those socialized into the warrior society. The inflated compensatory self-image must be defended, and the rage provides the fuel to do so.

Thus, within that system of honor, the criticisms from the abolitionists were experienced as intolerable insults. (The intensity of the South's reaction to the abolitionists, with their severe moral criticism of slavery, is in itself clear evidence that some deep wounded place had been touched, and a kind of traumatic response had been triggered.)

The man of honor does not accept an insult. Rather, he returns it, like the Old Maid in the card game. (The challenge to a duel is conveyed by the insult of a slap across the face with a glove.) A man of honor responds to an insult with an eagerness to fight on the field of honor. Revenge through violence is the goal. But even death is better than dishonor.

One can clearly see how, in the decades leading to the Civil War, this sense of insult, and the resultant impulse to defend an offended sense of honor, helped drive the shift in the balance of power between forces of wholeness and brokenness in the South.

The economic and political motivations for the defense of slavery were thus further inflamed by the deep passions coming from the psychological level. The combination of inflated pride on the conscious level and vulnerability to feelings of inferiority on the unconscious level—a clear manifestation on the psychic level of the pattern of brokenness—gave rise to a political response in the South that greatly magnified the power of the Spirit of Brokenness in the American political system.

Thus was the nation driven into a catastrophic Civil War. A war that, in a meaningful sense, can be seen as the duel on which the slaveholder-dominated South insisted, as the means to defend its/their wounded sense of honor. A war, it is fair to say, from which the nation has still far from completely healed.

> [NOTE: With permission, I quote from a relevant email to me from Professor James McPherson, one of America's most respected historians of the Civil War: "I think you are right about the South's resentment of the insult to their honor represented by the election of an antislavery president. That was certainly a motivating factor in secession."]

One more instance of how wounds in the human psyche, interwoven with a cultural system, can provide an entry-way for the force of evil to wreak still more destruction upon civilized humankind.

Terror of the Subordinate Role

Both the South in the lead up to the Civil War and the Republicans of today refuse to accept that in a democracy sometimes one wins and sometimes one loses. In both cases, one important meaning of that refusal is that people's experience in the dominant-subordinate relationship has made the weaker position so repellant and painful as not to be tolerated.

The election of Abraham Lincoln put the Southern elite in a position subordinate to an authority hostile to slavery, i.e. the institution about which they had already felt insulted. But that election was not the only indication that the tide of power was running against the South.

A great wave of immigration was coming to American shores, and these white immigrants were choosing to make their lives in the North, rather than compete against slaves. Thus, with the balance of population moving toward the North, so also would the political power in the American democracy.

Meanwhile, the North was industrializing, and this was yet another portent of that region's growing power.

In history, the power of peoples and regions has continually ebbed and flowed, and many have had to adjust to the loss of dominance. Some do so gracefully (e.g. Great Britain which, in the course of a century, went from being the world's greatest power to being a middling one). The South, by contrast, proved incapable of accepting that loss gracefully. And an important reason for this is what I call "the terror of the subordinate role."

Here is yet another way in which the force of evil could employ a pre-existing dimension of brokenness when a change of circumstance created the opportunity. Here, that pre-existing form of brokenness was the stark cleavage in the South between those on top and those on the bottom.

In a society based on slavery, the core of the relation between master and slave is subordination. As soon-to-be Vice President of the Confederacy Alexander Stephens declared: "the negro is not equal to the white man; that slavery, subordination to the superior race, is his natural and moral condition."

It is easy to understand how, in a society based on slavery, the idea of being subordinate would be terrifying. And the language coming out of the South, as that section lost its dominant position in the American political system, confirms that sense of terrible danger. Submitting to a power not their own was fraught with degrading connotations—like being turned into "slaves," and "a degradation to which a high spirited people should not submit."

The game of American power was fine with them so long as they came out on top, which they did to a remarkable degree for four score years and more—thanks to the three-fifths rule, clever political strategies, and Northern political divisions and weakness.

But when they were to be put into a position of "vassalage," as they saw it, they chose secession—even if it meant war—over submission.

That "terror of the subordinate role" seems relevant to the brokenness of our own time. While we in America today do not have an institutionalized nightmare of domination, like slavery, there are other ways of instilling in people a terror of being in a subordinate position. As children, we all grow up in a situation of weakness, and the psychology is well-established about how the lust for power can grow out of traumatic experiences of weakness.

The way in which today's dominant group apparently speaks of half of America as "takers" and "losers" seems further evidence of something absorbed regarding the meaning of being on the bottom of the hierarchical ladder. That, however, is speculation.

What is not speculative, however, is how much the Republicans of today re-capitulate the refusal of the Southerners on the eve of the Civil War to accept the prescribed American tradition of how to deal with losing an election conducted in a constitutionally legitimate way.

It has been more than thirty years since the Republican Party has accepted the legitimacy of a Democratic president. Rather than accepting that sometimes one's side will lose an election, and be consigned to playing a subordinate role, they have chosen to fight to destroy the power of their duly-elected opponent.

Democracy does not guarantee anyone permanent dominance. In a democracy, a fundamental principle is that we all agree to abide by the results of fair elections. That's what enables a society to deal with issues of power peacefully.

But those people who are terrified of the subordinate role—those for whom being the weaker party, even if temporarily, tends to trigger such feelings as humiliation, impotence, vulnerability, pain and rage—respect the democratic process only when they are triumphant.

Here is yet another way that we can see that "the spirit that drove us to Civil War is back."

Which brings us to the question, why is it that this force of brokenness has been able—at this moment in American history—to return again to a level of power sufficient to wreak great damage upon the American civilization?

Why Now?

Why at this moment in our history has an evil force been able to become so ascendant in the United States, in the absence of any huge and inescapable issue or any shattering national traumas? Three proposed pieces of an answer follow.

In our times, as in the era leading to the Civil War, the force of destructiveness has gained in power. Yes, in the 1950s (when I was young), there was McCarthyism, and the regime of racial segregation remained unbroken. (And women were more fully confined then to a position of enforced subordination.) But taking the American picture as a whole, I feel confident in saying, the balance of power between constructive and destructive forces was far more favorable then.

McCarthyism was a pathology that afflicted a particular dimension of our political process. Even while the paranoia around the "communist menace" was gathering steam, our national political system still had accomplishments of historic magnitude: the G.I. Bill, the interstate highway system, etc. The pathology at that time was localized to a particular slice of the nation's concerns. Now, by contrast, it pervades the whole system, and disables us from dealing with the whole spectrum of issues.

The segregationist regime was a terrible injustice central to the social order of one of the nation's regions, but it was not national in scope. Now, "the force that drove us to civil war is back" but is spread more or less nationally (even if its fortress remains in the South) and the brokenness is being played out nationally.

> (Besides which, it was in the post-war years that the United States finally began to complete the liberation—that the 13th, 14th, and 15th amendments were supposed to have accomplished almost a century before—of the descendants of the former slaves.)

The question then arises: why now? What has happened in America to account for this recent adverse shift in the balance of power between the embattled forces of good and evil?

It is not terribly difficult to imagine how the issue of slavery—on which so much hinged, and to which so much in the unfolding of America in the mid-nineteenth century was connected, and which so divided the nation—could blow open a hole in the American system through which the force of brokenness could enter the system and wreak its damage.

But in America in our times, there is no such inescapable division over a fundamental issue. Why then this rise in the power of evil?

Unlike in the Germany of 1914-1933, our nation has not suffered a sequence of great traumas. 9/11 can hardly compare with the four years of carnage in World War I, nor can our economic difficulties be compared to a time when a wheelbarrow full of Deutsch marks would buy but a loaf of bread. What then can account for the power of darkness ascending so markedly in America in our times?

I don't know what the best, whole answer would look like. But there are three hypotheses I would like to propose as possible pieces of an answer.

A Coalition of the Broken

Two major powers of brokenness that used to be divided in their partisan political allegiance—the spirit that drove the Slave Power, and the spirit of unrestrained corporatism—are now joined together within a single party (the Republican).

Power depends heavily on organization. A host of scattered actors cannot achieve nearly what they might if they came together, organized, and took concerted action. Thus we can see how the "selection for power" in the evolution of civilization drove civilized societies toward larger and more centrally controlled entities. (See Chapter 3 in *The Parable of the Tribes.*)

During the George W. Bush presidency, I perceived the rise of this evil force in terms of the confluence of several streams of brokenness that run through the history of American civilization: the imperialistic impulse, which had provided the impetus for the theft of land from the Native Americans, and which seems to have underlain the invasion of Iraq; the current of a particular kind of religion, which emphasizes the conflict of an "Us" against a "Them"; and the force of a kind of greed that is one of the downside tendencies of capitalism.

I still believe there is some validity to that image of a confluence of cultural streams.

Here is another very quick way of showing how the confluence of forces in America in our times might help answer the question: Why now?

Until recently, "the spirit that drove us to Civil War"—including the racist component of that spirit—and the spirit of greedy corporatism were on opposite sides of our two-party political system. That was certainly true in the post-Civil War era, when the Solid South was part of the Democratic coalition, and "big business" was part of the Republican coalition. The South remained part of FDR's electoral base, and it stayed aligned with that political party (the Democrats) that acted as a check against corporate dominance until the switch of the South from solidly Democratic to solidly Republican. As the South turned red, that spirit that had dwelt in the South came into coalition with the force of corporatist capitalism. (Not that this corporate force doesn't own a piece of the Democratic Party as well, but it's clear which party is the political ally of the Chamber of Commerce and the corporate lobbying organization, ALEC.)

Now, with the old spirit of the Slave Power and that of contemporary corporatism in a tight alliance, the power of evil in the American power system has been magnified.

A Sociopathy Built into the Structure of Our Corporate System

The publicly held corporation is structured so that no one can put any other values ahead of profit-maximization: the managers, who control the corporation, are obliged to serve only the owners; while the stockholders, who own, are mute and reduced only to their presumed desire for riches. The sociopathic implications of this structure has gradually marinated the corporate power in America.

It has seemed to me for a while that there has been an adverse change in the "spirit" in which America's powerful corporations are run. Whereas the corporations in the America in which I grew up had a sense of responsibility, nowadays it seems that the corporate system as a whole is almost uninhibited in its pursuit of more riches and more power. Or at least so I have imagined, and so I have written. I have imagined that if one were to read the transcripts of discussions in corporate boardrooms in the first couple of decades after World War II, one would find moral concerns being weighed a good deal more seriously than in the corresponding transcripts from our present era.

To those to whom much has been given, much shall be expected. That's an ethic I imagine had some power in the American corporate system of, say, 60 years ago that's pretty much missing now.

So I have believed, but haven't known how to test those beliefs empirically. At least now, Robert Reich has expressed a similar sense of a transformation toward amorality in the corporate system.

> A half-century ago, CEOs typically managed companies for the benefit of all their stakeholders—not just shareholders, but also their employees, communities, and the nation as a whole.
>
> "The job of management," proclaimed Frank Abrams, chairman of Standard Oil of New Jersey, in a 1951 address, "is to maintain an equitable and working balance among the claims of the various directly affected interest groups… stockholders, employees, customers, and the public at large. Business managers are gaining professional status partly because they see in their work the basic responsibilities [to the public] that other professional men have long recognized as theirs."
>
> This view was a common view among chief executives of the time. Fortune magazine urged CEOs to become "industrial statesmen." And to a large extent, that's what they became.
>
> For thirty years after World War II, as American corporations prospered, so did the American middle class. Wages rose and benefits increased. American companies and American citizens achieved a virtuous cycle of higher profits accompanied by more and better jobs….
>
> [While later,] Corporate statesmen were replaced by something more like corporate butchers, with their nearly exclusive focus being to "cut out the fat" and "cut to the bone."
>
> In consequence, the compensation packages of CEOs and other top executives soared, as did share prices. But ordinary workers lost jobs and wages, and many communities were abandoned. Almost all the gains from growth went to the top. http://robertreich.org/post/97357974470

A movement from a system that cares more about the whole of society compared to a system that serves only those on top: is that not a clear indication of a movement toward brokenness.

> [NOTE: Dr. Barry Castleman has expressed to me his skepticism about there having been a change of this sort in the spirit of corporate America, as Robert Reich and I are postulating. I give some weight to Dr. Castleman's views, for not only is he my friend since we were in fifth grade together, but he is also one of the world's foremost experts on the conduct of the companies from many industries using asbestos from the 1930s onward, and has delved deeply into similar examples of corporate willingness to sacrifice people for profits. It would be interesting if a way could be devised to test empirically the notion that CEOs acted *more* like "industrial statesmen" a half century ago than they do now.]

In addition to the clear and measurable shift in the distribution of wealth, the corporate world now manifests another, related aspect of societal deterioration. Power in America has shifted from the citizenry to the corporate system. The role of money in American politics—always a problem—has greatly expanded.

The pronounced movement from democracy toward plutocracy is yet another sign of brokenness.

As our democratic government becomes ever more an instrument of the corporate system, our nation's constitutional doctrine is being pried open ever wider to allow corporations the political rights of actual "persons."

As I put it in an op/ed piece I published in the newspapers of my overwhelmingly red part of Virginia: "We Americans should be asking, 'What kind of "persons" are these corporate giants whose rights and powers in our political system are expanding so dramatically?' The answer is not comforting."

To which, in the present context, should be added the question: Why is it that the moral nature of these corporate entities has apparently deteriorated so much over the past couple of generations?

As is so often the case when looking at the trends visible in the human world, a big part of the answer lies at the level of the system and the implications of how it is structured.

The American corporation—or more particularly, the *publicly held* American corporation—is structured to act like a sociopath.

Although the original idea of a "corporation" in American law was an entity that would serve the public good, our giant corporations today are set up in a way that virtually requires that they behave unscrupulously whenever their profit-making conflicts with the public good.

Those who run our publicly-traded corporations declare that their fiduciary duty is to serve the interests of those who own their companies. But while real human beings care about many things, the corporate system is set up so that the "interests" of the owners of corporations (i.e. stockholders) are reduced to purely financial terms: they are assumed to care only about maximal return on their investment. The ostensible owners have no effective way of registering other concerns.

From this it follows inescapably: the people who *run* the companies are declaring themselves to be *obligated* to maximize their profits, and not to allow any other values to interfere with the maximization of profits.

Given that structure, these mighty "persons" will behave like sociopaths, governed by selfishness unrestrained by conscience.

This sociopathic quality has been on display in virtually every case where industries have discovered that their products kill people.

The asbestos industry is still in courts around America and the world for hiding from their workers the lethal truth the companies knew full well. The result of their deception was that many thousands died terrible deaths from asbestos they had breathed on the job.

The big tobacco companies lied for decades about the connection between their products and fatal illnesses, maximizing their profits even at the cost of their customers' lives.

Now the hugely powerful energy industry is doing much the same, running a public disinformation campaign to sow doubt where science says there is none. In the pursuit of short-term profits, these companies work to keep us addicted to their products even if the disruption this causes to the earth's climate has a catastrophic effect on the lives of our children and grandchildren.

Now, this power without conscience is increasingly visible in countless decisions being made in our political system.

- We can see it in the laws that remove protections for the pensions that hardworking Americans earned.
- We can see it in the bankruptcy rules that favor banks over American families devastated by medical crises.
- We can see it in the weakening of the rights of workers in an era where the proportion of our national income going to wages is already way down.
- We can see it in the perpetuation of subsidies for a fabulously rich oil industry.
- We can see it in policies that revive the prosperity of Wall Street while Main Street still suffers. And on and on.

That's what we can see about how brokenness is being fostered by what our corporate system has become.

But the question still remains: why this change—why this adverse shift—from how American corporations behaved, say, two generations ago?

An important part of the answer, I believe, lies in that idea of a "lag time" between the introduction of a change and the realization of the full implications of that change.

> This was discussed earlier in the context of the founding of the American republic: our founders were doing something revolutionary in human history, but they were still under the influence of their cultural heritage. Thus they began our "democracy" by enfranchising only white (not of color) men (no women) of property (not those with less).

Mandatory sociopathy is structured specifically into *publicly-held* corporations. It is that structure that divides the decision-makers from the owners. Then all that is necessary is to reduce the "interests" of the essentially mute owners to the desire for greater wealth.

Even though the publicly held corporation is not a new phenomenon—and even though there was plenty of unscrupulous behavior from publicly held corporations more than a half century ago (e.g. the asbestos companies)—we are now a half century further along in the transformation of the corporate system from one which in owners—like Andrew

Carnegie and John D. Rockefeller—dominated, toward one in which the system itself (managers selected by boards, often in a self-perpetuating circle) dominates.

Those owners of old may have been, in many ways, an unscrupulous lot. But they were human beings. And even a robber baron like Andrew Carnegie was strongly motivated by values of wholeness, as is demonstrated by Carnegie's great philanthropy: far from seeking to undermine democracy, Carnegie spread the tools of democracy by endowing libraries in countless towns throughout the nation.

(Today's national Chamber of Commerce seems more likely to spread disinformation.)

A human being has many values. But a corporation set up on the basis of an alleged "obligation" solely to maximize profits does not. (We can find corporations, for example, like some coal companies, choosing to break the law when the calculation shows the extra profits will exceed the expected costs of their criminality.)

To return to the idea of the "lag time," what I am proposing is that two generations ago, the people (men) in the corporate board room brought more of the old culture—both the corporate culture and the more general traditional American culture—into their decision-making. The idea that maximizing wealth and power was the *only* goal was not yet as entrenched as it would become with time.

Time would take them further from the heritage of actual human beings who ran the corporations they created. And time would also allow the self-perpetuating, self-reinforcing corporate system to become more deeply entrenched, making sure that those who make the decisions had bought fully into the values built into the system.

This evolution of the American corporate system, I believe, is *one* of the important factors in the strengthening of evil in our cultural system. I don't know how big a factor it is, but obviously corporations are the most powerful actors in the non-governmental, private components of our civilization. And with these corporations increasingly taking over the governmental instruments of collective power, a decline in their moral nature cannot help but have a serious detrimental effect on the balance between good and evil in the American system.

Humanizing the Corporate Power

An essential challenge for humankind is to structure our systems so that we can rule them rather than having them rule us. I have a proposal for how the problems of built-in corporate sociopathy can be addressed in a way that honors the rights of private property far better than the current arrangement.

For human beings, the central challenge is first to understand the dynamics by which our systems tend to take us, whether we want them to or not, to a destination of their choosing. And second to get some control over how our systems evolve, so that we as a nation and we as humankind can arrive at a destination that we desire.

It is essential that we learn to understand these systemic forces of brokenness and that we devise ways to use the powers of wholeness to block the force of brokenness from doing its damage.

In this instance, such ways would include wise, fair, and efficient regulation of corporate activities where that's needed in both the economic sphere (such as rules limiting pollution) and the political sphere (like campaign finance reform that puts effective barriers to prevent the great financial power of the corporate system from being translated into ownership of—or undo influence on—the American government).

But, as we can see from the news of our times, there's a bootstrap, or chicken-and-egg problem about getting the necessary regulations instituted and enforced. Getting to that point may require instituting a remedy for this problem of structurally mandated sociopathy.

In my book *The Illusion of Choice: How the Market Economy Shapes Our Destiny*, I propose such a remedy. Inasmuch as this solution involves giving *more real power to the real legal owners* of these publicly-traded corporations, I can imagine it having some political potential. The capitalist system has invested so much "capital" over the generations in enshrining the "rights of private property" into the American value system, the corporate power system may well lack the antibodies to resist an argument that gives the OWNERS power over their property. My proposal*—with the name "Let the Owners Decide"—is found in chapter 11 ("Autopilot") of that book, and also in the "More Depth" collection at www.whatweareupagainst.org.

The Challenge of Affluence

Unprecedented affluence gives people unprecedented scope for acting on desire rather than obligation. Traditional morality has been based on a world of scarcity. The unintended consequence is that a mismatch between the sudden change of economic circumstance and the slower evolution of cultural guidance has weakened the power of morality in our affluent society.

At the same time as the growing influence of the mandated sociopathy of the corporate system has strengthened evil in America, an unintended consequence of the unprecedented rise, over recent generations, in the level of affluence in America has weakened the force of goodness.

One need not go back beyond living memory in America to find the great majority of people living at a much, much lower level of material wealth. Even if our economy has recently come upon hard times, and even if in recent decades the less wealthy half of the American population has stopped growing richer or even lost ground, nonetheless, the level of affluence for the population as a whole is far greater than that in, say, the early decades of the 20th century, or in any of the centuries before that.

The United States and many others of the world's advanced societies have experienced a dramatic take-off in material wealth, affording their citizens a "standard of living" well beyond anything ever experienced by the mass of the people anywhere in the history of civilization.

That is no small thing.

And in many important ways, it is a blessing. We no longer have our numbers culled by periodic famines. We enjoy a life expectancy a good deal longer than people in any previous human societies anywhere. Etc.

But as always, we civilized humans stumble into our future. Achieving one long-sought goal (a higher "standard of living") brings with it new challenges. These challenges are not always readily met, or even recognized.

In particular, the challenge of affluence consists of this: we are living in a new situation (being rich by historical standards), but for guidance in managing our lives we are reliant on a cultural heritage that developed over the millennia as an adaptation to the old, very different material situation.

That cultural heritage has at its core an ethic predicated on dealing with scarcity. Scarcity implies necessity. To put it another way, the closer one is to subsistence, the more one's life must be governed by what one *must* do. The less the margin for error, the more the culture—to be adaptive to the needs of the society and its members—will convey a moral structure based on obligation. People are taught to think of their duties, their responsibilities, what is required of them.

That's what the morality of scarcity is about: teaching people to focus on the question, "What must/should I do?" with little need to instruct them on how to deal with the question, "What do I want?" That latter question was something of a luxury, a relative rarity in the fabric of people's daily living.

Our traditional morality tells us to do our jobs. It tells us of the virtues of hard work and patience and loyalty and honesty. It tells us not to steal or murder, and to pay our debts. It tells us, in other words, what is required of us by the surrounding world.

As people become affluent, the question "What should I do?" remains a part of life, but a diminished part. No longer working from dawn to dusk like peasants of old, a member of the affluent society more likely works an eight-hour day, five days a week.

Meanwhile, for the members of the "consumer society," the question "What do I want?" takes up an increasing part of the landscape of daily life. We get to make more and more choices that are not about one's obligation to meet external demands but about choosing which of one's internal desires to satisfy.

- What do I want to do with my leisure time (now that I am no longer working from sun-up to sun-down, as so many of my ancestors had to do)?
- What do I want to do with my disposable income (now that I no longer have to spend just about every cent I have, as my ancestors did, to take care of the bare necessities of life)?
- What do I want to eat, and how much do I want to eat (now that I—unlike so many before me– have a wealth of different foods available to me, and enough of them so that I can eat until I choose to stop and not until the food runs out)?

This greatly widened scope for the satisfaction of desire has had an enormous impact on the lives of recent generations. Once again, we might imagine a lag time, as the cultural heritage of the past erodes under the force of the new currents. Thus baby-boomers—perhaps the first generation to enjoy truly widespread affluence—revealed both the loosening moral hold of the old order and also the persistence of the old order, imbibed from their parents under the influence of whose discipline (which had been sharpened by the stringencies of the Great Depression and the responsibilities of World War II) the baby-boomers grew up.

But meanwhile, they (we!) also gave us the counter-culture, the experimenting with liberation from moral constraint. "If it feels good, do it," was one expression of this ascendant ethic of "What do I want?" And as a member of the counterculture, I often encountered—even into recent decades—the insistence that one "should" not talk in terms of "shoulds." (Nothing should be judged but "judgmentalism.")

But if the baby-boomers still had internalized a degree of discipline, the moral erosion continued after them, as the implications of the new situation continued to play out.

As the strength of "What is required of me?" diminishes, as that question occupies less of the individual's mental process, the question "What do I want?" meanwhile is confronted in a comparative moral vacuum. The traditional morality was not geared toward the regulation of desire, except to suppress it so that duties got met and commandments of the "thou shalt not" variety got obeyed.

But how one answers the question, "What do I want?" has major moral implications.

The Need for an Ethic of Wise Choices

With traditional morality an insufficient guide for our present circumstance, and with consumerist society teaching people to seek fulfillment through what can be bought and sold, the danger grows that people will not be able to distinguish between right desire and wrong desire. A wise moral culture addressing that distinction must be developed to close the present gap through which the force of evil can gain power.

Lacking a profound tradition to provide wise guidance for our relationship with desire, we Americans have been sliding into lives diminished by self-indulgence. Without a discipline to orient our choices toward some notion of the "Good," the continual choosing of mere gratification can make us slaves to our impulses. Without a morally adequate perspective on the consequences—for good or for ill—of our ways of pursuing happiness, our culture's adventures into affluence have caused a general loosening of our hold upon the moral vision.

This loosening begins in our private lives, but then—because of the gradual replacement of the old habit of responsibility by the new habit of self-indulgence—that increased laxity inevitably moves outward into the wider world, eroding the allegiance to the good even in the realm—with its shoulds of duty, responsibility, service to something beyond ourselves—in which our traditional morality has held sway.

The choices we make have consequences.

At the first level, the choices we make—even in matters that seem to bear only upon the person making the choices—affect what kind of person we become.

So goes a Cherokee legend:

> An old Cherokee is teaching his grandson about life. "A fight is going on inside me," he said to the boy.
>
> "It is a terrible fight and it is between two wolves. One is evil—he is anger, envy, sorrow, regret, greed, arrogance, self-pity, guilt, resentment, inferiority, lies, false pride, superiority, and ego." He continued, "The other is good—he is joy, peace, love, hope, serenity, humility, kindness, benevolence, empathy, generosity, truth, compassion, and faith. The same fight is going on inside you—and inside every other person, too."
>
> The grandson thought about it for a minute and then asked his grandfather, "Which wolf will win?"
>
> The old Cherokee simply replied, "The one you feed."

So, if we respond to an abundance of food by over-eating, we may become obese. Thus the much-reported rising epidemic of obesity—and of other unhealthful conditions associated with our over-indulgence of the foods containing excessive amounts of sweeteners, salt, and fats—stands as an emblem of how we can hurt ourselves with unwise, undisciplined choices.

If we respond to the abundance of media options by choosing those that appeal to our baser selves—spending our time with the most sensationalistic and coarse of cultural expressions—we train ourselves to yield to our lower impulses. We fail to embody the ideal of our best potential.

And this lack of distinction between right desire and wrong desire is systematically encouraged by the market in the consumer society. It is part of the "ethic" of mainstream economics NOT to distinguish between different choices: "utility" is what is good, and any dollar spent is presumed to buy an equal amount of utility.

Our consumerist economy unleashes a systemic force indifferent to what kind of impulse we gratify—so long as we seek our fulfillment through what the market deals in. The market grows stronger the more people focus on what can be bought and sold, and so the distinction that the system promotes is not between right and wrong desire, but between what can be marketed and what cannot.

Thus over time, like the iron filings in Oscar Wilde's little fable, the people living in such an environment will gravitate toward seeking their fulfillment through market transactions.

(For more on this, see the chapter, "In the Image of Our Creator" in *The Illusion of Choice*, and in the Chapter "Guiding Voices" in my book *Fool's Gold: The Fate of Values in a World of Goods.*)

Our individual choices, therefore, take place within a field of forces that create society-wide trends. These trends can strengthen or weaken the forces of wholeness and brokenness.

A telling trend can be discerned, I believe, in some of the major cultural expressions of American culture: i.e. in the television programs, films, and popular music of the past six or so decades. In these forms of popular culture—which can be seen as both reflecting and shaping the moral structures of everyday American consciousness—there is discernible a movement toward the glorification and satisfaction of some of humankind's darker and least desirable inclinations.

For example, as a movie buff, I have had the chance over the years to compare the movies of different eras. This is one way of getting a sense of our society's moral evolution. What I've noticed is that films from the 1930s and 1940s—though they deal plenty with wrong-doing—are permeated with a concern with what's right, with an aspiration toward the ideal. With the passage of the decades, starting to accelerate perhaps in the late 1960s, that implicit orientation toward the ideal seems to melt away, as increasingly our films pander to our basest impulses.

A movie today is more likely to be about some serial killer than about anyone worth admiring. The admirable is no longer the central concern it once was.

> In one of the recent *Batman* movies, our hero interrogates someone by holding him off the roof of a six-story building, threatening to drop him unless the fellow will tell him what he wants to know. And the film shows no sign of concern that there is something problematic about our hero's using this method of torture. It is completely unthinkable that a hero in the films of the 1950s would have engaged in such conduct. The hero might have wanted the information, but he was bound by moral rules. It was the Gestapo, not Americans, our movies used to tell us, who did things like that.

This unraveling of old moral ideals is one of those cultural developments that has diminished the power of the forces of goodness to resist the advance of the opportunistic force of brokenness, working to expand its empire.

The children and grandchildren of people for whom striving toward an ideal occupied a major aspect of their consciousness about the meaning of human life have trained themselves—and have been trained by the culture—to imagine that the satisfaction of desire, of impulse, of appetite is life's most fundamental purpose.

If we use our discretionary income to buy ourselves things that titillate but do not elevate, that we choose out of impulse rather than need, that are only about comfort and not about growth, then we diminish ourselves.

And so, in America, the capacity of moral structures to channel human choices has weakened.

And, thus, America has now moved into a time of moral darkness. For the transformations of consciousness brought on by a lifetime of unguided choices ultimately impact also the wider world.

The habit of self-indulgence—of answering the question "What do I want?" in terms that make no distinction between "right desire" and "wrong desire"—cannot stop at the borders of the realm of the purely individual. It inevitably erodes also that other realm, the realm in which the tradition worked for centuries to discipline people to consider their responsibilities to others and to the good itself.

Here's how I described what I believed to be some of those consequences during the presidency of George W. Bush:

> The ethic of self-indulgence enables people to saddle their descendants with their own debt, running up huge deficits in the national accounts. [This refers to the near-doubling of the national debt during years of reasonably good economic times under George W. Bush, not the necessary deficit spending called for in hard times, as in our recent Great Recession, when the economy suffers from an insufficiency of aggregate demand.]
>
> The habit of yielding to baser impulses makes it easier to support baser policies in the collective realm—e.g. wielding great national power without being constrained by a sense of obligation to provide reasoned justification, or to obey the accepted rules of conduct among nations.
>
> The failure to distinguish between those desires that are worthy of being satisfied and those that should be held in check by moral discipline can lead to a pervasive cynicism in society, a belief that human beings can never amount to anything anyway, thus opening the door still further to mere selfishness.
>
> And now moral anarchy has opened the door to evil. The general weakening of moral structures has loosed the wolf from its cage. America slides toward fascism, in which the darkest impulses of greed and the lust for power, thinly disguised under a false righteousness, govern from the nation's highest places.

The Bush II presidency has been replaced by another. But that same force that gave us the Bush presidency is at work from its new vantage point wielding the Republican Party now in opposition—systematically sacrificing the nation's good in the quest for power.

Not all our impulses are good. Particularly in a broken world. A culture that is both affluent and unable to make the necessary distinctions between right desire and wrong desire opens the door to the force of evil. As we see in America in our times.

A Cultural Karposi Sarcoma

> *Earlier, I wrote: "Dark patterns lurk in the system, like some dormant virus, ready to erupt when the culture's immune system weakens."*

Our level of affluence has changed far more rapidly than the ability of our culture to adjust. Under circumstances not of necessity but of abundant choice, the weakened power of the moral habit of asking, "What *should* I do?" has weakened the culture's immune system.

As a kind of cultural AIDS weakens the cultural immune system, a destructive force, like some cultural "Karposi Sarcoma," erupts within the system.

As the force of the good diminishes, the old dark pattern, having lurked in the system for all these generations, gains in power.

INTERLUDE IX:

Moral Endo-skeletons and Exo-skeletons: A Perspective on America's Cultural Divide and Current Crisis

The following was written early on in this mission, in 2006, at a time when George W. Bush was president, the war in Iraq was grinding on in its ugly way, and darkness occupied the pinnacle of power in America.

❋ ❋ ❋

In the months after the 2004 election, when the Red States were said to have voted on the basis of their "moral values," it was noted by many observers that the parts of the country where sleazy TV and movies get their highest ratings are the very same as those most populated by those traditionalist and Christian conservatives who most energetically denounce such entertainments. (It was noted, as well, that some of the family pathologies that traditionalists decry are found at high rates among these most vocal proponents of "family values.")

Some took this as a clear indication of the hypocrisy of the conservatives: what they denounce, they also secretly enjoy. They are not as concerned about morality, this critique declared, as they pretend to be. They assume a posture of righteousness, it was said, all the while indulging forbidden impulses in hidden ways.

Jimmy Swaggart writ large.

But I don't think "hypocrisy" is the most illuminating way of seeing this phenomenon. Not if hypocrisy is understood as a form of deliberate dishonesty.

Different Structures of Morality

Many people on the right feel a need for an external power—the community, or the state—to enforce the morality that they want to live by. Many of our political conflicts over "culture war" issues derive from this reliance on a moral "exo-skeleton." It behooves liberals to understand how threatening it is for some people to be compelled to rely only on themselves to walk the straight-and-narrow path.

From my many years of discussing morality with religious traditionalists on the radio, I've gleaned that many of them assume that people who do not share their firm moral structures—who do not believe in God, or in the Ten Commandments, or in inviolable and absolute rules of moral conduct—must be living lives of sin and debauchery. They cannot understand—and often seem unwilling even to believe—that people like Unitarians might be living well-ordered lives, that they might be as responsible and dedicated family people, as they themselves strive to do and be.

Their failure to understand how non-believing "liberals" can live moral lives is actually the reverse side of the same coin from the liberals' imputation of hypocrisy to the red staters who watch "Desperate Housewives" and may also have disordered family lives.

These misunderstandings derive from the two groups' having different moral structures.

It was a student of mine (in an adult education class about "America's Moral Crisis") who came up with the apt image. It didn't matter much to her, she said, whether her society has a lot of enforced rules. She's got her moral beliefs firmly inside her—a kind of endo-skeleton, she said.

We had been talking about the distress American traditionalists have felt at the erosion of a social consensus about the straight-and-narrow path. Morality for them, she said, seemed to be a kind of exo-skeleton. This was her image to capture their reliance on external moral structures—laws, punishments, etc.—to keep them within the moral confines in which they believe.

In that perspective, some of what might seem anomalies—or hypocrisies—of some traditionalists make greater sense.

It becomes clear why such people—with intense moral concerns combined with a reliance on external moral structures to keep their own forbidden impulses in check—would support a state that enforces moral rules and a social culture that stigmatizes those who violate those rules. It is a genuine threat to them—- a threat to their own inner moral order—when the society around them fails to be clear in its rules and strict in its enforcement.

For those whose moral structure is cast in that exo-skeleton form, the absence of external moral authority seems necessarily to imply the outbreak of moral anarchy. That's the logic implied by that famous line, from a character in Dostoyevski's *Brothers Karamazov*, that "if there is no God, everything is permitted." That's what lies behind that fear that—- if gays are allowed to marry—marriage generally would somehow be threatened, including the sanctity of one's own marriage.

To someone, with the endo-skeleton structure, both of those beliefs—that without God there could be no morality, and that allowing same-sex marriage would threaten the marriages of others—seem like logical non sequiturs. And logically, perhaps they are. But they bespeak a psychological reality. If the outside structure breaks down, who knows what I might do? (It's like that writing in the mirror in the movie, "Stop me before I kill again.")

Liberals have often failed to understand how genuinely threatening it is to the moral order of those with the exo-skeleton structure if there is a loosening of society's moral standards, rules, and sanctions. Liberals have not appreciated the plight of people who deeply want to toe the line, and need help in doing it.

Likewise, many liberals have responded with anger, unleavened by understanding, to the tendency of some traditionalists to try to impose their moral views on others. It is their dependence on the strength and integrity of the external moral order that drives many "exo-skeletons" to crusade to make the whole world around them conform to the moral system to which they themselves are striving to adhere. The unspoken—- and generally unacknowledged—need is: please, society, be morally strict enough to keep me on the straight-and-narrow path.

Integrity and Hypocrisy: The Challenge to Exo-Skeletons

Part of the brokenness involved in the world of the "exo-skeletons" is that they identify with only a part of themselves, while denying those parts that are in conflict with their morality.

These fears of exo-skeleton traditionalists reflect a lack of integration: their morality is not fully integrated into the psyche.

St. Paul lamented: "For the good that I would, I do not: but the evil which I would not, that I do." Truly, he wanted to do the good. But it is not entirely true that the evil he did was something he wanted not. For a part of him did want it, or he wouldn't have done it.

So was Paul a hypocrite for doing what he declared himself to be against? And are the red-staters hypocrites if they indulge—- perhaps more even than the liberals—the forbidden desires?

Well, yes and no. Yes, in that they are not practicing what they preach. And that does represent a kind of lack of integrity. But the "dishonesty" involved is not about lying to others so much as it is a natural outgrowth of the identification with only a part of the self, the moral part, with a concomitant sense that the other part, with the forbidden desire, is the not-I.

So that is the hypocritical part: the failure to embrace the whole truth about the self—that is comprised not only of the "righteous" part but of the "sinner" part as well.

If the moral order of the surrounding society weakens, the person with a moral exo-skeleton is genuinely threatened—- not just regarding his conduct, but also even regarding his identity.

The Dangerous Blindness of Some of Us Moral Endo-Skeletons

A problem among the "endo-skeletons"—exemplified by many of the middle class youth in the 60s "counterculture"—has been the failure to recognize how much moral structure they have internalized. The result of that blind spot has been the fallacy of believing that society does not need to exert some kind of moral force.

Those of us with the endo-skeleton structure—who can live moral and orderly lives even if we live in an "anything goes" society—can reasonably be tempted to feel superior to those others with the exo-skeleton dependency on the moral sanctions of a more straight-and-narrow society.

And indeed there are theories of moral development according to which the internalization of moral order is a more "advanced" form of moral development.

But, at this point in American history, it can be seen that the quest for advanced consciousness has many dimensions, and neither side of America's divide has aced the course. This is part of the cost of our cultural polarization—two forms of moral blindness, very different but also two sides of the same coin.

Just as the cultural right has damaged America because of its failure to acknowledge its inner sinner, the left has damaged America through its failure to recognize its inner moral structure.

This was one of the greatest shortcomings of the counterculture that arose in the 60s. We—- and I was a member of that tribe—simply tore down a great many of our society's moral structures and assumed that all would be well. We had half-baked theories of human nature, and of society, that justified "letting it all hang out" and "doing our own thing" and "if it feels good, do it."

History has shown that we were naive. Not all has been well. Indeed, I would argue that this naive miscalculation is part of what has led, ultimately, to the rise of the dark and destructive forces from the right embodied by the [then] current dangerous Bush II regime.

Living Off Our Moral Capital

In American culture, liberalism has helped loosen the moral cages that kept disorder at bay. Some of that disorder is bottom-up—like the huge increase in the number of children born outside of intact families—and some of it is in the realm of top-down power, where the wolf of rage and the impulse toward vengeance has escaped from its cage and gained power over our politics.

What many in the counterculture did, I believe, was to look at themselves—in what they took to be their "liberated" state—and imagine that they saw human nature in its pristine state. But in reality, many of the middle class youth—brought up in the 1940s and 1950s—who comprised the counterculture had already internalized a great many of the disciplines—moral and otherwise—of traditional American culture.

That's why they could engage in the cultural revolution of liberation, and then go on to become effective middle class professionals, and the kind of liberals with well-ordered lives that I meet when I speak to Unitarian groups.

The loosening of the moral structures of American society did not, indeed, greatly disturb the lives of most of us middle class American youths of the counterculture, because the necessary structures were already inside us. Our endo-skeletons made the social enforcement of norms and standards and morals unnecessary.

Unnecessary for us, that is. Meanwhile, much of the rest of society was not identical to us endo-skeletons. And there, the costs of the cultural loosening have been more visible.

For one thing, there are elements of American society in which the disciplines of moral order were less firmly established than in the white middle class. And for them, the loosening of the moral fabric of the overall cultural system led to disastrous results, such as a steep increase in the rate of illegitimate births and a general deterioration of family structure.

(This picture is painted plausibly in Myron Magnet's *The Dream and the Nightmare: The Sixties' Legacy to the Underclass.* I continue to believe that there was much that was valid and right in the counterculture, whereas Magnet is basically a conservative counter-revolutionary; but I nonetheless think it is important to recognize the truth of valid critiques even—sometimes especially—from people who are in many ways adversaries.)

In addition to the effects of the loosening of our culture's moral structures on the underclass, there is also the impact that the dissipation of our culture's moral capital has had on our heirs, the young.

The youth coming up did not form their characters in the tighter environments of the 1940s and 1950s, but in the culturally looser decades since. And one has been hearing from veteran teachers for a long time now that each successive wave of students shows signs of a loosening of discipline of various kinds. The culture has grown trashier, the demands of society have become less stringent, the culture of indulgence has grown deeper—and all this has led to a visible cultural decline. Many of the children of those who carried with them the older structures have managed to raise children whose lives are also fairly well-ordered. But even there it is a diminishing cultural capital that we are living off of. And I expect that the necessary forms of moral structure (and other disciplines) will attenuate in time—unless we have some kind of cultural renewal.

But it is on the other side of the cultural divide—in the realm of the exo-skeletons—that the loosening of the moral order has proved most dangerous.

It is not only that the cultural right, more dependent on external restraints, becomes more likely to succumb to forbidden impulses— like sailors come to port.

More dangerous for the society is that the particular nature of the right's moral vision—being relatively harsh and punitive—transforms the impulses of the human animal into something darker. [See above in Chapter 6: "The Coherence of the Force: How "Evil" Transmits Its Pattern of Brokenness in Shape-Shifting Ways."]

Fragile orders tend also to be harsher—tyranny is the surest means to avoid anarchy. And, accordingly, a moral order that is less internalized, being more fragile, tends also toward harshness.

Thus the morality of the exo-skeletons tends to denigrate the human nature it seeks to control. This morality also tends to be more punitive in its approach to control—glad to invest big sums in a brutal prison system (whether or not such punishments actually serve society best, as with drug offenders), passionately committed to the death penalty, and building its worldview around a highly punitive figure as Lord of the Universe.

And the harsher the morality—the more conflictual the interaction between cultural demand and human nature—the darker become the feelings inside the human creature socialized in that morality. The more the feelings inside the human creature then turn toward rage (at the wounds inflicted). The result is an intensification of the desire for power (to counteract the powerlessness of being small in a world that has declared war on you) and fueling of an impulse toward vengeance (for all the punishment and rejection inflicted).

The harsh morality of the cultural right thus engenders within the human spirit a kind of wolf. It is a wolf such as Shakespeare described in *Troilus and Cressida*:

Then every thing includes itself in power,
Power into will, will into appetite;
And appetite, an universal wolf,
 So doubly seconded with will and power,
Must make perforce an universal prey,
And last eat up himself.

The same harsh morality that goads this wolf into life will also—when it is intact—help confine that beast its cage.

That wolf—the lust for power and the rage for revenge—has always been there, and it has played a role in the dark parts of American history. But it was largely, more than now, kept from running rampant.

The loosening of the cage of America's social morality had one meaning, therefore, among America's endo-skeletons, but another darker meaning among America's exo-skeletons. It is as though a boat was tipped by the left, but it was the right that got wet.

It was not just id that was loosed on the cultural right, but also unleashed were those impulses that their sub-culture's harshness had made dark. (One thinks of that famous passage in Carl Jung, written in the years before the rise of the Nazis, about the "blond beast stirring in its subterranean prison… threatening us with an outbreak that will have devastating consequences.")

The wolf has now broken from its cage. We in the counterculture who wanted to liberate, for example, the natural sexual energies of the human creature also, unwittingly, weakened the checks on the lust for power, on greed, on self-aggrandizement.

Morality, it turns out, is of a piece. And so is our culture.

"Make love, not war," we chanted. But now [during the Bush II presidency], being undisciplined in our approach to the moral issues of making love, we live in a country that defies all international laws in its making of war.

It is a time when the wolf rules America.

Turning Back from Fascism

In moral terms, people on the liberal side tipped the boat and the people on the right got wet, unleashing a force of moral anarchy

> *into the American power system. To help put the wolf back in his cage, liberals need to recognize—better than many in the counter-culture did—that a healthy social order depends upon some kind of moral structure.*

Fascism arises from the sense that the choice is between its tyranny and mere anarchy.

Never mind that the fascists merely bring the anarchy of the enraged wolf, hiding under the national flag, to prowl around society. They do it from the precincts of power, and they fool enough of the people into thinking that what they are bringing is order.

But there are, in any event, better options than either tyranny or anarchy. They require good effort, however, to be achieved. Good order in the human realm does not happen except through wise and hard human effort.

That achievement was the great glory of those who founded the American democracy

The task then is two-fold. It is not only to remove that wolf from power, but it is also to help reconstruct the cage—those structures of morality—that previously was able to keep it in check.

Ideally, we'd do much better than merely "reconstruct" the moral cage of an earlier era. That would be an improvement over this loosening, which has unleashed these dark forces. But still better would be to find a better means of containment, even a more harmonious form of domestication that does not need to abuse the creature it brings into the social fold.

That old order was far from ideal.

That much the counter-culture recognized, but it failed to realize that a truly beneficent revolution is not accomplished by storming the Bastille. And it failed to recognize that the movement of a culture to its next, more advanced form is a long-term and difficult process.

What is needed this time around is not a wanton rejection of the old structures, replacing them with nothing. We endo-skeletons must understand more fully the structures that hold us together. We must understand, that is, that the order of the endo-skeleton is not an absence of order. It is the internalization of the order the growing creature encounters around him/her.

And no skeleton at all is a recipe for falling apart.

Chapter Ten:

The Reality of the Abstract

Is Only the Concrete "Reality Itself"?

In a world that is shaped by forces and patterns, what would it do to our connection with the real world to regard only the concrete embodiments of those forces and patterns as "reality itself"?

Earlier I wrote that we tend to live our lives in "the immediate and the concrete." By contrast, I am asserting here that our destiny is largely shaped by the battle between two sets of vast but subtle forces—"the battle between good and evil"—that powerfully shape the concrete reality we experience in an immediate way.

The question reasonably arises, How *real* are such forces? This, in turn, is part of a still larger question of how real, in general, are those supposed "things" that are abstracted from concrete realities?

My position is that well-conceived abstractions are very real. Or, to put it another way, are as important for our perceiving our reality as anything else.

What appears to be a dramatic challenge to that position can be found in Richard Ned Lebow's *Forbidden Fruit: Counterfactuals and International Relations.*

In the course of exploring some of the philosophical issues raised by his "counter-factual" explorations, Lebow takes the position that when we talk about society and politics, we have departed from "reality itself" as soon as we get away from "first-order 'facts.'" Our concepts are "ideational and subjective" and somewhat "arbitrary." Our theories are reflections of "social construction," and "can only be true by convention." They "tell us more about our view of the world than about the world itself." "Social 'facts' are reflections of the concepts we use to describe social reality, not of reality itself."

In a statement that seems clearly to reject the reality of our abstractions about the human world, Lebow declares: "There is no such thing as a balance of power, a social class, or a tolerant society."

(By the way, it is not only in the social realm that Lebow sees this issue: "Temperature," he says, "is undeniably a social construction, but is a measure of something observable and real: changes in temperature measure changes in the energy levels of molecules." I do wonder, incidentally, whether the notions of "energy levels"—or of "molecules," for that matter—are any more factual than that of "temperature.")

If Professor Lebow were correct, that would greatly diminish the status of the "forces" that I'm declaring here to be perhaps the major actors in the human drama. Mere "constructions." But I do not believe that Lebow's assertion is correct that "real" must mean "concrete," and that whatever is abstracted from the concrete is less real or even not real.

I would maintain, contrariwise, that these forces—of wholeness and brokenness, good and evil—are deeply and importantly real, perhaps even more importantly real than the concrete "first-order" facts.

Here are some of the challenges I would pose to Lebow's position:

What's more real, a particular fireworks display in some small American town on the 4th of July, or something that could be called "the American tradition" of exploding fireworks on the 4th of July?

Walking along the street, one hears two people having a conversation. They are speaking in English. Is the exchange of words, or of sounds, that constitute that conversation—what I imagine Professor Lebow would call a "first-order" concrete fact—more real than "the English language"?

Getting still closer to the nature of that "integrative vision" I've been presenting here as an important dimension of how things work in the human world, I'd ask two other questions:

First, there are a great many human beings walking around on this planet. Are the individual organisms more real than "the human genome"? (I'd say that in some ways, the genome is a more fundamental reality than any of us who are temporary embodiments of it.)

The other question: If we know an individual, and observe a wide assortment of his actions and statements, which manifest a degree of consistency in their nature and quality, can we speak of this person's "character"? And is that character less real—or is it perhaps more real?—than the various individual behaviors from which we inferred the underlying "character" of the man?

When the integrative vision being presented here infers the existence of something large and deeply interwoven into the concrete level that we perceive, and for that reason "abstracted" from that concrete level, it employs concepts and ways of thinking parallel to the more abstract elements of those four questions, above.

As with the fireworks tradition, and the English language, the ideas presented here focus on the patterns that get transmitted through time in cultural systems.

As with the genome, this "integrative vision" argues that the pattern is more fundamentally real—because it is a more fundamental determinant of what happens in our ongoing reality—than its temporary embodiments.

It has been said that a hen is an egg's way of making another egg. I would propose that this observation be altered to say that both the hen and the egg are a genetic pattern's way of perpetuating itself. Similarly, a human being can be regarded as a culture's way of perpetuating the culture.

As with the issue of an individual's character—the "spirit" that's expressed in the various particular behaviors of the person—the notion of good and evil forces identifies elements of "spirit" that operate in cultural systems through the generations, showing consistency in the nature of what they impart.

These forces involve patterns whose mechanisms and character and effects can only be inferred from their imprint on many more specific events. They exist, therefore, at a level "abstracted" from that of our usual daily perception.

Abstracted, but not less real for that.

Realities versus "Mere Concepts"

Not all concepts are "real" in the same way. Some have a reality through the fact that people's thoughts and actions are shaped by

> *the concepts in their minds. But others—like "biological evolution," and "the battle between good and evil"—are real whether or not people perceive them, or think in those terms.*

This is not to go down Plato's path toward the notion of an ultimate reality consisting of Platonic Forms. The key question here is not about our minds, or the categories that exist in it, but about what it is that shapes our world.

As I recall the Platonic argument, it asserted that because a great many things are called "table," there must be an ideal Form of a table of which each table is but an embodiment. If I recall, also, these Forms are supposed to be eternal.

So are we then required to believe that that the Form of a "table" existed for some 13.8 billion years before there existed a creature who wanted a table, conceived of a table, and constructed something that would serve as a table?

Yes, the concept of a table, or a "*Tisch*" (German) or a "*stol*" (Russian) does have a reality in that in much of the world there are cultures and minds that employ the concept. And that concept does have an impact on the world, as people think in terms of "table" as they design, construct, buy, and use certain pieces of furniture.

But in such cases, the category gets its reality from *the impact on the world of people having those concepts in their minds.*

It is different with what I am talking about here regarding "the battle between good and evil." The contention between the forces of wholeness and brokenness has a reality, I maintain, that is not dependent upon people perceiving it or thinking in those terms.

Similarly with the evolution of life. Life was being shaped by an evolutionary process—involving mutation and natural selection—for 3.5 billion years before Darwin et al. came to understand the nature of the forces at work in shaping the living world in which we are embedded. That evolutionary process did not need Darwin in order to become a real and important part of the earth's story.

Consider also the "panics" that brought serious collapses of the American economy during the 19th century and up till the inauguration of Franklin Roosevelt in 1933. The the events of those times—such as the runs on the banks—could not be understood at the most concrete level of individual decisions to attempt to rescue their money. It was something systemic, collective, contagious—therefore abstract. If that collective "panic" wasn't real, how come so many lives were adversely affected in such important and concrete ways? Something must have been real at the collective level to produce such a pattern of human distress.

To see things in terms only of the pieces is to miss the essential dimension of interconnection so densely woven by the interplay of cause and effect. To imagine that all our concepts are mere "constructions" is to deny the claim on our heartfelt allegiance of the basic values at stake in our human drama.

Our abstractions may not capture reality perfectly, but to conceive of the really real as only what we can concretely perceive is to deny the multi-layered richness of the world we live in. "Reality itself" consists of far more than the concrete.

The Water and the Wave

Here's an analogy for the different levels of our reality, from concrete to abstract. Something real is moving across the water in a wave. But it is not the individual drops of water whose movement makes the wave. Those drops of water just move up and down. The water is what a force uses to transmit the wave.

Here is a metaphor for the multi-layered character of our reality.

Consider humanity at the concrete level as so many drops of water making up a sea. If we look at the water drop by drop, what we see is that each one bobs up and down. If we step back and look at the larger picture, we see something quite different: we see waves moving across the surface of the sea.

It is the wave that makes each bit of water rise and fall. And the movement we observe across the surface, with the rolling wave, does not involve the water flowing, as in a river's current. In the crosswise direction of the waves' motion, each bit of water is essentially stationary. Only the wave moves.

But isn't the sea—and isn't the wave—made up only of the water? Yes, at the concrete level of the molecules of H2O. But the wave is a different level of reality. It is a force that operates, affecting the water, but existing on a different plane.

So it is with the operations of the patterns and forces in the human system over time. We can look at the actions of specific individuals, or specific generations, or specific societies—and those movements will make sense within their own framework. But to understand truly the reasons for those movements, we need to look at the waves moving through the system of concrete actors, moving those actors and shaping the overall drama being enacted.

So when I say, in my definition of evil, that I am talking about a force (or pattern, or spirit) that moves through the human system—and when I do not talk about "evil" in terms of evil people—I am talking about the wave, and about how it moves the water but is not the same as the water.

We Are Not Dwellers in Plato's Cave, But...

In addition to the reality that is visible to us in our daily lives, there's a profound reality of powerful forces operating around us. The better we understand the mechanisms of those forces, the better our chance of controlling them instead of being controlled by them.

Not long ago, while floating between being awake and asleep, I was powerfully struck by an image. It is not easily conveyed, but I will try.

I saw myself crouched on the earth. I understood myself to be representing humanity. The important action, however, was not with me, down on the ground, but in the sky above. Actually, the sky itself was only partially visible, filled as it was with great metallic spheres and intermeshing gears of bronze rotating this way and that, like spherical astrolabes. In that instant, I understood that as much as we move around down here on the earth, the gyrations of those spheres, and the meshing of those gears, were playing a powerful role in shaping the world in which we operate.

It occurs to me that this is my substitute for Plato's famous image of the cave, whose dwellers imagine that they are seeing reality when what they behold are but the shadows cast by the source of the real light onto the wall of their cave.

In my image, there's nothing illusory about what the mass of humanity considers reality. But that reality—the concrete, down-to-earth level of things—cannot be well understood on the level we can perceive. We are enmeshed in a world of great forces—those discussed here and others as well—that can be seen only when we raise our gaze to a higher level.

The movement of these great spheres shapes both us and our world. And the better we understand the mechanics by which these forces operate, the more chance we have of controlling them and not just being controlled by them.

Something Worth Calling "Spirit"? The "As If" Factor

There are reasons why, even when regarding these contending forces of good and evil in purely secular terms, it makes sense to speak of those forces in terms of "spirit." That's because in many ways they act as if they were vast spirits with a kind of "intent," and because their impact touches something of the "spirit" within the core of our being.

Language is a funny thing. Words have history, and history instills into words a set of connotations. When a word is used to mean something that varies to some degree from its historical usage, the question can legitimately be raised as to whether it is more illuminating or misleading to use the word.

The phenomenon that I have called "evil" raised that question. For some, the word calls to mind Satan and his minions—which is not what I intend. For others, it brings up images of bad people, or inborn aspects of human nature—which is also not what I had in mind.

Nonetheless, the phenomenon I described has so many of the essential characteristics associated with the word—and the power and resonance of the word seems so appropriate for conveying *what we're up against*—that I believe it is very much the right word.

A similar set of questions arises with respect to the word "spirit," which I propose to use as equivalent, in some contexts, to the word "force." If an evil force is something that moves the world in the direction of brokenness ("imparts a pattern of brokenness to what it touches"), that in itself connects with one of the main connotations of "spirit" in our language.

Spirit has long been understood as something that we cannot see directly, but that we infer from the way the things we do see *move.* The word derives from words for breath (inspire, expire) and wind. And spirit is indeed like the wind.

We do not see the wind, but looking through our window we know there's a wind from the swaying of the trees. To be "in-spired," for example, is to be *moved by something.* When a team is infused with "team spirit," there is something shared by the team members that enables them to act as a team to achieve their common goals.

Not visible: that's part of the essence of the meaning of spirit.

Consider "the Spirit of '76"—referring to the collective passion/ideas/values/goals that rose up among a substantial portion of the population of colonial America in 1776, and that gained expression in the Declaration of Independence and in the willingness of a great many people to risk much to gain independence from the mighty British colonial power.

Such a thing as this "Spirit of '76"—which persisted in a powerful way as an ideal that inspired and moved Americans for generations after the nation was founded—surely has many of the properties of an entity. It is not "just an abstraction." It moves things in the world.

Our world cannot be properly understood in rational and empirical terms without reference to such invisible forces. One cannot "see" love or rage or panic, but they nonetheless move things in the world. One cannot see patriotism or "Christian ethics" or the spirit of hope in the crowd in Grant Park on Election Night, 2009. But we can see that things in the world move differently under their influence.

Two other properties might make it appropriate to speak of an invisible force in terms of "spirit."

Speaking that way makes sense if that "force" "touches" that part of human beings that we might consider "of the spirit." When the impact of a force is felt directly on the core values of our humanity, when it consistently either enhances life or degrades and destroys it, that force is itself "of the spirit."

> When Rush Limbaugh, for example, works for a generation to weaken the force of "kindness" in America—as his hate-mongering rhetoric surely has succeeded in doing—we can rightly say that the force that is working through him is expressing a dark "spirit."

When we behold such spirits "animating" the way things are moving in our world, toward good or evil, we are likely to be moved in profound ways that call forth deep energies that might be called "spiritual" passions.

[NOTE: Think of how we, as an audience, feel when we witness the contrast, in *It's a Wonderful Life*, between two scenarios for our characters' society: one called Pottersville, shaped by the spirit of selfish greed; and one, called Bedford Falls, shaped by an altruistic caring for others. Think of the words in the "Battle Hymn of the Republic"—"as he died to make men holy, let us die to make men free"—with which Union soldiers in the war that ended slavery went off to battle.]

So there is an aspect of spirit to be found in ourselves, and a corresponding aspect referring to vast forces at work in our world.

And that brings us to the second property that makes use of the word "spirit" especially fitting in speaking of a force: that is when the force can be seen to be working AS IF it had an intention or purpose bearing upon those deep values core to our humanity and our fulfillment.

(Of the ideas in this book, this—involving envisioning a force acting "as if" it were purposeful—is the one I find most challenging to wrap one's mind around.)

To be clear, I am not suggesting that any kind of conscious being, an entity with feelings or desires, is involved when an "evil spirit" is at work. However, the workings of this network of elements—woven together into a "coherent force" through cause and effect (as described in Chapters 5, and 6)—does operate remarkably *as if* it were a malevolent force at work.

And it is here especially that we can benefit from making use of that ancient, resonant, fraught word, "spirit."

Where history provides a glimpse of a relatively "pure case" of a force of brokenness—and in America today we have the dubious privilege of witnessing such a force unambiguously aligned with brokenness—one can see a kind of "opportunism" at work. Where the forces of wholeness have weakened, the force of brokenness advances through the breach—as if some spirit of darkness were looking to expand its empire.

But this should be understood as, basically, the same kind of "as if" as when we speak of water "seeking" a lower spot to flow to.

During the presidency of George W. Bush, when America was being damaged almost across the board in terms of its values and its institutions and, eventually, its power and material condition, I wondered: If there were some diabolically clever Evil Being that wanted to damage the nation, how much more effective a course of demolition could it devise than that being enacted on an ongoing basis by the force then animating that presidency? The answer seemed to be that the damage being inflicted by the force operating through that presidency was nearly as great as a conscious "spirit" with intelligent strategy could have accomplished.

Again, I posit no such Evil Being. But I do perceive that the forces of brokenness and wholeness—though they can be explained in naturalistic, rational, secular terms—are so vast and enduring, so subtle and transcendent and opportunistic in their operation, that they do seem of a spiritual nature—acting as if they were animated by benign or malign intention.

Finally, I believe it can be useful strategically to employ the word "spirit" in talking about these forces. For one thing, it alerts us to the intellectual challenge it represents to comprehend these phenomena that are so far removed from what is immediately visible, yet so powerful in shaping out world. And in addition, it invites us to relate to them with the same kind of moral and spiritual passion that centuries of our forebears brought to their relationship with good and evil.

It is "spirit" of a wholly secular sort. But our world is not without its vast unseen forces, including those for good and evil. And our inner experience regarding this "battle between good and evil" is not without spaces of a deep and numinous kind.

INTERLUDE X

Butterfly Wings Beating in the Jungle: Inevitability Versus Contingency in History

We are obligated to act as if what we do may prove important. That squares with the "inevitability" of which I spoke earlier in two ways: 1) the knitting together of a world civilization opens up new possibilities of escaping from the reign of power; and 2) the "butterfly effect" applies also to history, as sometimes very small things have very large consequences.

In Chapter Seven ("The Battle Between Good and Evil"), I wrote: "It is a battle in which the stakes are, literally, life or death. And we are all obliged, I believe, to see that battle as hinging on what we ourselves do."

At a superficial level, it might seem incongruous for me to say that the outcome of the human project may depend on what we—you and I—choose to do. After all, did I not argue (in Interlude VI) against the idea of "free will"? And have I not stressed (in Chapter Five) that the troubled course of the evolution of civilization was "inevitable"?

But the incongruity is only apparent.

The "free will" issue is quickly disposed of. Whatever set of forces made me into the person who chose to write this book, and to issue a call to action to my fellow citizens, there is nothing standing in the way of my executing that choice to the best of my ability. And whatever fashioned you into a person who would or would not respond to that call to action, the choice is yours. The level at which free will is illlusory pertains only to the issue of "malice toward none," and not to our ability to chart our course into the future.

More interesting by far is to look at the apparent contradiction between my speaking of *inevitability* in one context and of *uncertainty of outcome* in another. It was the overall direction of the course into which civilization led humankind that I called inevitable. And it is the ultimate outcome of the whole human project that I said was uncertain, thus obliging each of us to try to affect the outcome of this ongoing battle between good and evil.

Is there a contradiction between these two ideas?

Both are true, but they operate at different levels. Additionally, what has previously been inevitable for civilization so long as the system was fragmented becomes less and less inevitable as global civilization gradually gets knit together. As alternatives to intersocietal anarchy become conceivable, a greater range of possibilities opens up for humankind.

Let's look first at the different scales at which history unfolds. For in many ways, at the small scale the course of history has always been unpredictable. That is because small and contingent events can produce large effects.

At the largest level—and for thousands of years—the selection for the ways of power was inevitable. And as is demonstrated by the parallels in development of all the pristine civilizations (as pointed out by the anthropologist Julian Steward, cited here in Chapter Five), the emergence of civilization wherever it occurred was going to manifest certain basic and important characteristics.

So long as intersocietal anarchy obtained, and thus power was unregulated, this would be the fate of the civilized creature.

But on the more human, smaller scale, a study of history shows just how much can hinge on very small things. A woman in Palm Beach County, Florida, unintentionally designs a confusing ballot in 2000, and the results include the Iraq war, and significant damage to the American political ethos.

The history of Abraham Lincoln, for example, shows how extremely improbable it was that he would become president of the United States. But he did, and one might readily surmise that with some other president, a very different history would have unfolded in that crucial era.

[NOTE: In addition, an alternative history that greatly interests me is how much different—how much better—the post-Civil War history of the United States would have been had the presidential box at Ford's Theater that night in April, 1865, been better guarded, and had Lincoln survived to oversee the reconstruction of the Union, with his marvelous combination of "malice toward none and charity for all" along with his resolute will to assure justice for the former slaves whose freedom he had won at such a price.]

Likewise, with the study of Winston Churchill's life. In the years before he was brought out of the figurative wilderness at the age of 65 to lead his country, the possibility of his becoming Prime Minister seemed to have been foreclosed. So many ways it could have not happened! Furthermore, had Churchill *not* become Prime Minister at that perilous moment, when it was almost too late to save the nation from Hitler's advancing forces, it is quite possible that Great Britain would have made a separate peace with the Nazi regime. (As it was, most of Churchill's own cabinet was so inclined.) That would likely have taken world history down a very different path.

And what would have happened if, in 1933, the assassin's bullet which killed Chicago Mayor Anton Cermak, had instead killed his intended target, the newly-inaugurated President Franklin Roosevelt, making Texan John Nance Garner president? How would the course of 20th century history have been different?

The idea of alternate history is controversial: After all, what happened, happened—so what does it mean to say it could have happened otherwise? And how can we know what would have happened otherwise "if only" a different fork in the road had been taken? But I think such exercises are quite useful for illuminating the nature of the historical process.

History in many ways unfolds in entirely unpredictable ways.

An excellent book (cited earlier as arguing against the reality of abstractions), *Forbidden Fruit: Counterfactuals and International Relations* by Richard Ned Lebow, explores this idea of how really big forks in the figurative road can hinge on extremely minor matters.

The most serious of these scenarios that he explores involves the assassination of Archduke Ferdinand in 1914—the event that precipitated the cascade of events leading to the carnage and upheavals of World War I. Lebow shows convincingly that the assassin succeeded only because of a set of very small contingencies that just happened to play out in a quite improbable way. Lebow also posits that had there been no assassination that day, there would have been no European war. (On that score, I am less convinced.) If no World War I, then likely no World War II, etc.

A real fork in the historical road, hinging on the smallest of happenstances.

(Lebow also spins out a more whimsical, but interesting, hypothetical history based on the idea of Mozart living well beyond his thirties and being thus able to lead what became the Romantic movement in a very different direction, altering—so Lebow proposes—the course of the history of Europe in the 19th century.)

History can be both the fruit of very large forces that carry the overall thrust of the evolution of civilization in some inevitable ways, and of small contingencies that determine which of highly divergent possible paths the unfolding of particular bits of history might take.

Perhaps this combination of apparently contradictory elements can be likened to the contrast between *climate* and *weather*. There are large-scale movements in the earth's climate, and then there are also rather short-term movements in the weather. Large-scale movements include the annual cycle of the seasons: we know that the temperatures in Minnesota during the winter will be notably colder than those in the summer, even if we don't know even within 20 degrees what the temperatures will be on a given day a month from now.

Meanwhile, the science of *chaos*—with its famous Butterfly Effect—says that within the earth's highly complicated system of weather, very small perturbations in one part of the system can bring about very large differences in the weather. The beating of the proverbial butterfly's wings in the jungle could affect the development of a storm elsewhere on the planet—in the same way that if Archduke Ferdinand had stuck with his assigned parade route, he would have avoided assassination and the world would have escaped all the storms that the assassination set in motion.

But there is also an important difference between the butterfly effect in climate, and how small changes can have large effects on history. The butterfly might affect the short-term weather, but not the long-term climate. In human affairs, by contrast—and especially in the circumstances of the civilization of our times—changes can yield *enduringly* large effects.

That was probably true in the Cuban Missile Crisis: if a different move by Kennedy or by Khrushchev had precipitated a massive exchange of nuclear weapons, the whole human experiment might have failed then and there. That's a lot more than just "weather."

Then there is the way the inevitability described by "the parable of the tribes" (Chapter Five) steadily diminishes as new opportunities emerge for civilization to end the intersocietal anarchy that has been the root of the problem. As humankind has a chance, in coming generations, to create an order to contain the rule of power, it becomes conceivable that the long-echoing impetus of brokenness that has marred human history could gradually be dissipated.

It is therefore conceivable that some seemingly insignificant fork in the road could spell the difference in the destiny of humankind between the triumph of good over evil, or evil over good, in determining the outcome of the human experiment.

It seems quite probable to me that, in the coming several centuries, *either* humankind will have made a significant turn toward a far more whole kind of civilization —e.g. living in harmony with the earth, maintaining an order among societies that preserves peace and assures justice (displacing the order of "might makes right" that has prevailed since civilization first emerged)—*or* the continued escalation of human powers will bring about disorder and destruction of such magnitude as to make brokenness the ultimate victor in the battle over human destiny.

So as history approaches a possible climax, as the powers of both good and evil in the human system escalate, and as the grip of inevitability is loosened, the importance of the contingent grows greater.

What we do or don't do *might* matter hugely.

This is especially true in America today. Of course it matters to us Americans, for at stake is what kind of country we will be. But the stakes are likely much bigger.

How this crisis plays out in the United States—"the world's leading nation," or what former Secretary of State Madeleine Albright quite plausibly declared to be the "indispensable nation"—could very well be crucial to the outcome of the human experiment as a whole.

Much may hinge on whether—in the face of the rise of this force of brokenness—those whom the nation needs to defend wholeness will continue to be blind and weak, or will rouse themselves to fight and win the battle.

Hence the obligation, as I see it, even for those of us who are not mighty, to beat our wings so as to generate the kind of storm that will help successfully resolve America's present crisis.

In Part III, I will take a new look at our predicament and propose why and how we can find a successful way out of it.

Part Three

Part Three

"The Emperor's New Clothes Project": A Strategy for Fighting Evil in a Democracy

Chapter Eleven:

See the Evil. Call it Out. Press the Battle.

Many Liberals Don't Like the Idea of Battle, But the Alternative in America Today is Much Worse

Although it is a sign of emotional and spiritual health not to prefer a life of combat to one of peace, sometimes the only alternative to battle is to allow all that one holds sacred to be damaged or destroyed. At times throughout history, people have faced such a choice. For Liberal America, this has been such a time. It is time we rose to the occasion.

In America right now there's a battle that needs to be fought and won in our political arena. It's a battle over what kind of country, and what kind of planet, our children and grandchildren will live in.

At its heart, this book is a call to battle.

Although some people like waging battle—some even insist on it—most liberals I've known are capable of living richer, more balanced and fulfilling lives. Most of us liberals would rather lead those better lives than focus on political combat.

But let's review the perilous state of America in our times.

Over the past decade or two, while we've been living our fuller, more rounded lives, we with the more humane set of values have been out-organized, out-fought, out-messaged by a relentless force that has taken over the right, and that

- turned our politics into a kind of war,
- hollowed out the middle class,
- debased our public discourse,
- brought out the worst in our decent conservative neighbors,
- undermined the rule of law,
- placed our descendants in greater peril of ecological catastrophe,
- embroiled us in needless wars,
- besmirched America's good name in the world,
- drove our economy into a pit,
- and helped corporate power steal our democracy.

The response from Liberal America to this ugly, destructive force on the right, as I have been arguing here from the outset, has been woefully inadequate to protect the nation. Close to a forfeit.

The combination of a destructive force and a weak response to it has created one of the most profound crises in American history. If our nation is going to stop its descent, and to regain the ability to deal constructively with the challenges we face, this dangerous political dynamic must be changed.

Sure, we'd rather live our healthier, more fulfilling lives. But history does not always give people the choices they prefer.

Throughout history, peoples have been forced to confront others bent on dominating them. The undesirable choice has been either to be subjugated by those aggressors, or to achieve the power necessary for defending what they hold dear. (This, it will be recalled from Chapter Five, is a major implication of "the parable of the tribes," which examines the problem of power in social evolution.)

Even though we might prefer the option of going on as before and have everything be all right, that option simply does not exist anymore.

In plain sight, the relentless force that has taken over the Republican

Party is working against pretty much everything we believe in: justice to protect the people, truth in our democratic deliberations, compassion for our fellow citizens, and care for the integrity of the living systems on which we all depend for our survival.

That's the nature of what we're called to fight and defeat. The stakes could hardly be higher.

We're not the first to be required by the luck of the historical draw to be called to a duty we'd not desired.

In the 1940s, my father's generation had to set aside the lives they would have preferred to lead—lives richer and more humane than fighting their way across France or the islands of the Pacific—because it was necessary to defeat a destructive force that had arisen in Europe and Asia.

Likewise, the present generation of Americans has a moral responsibility to sacrifice our ease and comfort to defend the same values by fighting—resolutely, but by non-violent democratic means—here at home.

Analyzing the Dynamics of the Battle

Defeating the force that has arisen on the right will require unmasking it in the eyes of those who have supported it. The impetus for that will have to begin in Liberal America. That impetus requires a change in liberal understanding that is not superficial and thus will not come easily. Nonetheless, a coherent strategy for victory is possible.

Earlier, I asserted that the central dynamic of our crisis had two main parts:

1. The Republican Party has become the instrument of an evil force; and

2. The response from Liberal America to this threat has been woefully weak.

Correspondingly, the saving of America has two components:

1. The power of this force that's taken over the right needs to be reduced. And

2. The intensity and strength of Liberal America in this battle need to increase.

It would be simpler for us if America's problem were confined to this or that part of the body of American civilization, but this deep-seated crisis shows that the pathology gripping our nation permeates the whole. While this pathology manifests itself differently in different components of the American body politic, the challenge of making America more whole again requires that all the components of our present systematic pathology be addressed.

Is there a coherent strategy for addressing the defects on both the right and left side of our political divide? This book says yes.

In our still-democratic polity, the destructive force that has arisen on the right depends for its power on the support of millions of our fellow citizens, as expressed at the polls. As powerful as Big Money is, that power still has to translate into votes. (A generation from now, that might not still be the case.) Taking power away from this force, therefore, entails prying away enough of the supporters of that force that it loses its clout to greatly influence the nation's course.

How can this be done? If all those supporters of today's Republican Party fully understood the nature of what they are supporting, that task would likely be impossible. But the support of most of these Americans has been gained through a successful con job. (See* "The Fraudulence of the Republican Party and an Adverse Shift in the Balance Between Good and Evil in America.")

A substantial number of Republican voters—at least in my part of Virginia—are basically good, decent people who have no idea that the force they are supporting is far from being either good or decent. Thus, in a nation like ours the only way a force like this can gain power is by deceiving large numbers of people into believing that it is something it is not.

That lie is both this force's source of power, and its Achilles' heel. The question, "How can the force on the right be weakened" can therefore be reframed, "How can those good, decent conservatives be awakened to the truth about what they are supporting?"

Given what a closed, rigid, doctrinaire culture the right-wing world has become, such awakening will have to come from a powerful and sustained campaign of truth-telling from outside its boundaries. (See* "The Uncracked Nut.")

That powerful campaign is not now in evidence.

The saving of America must therefore begin with addressing whatever in the liberal part of the American body politic has made it so weak, so slow to rise to the battle, so little capable of providing the necessary jolt to the "uncracked nut."

Wouldn't it be nice if the problems in Liberal America were superficial and easily remedied? Wouldn't it be nice if it sufficed to argue, as I did above, that we have "a moral responsibility to sacrifice our ease and comfort" to defend our sacred values.

But, regrettably, the problem is not superficial. The dynamics of this crisis did not arise overnight, and therefore are not apt to be changed overnight.

This book is an attempt to illuminate the nature of the problem and to begin addressing it. The response from Liberal America has been weak, I am asserting, because we do not see that *what we are up against is an evil force.* If we saw the reality before our eyes for what it is, I've proposed, we would be inspired to respond to it more in the way our heroes do (like Luke, Frodo, and Sully).

Accordingly, I've tried to make that reality of what we're up against—the reality of an "evil force"—visible.

This effort has had two components: 1) *showing* the evil force that is right before our eyes, and 2) explaining—in secular, rational, empirical terms—how such a thing can be, how the human world is and has long been a stage on which a drama that warrants being called "the battle between good and evil" has been enacted.

"See the Evil" is the first step in generating the change America needs. You can't hit what you can't see.

But this "seeing the evil" requires an awakening of its own. For in much of secular/liberal America, to *see the evil* would imply, for many, a change in worldview. And changes at that level do not come easily.

Both sides of our politically embattled nation, therefore, have to undergo important transformations. Neither transformation will be easy. But so great are the stakes in this battle—will our nation be shaped by the forces of wholeness or of brokenness?—that we cannot allow ourselves to be daunted by the magnitude of the challenge.

At the Deepest Level

It is at the spiritual level that both sides of our divided nation are making a fundamental error. The people on the right have mistaken the evil for the good, while those in Liberal America have failed to recognize that those forces of good and evil are a vital part of the human drama.

Whether or not one can *see the evil* is but the visible tip of a very deep iceberg. That question of seeing the evil, affords an entryway into a whole realm, into that deepest level of our understanding of our reality—i.e. into what might be called "the level of the spirit."

Our nation is divided, but the two sides have in common that people on each side of America's political divide are making a fundamental error at the level of the spirit. And it is these two errors that, together, have plunged America into this dangerous condition.

The two sides are making very different errors, but both their errors involve a failure to recognize a fundamentally destructive force.

1. On the right, the error is mistaking the evil for the good.
2. On the left, among many with a secular/rationalistic worldview, the error is failing to recognize the reality and centrality in human affairs of the forces of good and evil.

No wonder our nation is in such a dangerous situation, with vast numbers of Americans making serious errors concerning what might be called the force of "evil"—a phenomenon so vast, so subtle but mighty, so fundamental to the contest between life and death, between wholeness and brokenness, in the human world.

Our battle appears to be a political one, since it is being fought out in the political arena. (Not surprisingly since, as "the parable of the tribes" suggests, the force of brokenness emerges primarily out of the problem of power, and because it is the nature of this force that it swarms around power like flies swarm around a pile of steaming excrement.)

But more fundamentally this battle is in the realm of "spirit" (as "spirit" was described at the end of Chapter Ten), the vast forces embattled over the destiny of our civilization.

Healing America requires addressing those errors at the level of the spirit.

Weakness as a Result of a Disconnection from the Spirit

Those who believe that there was nothing President Obama could have done to prevail over the disgraceful Republican obstructionism he encountered reveal a lack of awareness of the dimension of "the spirit." This is symptomatic of the underlying malady that has made Liberal America too weak to protect the nation.

The brokenness in Liberal/secular America could be characterized as a loss of connection with a deep level of our reality, and of the humanity within us.

It is not only in the failure to see the evil that the spiritual disconnect in Liberal America can be perceived. That disconnect weakens Liberal America in other ways as well. Here's an example.

In the fall of 2014, Paul Krugman—whom I consider one of the heroes of our times—published in the *New York Times* an op/ed with which I took issue. Krugman, previously a tough Obama critic, was declaring Obama "one of the most…successful presidents in American history." I, originally an Obama enthusiast, took issue. In a piece titled "Sorry Professor Krugman: Obama Came to Office Holding a Royal Flush, and Then He Declared His Hand 'Ace High,'" I made the case that President Obama's failure to call out the disgraceful and unprecedented conduct of the opposition had not only prevented him from accomplishing more but had also allowed the degradation of our polity to continue apace.

(Lest anyone imagine that came only lately to that critique, I cited an "Open Letter to the President" I published* in the *Baltimore Sun*, in 2009 while President Obama was still in the first year of his presidency. In that column, I described the ways in which the president had given his power away to his enemies, and ended with this: "Your opponents are relentless, single-minded and ruthless in their efforts to weaken and destroy you. This is a continuation of the same struggle for which Americans chose you to be their champion. It's your job not to ignore the battle but to fight and win it.")

My 2014 piece disagreeing with Krugman prompted an online discussion which showed the spiritual problems in Liberal America from another angle.

A number of my interlocutors declared that, given the determination of his Republican opponents to make him fail, there was nothing Mr. Obama could have done. There was no real "bully pulpit" available for the president, it was said; and there was no way that the president could see to it that the Republicans were punished, rather than rewarded, for their dishonest, obstructionist, and downright unpatriotic conduct.

What matters about this now is not about President Obama, who will soon be part of our historical past, but about Liberal America, and whether it has the vision and thus can muster the power to safeguard America's future.

My interlocutors were good liberal activists, the kind of people who migrate toward the front lines of our political contests. Think what it means when people with those important qualities believe that, in the battle for public opinion, the President of the United States was helpless against a political force that was dealing in blatant lies, trampling on our national traditions and ideals, thwarting the expressed will of the people, and showing utter disregard for the public good!

To believe that is to have a terribly constricted vision of the potential forces that can work in the world. In particular, it shows an inability to perceive the potential power of the spirit.

If Martin Luther King could accomplish what he accomplished from the very modest position from which he began—the pulpit from which he started was far more modest than the president's "bully pulpit"—what should we be able to envision that a President of the United States could achieve from his most prominent place of leadership?

And let us remember, Obama began as not just any president. Let us remember the Colossus that Barack Obama was at the time he took office.

Remember the illuminated faces—alight with the passion of hope for the light-bearer coming to power after a time of profound darkness in America—in Grant Park in Chicago on the night Obama won the election. Remember, too, the worldwide enthusiasm for this new president—the huge and enthusiastic throng in Berlin not long before Obama was elected, and the Nobel Peace Prize awarded him not long after.

At that beginning, he loomed large over the landscape specifically because of the spirit that he seemed then to embody and that then swept him into office.

A deep well of spiritual force was there to be tapped into. It was this deep force of the spirit that had imbued Obama, whether deservedly or not, with a profound aura of moral authority throughout the world.

Call it Out

When the force of the spirit enters into human affairs, unexpected things happen. Examples of the seemingly impossible happening include what Gandhi achieved for Indian independence, what Mandela did in ending the apartheid regime without bloodshed, and what Churchill did in rallying Britain to hold off Nazi Germany.

Had the president tapped into that moral authority, and that power of the spirit, and called out the disgraceful conduct of the Republicans, how could they have persisted in that scandalous conduct and survived politically?

When the power of the spirit enters into our affairs, surprising things become possible. But so far, it is the evil spirit on the right that has unleashed a surprising amount of power, dismantling what's best about America with a speed few could have imagined possible a generation ago.

But my interlocutors, who stand against that evil spirit, maintain that Mr. Obama's prevailing over a disgraceful opposition was impossible.

Many things seem impossible within a worldview which fails to include the deep forces of the spirit.

Had there been no Gandhi, those with no vision of the potential power of the spirit would have claimed impossible the path India took to independence.

Before Mandela re-entered the scene in South Africa, the "realists" declared there was no way that the apartheid regime in South Africa could be ended without a bloodbath.

(This one I know for a fact from my work, in the early 1980s, at the Center for Strategic and International Studies in Washington, D.C.

My job there was to distill and articulate the expectations of that organization's community of experts on what developments in international affairs the United States might have to deal with in the coming years. CSIS called that effort the "Contingencies Project." And the "riding on the back of a tiger" dilemma in South Africa was a frequent topic of discussion.)

Had there been no Churchill, and if Britain had made a separate peace in 1940 with the Nazi power (already looking to strike across the English Channel), some would have declared that no better outcome than accommodating Hitler was possible for Britain.

But each of those leaders tapped into a great force of the spirit—- expressing itself non-violently in some circumstances, expressing itself as a determination to resist evil by all means available in others; sometimes as a call to reconciliation, sometimes as a call to battle—- and turned the tide of history in unexpected ways.

I expect that some will regard it as odd that I would include the pugnacious Winston Churchill together with the likes of Gandhi and Mandela. Is not the spirit of Wholeness, it might be asked, a spirit of peace?

Ideally, yes. Ultimately, yes. But sometimes, in this less than ideal world, we can reach our ultimate goals only by means other than what we would ideally choose. Sometimes the spirit of Wholeness—the force of the good—needs warriors, lest evil be allowed to rule the world.

Churchill's "spirit," as many of the quotations from that era showed, brought to the fore the best of the spirit of the English people—their courage, their fortitude, their willingness to sacrifice to preserve liberty and decency for their children—and the power of that spirit helped prevent Europe from falling for years, conceivably even generations, under the boot of the evil force of the Thousand Year Reich.

Spiritual Truth to Win a Spiritual Battle

The theme of this book—that what we are up against is an evil force—offers us a coherent strategy for addressing both sides of our national crisis. It addresses the previously mentioned "spiritual error" of both sides—the side that has mistaken the evil for the good, and the side that has failed to recognize the reality of good and evil. Two birds with one stone.

But of course, to save our nation, we have no need for sacrifice on the field of bloody and violent battle. Not yet anyway. We do, however, have a need for fighters.

I've encountered the objection: If we fight, aren't we just sinking to the level of our opponents.

To which I reply: if our opponents are fighting with the Lie, we do not sink to their level if we fight back with the truth.

The truth versus the lie is a moral and spiritual battle. And that is, fundamentally, what we are engaged in. The fight is between the force of wholeness and the force of brokenness. While the weapon for the force of brokenness is the lie, the weapon for the force of wholeness is the truth.

Our crisis can be measured by how often—under the presidency of George W. Bush, and in the triumphs of Republican obstructionism during the Obama presidency—the lie has defeated the truth.

And this battle can be turned around to the extent that Americans—on *both* sides of the divide—can grasp and respond to one vital truth. It is the truth that what we are up against, what has arisen on the right in our times, is an evil force.

If the good *people on the right* can be brought to see enough of that truth, this will correct their spiritual error—i.e., mistaking the evil for the good. And their response—requiring that their party change or be repudiated—will drain away from that evil force the power to damage our nation, either by separating the once-respectable Republican Party from the evil spirit that now possesses it or, if the grip of that force on that party cannot be broken, by driving the Republican Party into oblivion.

And if the thoughtful people in Liberal America can be brought to see that same truth, that will correct *their* spiritual error—i.e., not seeing the reality, in the human world, of "the battle between good and evil." And their response to that truth—to act more like our heroes in response to such a force—will fortify Liberal America for this battle that must be fought and won.

The same truth—the central message of this book—thus imparts to both sides of our fractured polity the impetus to move in the direction each needs to go.

So what we have is this:

- A two-fold dynamic to our national pathology.
- Two different directions to move the two sides.
- Two different errors of the spirit.
- But one message to accomplish both tasks.

Two birds with one stone.

Can a way be found for this stone to be thrown hard and far enough to hit those birds in a way that makes a difference? The tale of my experience on this mission might help to illuminate both the reasons I'm hopeful the answer is yes, and the reasons I am sober in those hopes.

I Can Do No Other

My efforts to sound the alarm about this force that's taken over the right, starting in 2004, have gone through phases. (This book is the fifth.) Here is a brief description of the first three, of which two can be described as "swinging for the fences, hitting a clean single."

For me, "seeing the evil" was a life-changing experience.

It was in early September 2004. I was watching the Republican National Convention on television. And it hit me. I saw the darkness that had come to power in America, and I was electrified. I mean, in terms of a galvanizing of the spirit, it was as if I'd stuck my finger into an electric socket.

Since that moment, I've been fighting against that force I saw. It would not feel correct—not true to how I've experienced it—to say that I CHOSE to fight it. It has really been an "I can do no other" kind of thing.

This book is the fifth stage of that fight.

In the first phase (up until spring 2005), I appealed, one after the other, to two prominent Americans with the standing, reputation, and skills I thought would enable them open the eyes of the American people to the dangerous force that was threatening our civilization. To each, I offered to help in any way I could, without pay. Both experiences were positive and interesting, but my effort failed: neither of these important Americans wanted to take on the job.

So in the second phase, I took on the job myself. It would have been better to have had someone with a big platform rather than a relatively unknown person like myself, but better someone, I figured, than no one. I began writing on a new website of mine (www.NoneSoBlind.org), and sometimes these writings would appear also on other more prominent sites.

I launched this effort with an article titled, "What America Needs Now: A Prophetic Social Movement." I concluded this piece, after explaining how the dark forces then ruling could gain power "only by selling their false image of righteousness to good, conservative Americans," in this way:

> By skillfully speaking the moral truth, we can help unite the good people of America, and end the polarization that our amoral leaders have worked to foster—helping America's conservatives to remember how better to tell the difference between good and evil, and helping America's liberals to remember how absolutely vital—and real—that difference is.
>
> Let us then speak to America out of our faith in a venerable idea deeply embedded in the Western religious tradition: the idea that the material power of the bad ruler can be overcome by the power of moral truth boldly spoken. Let us launch, then, a 'prophetic' social movement to re-establish the power of real righteousness in America.

For the main job of the prophets, in the Biblical tradition, from Elijah to John the Baptist, was to *call out evil power by speaking the moral truth.*

Although my writings during this six-year phase had a daily readership of several thousands, the "prophetic social movement" did not emerge. Swing for the fences, hit a single.

When, at the end of 2010, I concluded that our new president, in whom I'd placed so much hope, was not going to fight the battle that needed to be fought—that he was not going to call out the Republican opposition for its disgraceful conduct—I surprised myself by jumping into the political arena as a candidate for Congress.

I began my campaign with the slogan, "Let's Talk About the Elephant in the Room." That image calls attention to the two-sided nature of the problem: the presence of the elephant (the dangerous thing that needed to be talked about) and the failure of the others in the room to call out the problem. I eventually changed the slogan to "Truth. For a change." And I campaigned by calling out my opponent for all the falsehoods by which he obscured what he and his Party were doing with their power.

Unsurprisingly, in this 2:1 Republican District, I did not win. What was surprising to me, however, is how determined the conservative voters were to avoid hearing any message that did not accord with their orthodoxy. As described in the article* "The Uncracked Nut," it turns out that a generation's worth of unanswered demonization of "librels" had succeeded in making the idea of listening to *any* Democrat unthinkable to many good people. That was disappointing.

But there was one important way in which my campaign really did succeed. The message of moral truth—the calling out of the "evil force"—did light something of a fire on the liberal side.

This is visible in that previously mentioned six-minute video of a speech I gave to a banquet attended by 350 Democrats on the eve of Labor Day, two months before the 2012 election. It is gratifying to me to be able to demonstrate, with that video, that *this message*—a version of what this book says—*can have an impact.* The speech seemed to ignite the people there, and the video of that speech quickly took off on the Internet.

> (The man who, just accidentally, videoed my speech because he didn't turn off the camera after the speech of his wife, a candidate for local office, posted the video on YouTube, and it was discovered there by a Daily Kos blogger who posted it there under the title, "Video: A Real Democrat Gives One of the Best, Most Kick-A** Political Speeches I've Ever Seen!," and from there it took off.)

That was my one foray into electoral politics, and a wonderful experience it was—both for me and for my wife (April Moore), whose many virtues helped neutralize my own shortcomings in the hail-fellow-well-met department.

The campaign did not achieve all my goals—my opponent, Bob Goodlatte, then a twenty-year Republican incumbent, is now chairman of the House Judiciary Committee, where he obediently serves the dark force that owns his Party—but it has never felt like a failure.

Swing for the fences, settle for a single.

Through the campaign, I had developed a good relationship with a number of press people in my congressional district. And in the wake of the election, I was able to establish a niche for myself as a regular contributor of opinion pieces to a handful of the newspapers in the district. By that means, I have been able to keep "calling it out" to the mostly conservative readers of these newspapers.

Press the Battle

In the years since my campaign for Congress, I have worked to model my proposed strategy of pressing the battle by publishing a series of op/ed pieces in my very conservative District. Here is a sampling of those pieces, through which I seek to awaken those on the right who have been deceived about the nature of the force they are supporting.

These op/eds are the main place where I get to engage with *what we're up against*—by speaking directly to the kind of people who, on a national scale, are the electoral power-source for this evil force. It is the good people among them who are my target audience, the people whom I have in mind when I decide what to write about, and how to make the case. That is because these are the people who would withdraw their support from that force if they knew the truth.

Let me present a few of these pieces here to illustrate my own effort to practice the strategy I am proposing for fighting and winning this battle: after *seeing the evil*, one raises one's voice to *call it out*, and with the truth as the weapon, one *presses the battle.*

This piece ran in newspapers around my District in the summer of 2013.

Think Horses, Not Unicorns: The Incredible GOP Line on Climate Change

In medicine there's a saying, "When you hear hoof beats, think of horses not zebras." Whatever's going on is far more likely to be the usual than the extraordinary.

But when it comes to climate change, the Republicans are telling Americans not to think horses, or even zebras. They're saying, think unicorns. Republicans want Americans to believe that the alarm about climate change is based on a scientific hoax.

Republicans used to claim that the science was inconclusive. Fifteen years ago I was on television in Virginia debating the issue against a local Republican official who took that party-line position. But with so powerful a consensus among the experts--97%—the Republicans have taken the fall-back position that climate science is a hoax.

This hoax would have to be beyond extraordinary. Over the course of history, there have been hoaxes in science—a scientist or two creating false evidence. But if any scientific hoax has involved more than two or three people, I have been unable to discover it.

The scientific studies that show the disruption of the earth's climate due to human activities have been the work of thousands of scientists, from nations all over the world, conducted over decades.

A scientific hoax of that magnitude is beyond improbable.

If we ought not to believe in this unicorn, is there a horse around to explain the hoof beats?

In fact, there is. We have an industry doing what other industries have done in similar situations. And we have a political party doing what it has done again and again.

The 97% of climate scientists who agree that there's human-caused climate change also say that it would be irresponsible for civilized societies to fail to take action to avert—or, by this time, simply to lessen—the possible disasters ahead. Taking action, in this case, means weaning ourselves from our addiction to fossil fuels.

It's not all that long since science discovered that another powerful industry's addictive products were having deadly results. That industry worked for decades to sow doubt where there was no good reason for doubt. Eventually, it was revealed that the industry had known the truth for years.

I'm talking, of course, about the tobacco industry.

But it's not just tobacco. Whenever industries have discovered that their profits depended on sacrificing other people—like for example, the asbestos and chemical industries—they've done their best to hide or deny the truth. Is there an exception?

For the energy companies to protect their profits by persuading millions of people to reject science would be nothing unusual. The stakes may be unprecedented, given the potential catastrophes we may be unleashing, but the choice of greed over caring for the greater good would fit a pattern.

It has been documented for well over a decade that climate change denial is largely funded by energy industries. Like the tobacco company executives all claiming that they did not believe nicotine was addictive or that their products were killing people, oil companies know better than what they tell the public.

(I was told by two inside sources that by the time of the George W. Bush presidency, the oil companies were acknowledging behind closed doors that the scientists' warnings were correct, but were resolved to maintain their campaign to prevent the American public from knowing the truth.)

Corporations protecting profits even at great cost to the greater good is no zebra or unicorn, but a common horse.

Then there's the relationship between the politicians and these huge energy corporations, among the richest and most powerful organizations in the world. The Republicans, especially, have a history of doing their bidding,—shouting "Drill, Baby, Drill," protecting the subsidies we taxpayers still pay out to oil companies long after the original reason for them vanished along with $15-a-barrel oil. And now they support this campaign to discredit the urgent warnings from the scientists that there's big danger ahead and we'd better start steering our ship away from that iceberg.

No surprise that the Republican Party—no longer the Party of

> Teddy Roosevelt or even Richard Nixon when it comes to the environment—would choose to protect not the stability of our climate but the interests of the corporations who are their political partners.
>
> There's a choice. One can believe that we have a huge conspiracy to commit a scientific hoax—bigger by many orders of magnitude than anything ever seen before. Or one can believe that we have powerful corporations and the political party that serves them following a well-established pattern of deception for the sake of profits.
>
> With the issue of climate change now front and center in our political arena, it's about time Americans approached it from a shared reality. It really shouldn't be that hard.
>
> Think horses.

It's pretty straightforward what I'm doing in this climate change piece: I'm trying to confront the conservatives who read these newspapers with a reality check. "Which is more likely…?" Why believe something incredible and unprecedented when there is a highly plausible alternative?

Research has shown, I realize, that when you confront people—especially conservatives, but not only them—with logic and evidence that contradicts their previous beliefs, it has the effect of making them cling all the more adamantly to those beliefs, rather than change them in accordance with facts and logic.

But I suspect that altogether too much can be made of those findings. My doubts have to do with the question: How much time elapsed between the challenge to the people's beliefs and the post-challenge check-up to gauge the impact on those beliefs of the challenge they've heard. It is doubtful that the researchers waited around for months or years to measure their results. But immediate resistance to change, while predictable, is not necessarily indicative of the longer term impact of a strong challenge.

I'm reminded of a scene from the 1957 movie, *Fear Strikes Out*—a biographical story of a famous baseball player of the era, Jimmy Piersall. Piersall suffered from a mental illness for which he was hospitalized. In a crucial scene, a session between Piersall and his psychiatrist, Piersall becomes enraged at the therapist for trying to get him to look at the destructive aspects of his relationship with his father. At the end of an angry diatribe defending his father, he shouts out that if it weren't for his father, "I wouldn't be where I am today!" Then, looking around at his surroundings—a mental hospital—he realizes the meaning of what he has just said, and storms angrily out of the room.

Resistance is a well-known part of the path to change. Change does not come easily—that's because it has experiential costs. Imagine what kind of painful ripples it would make in the minds of the "good, decent conservatives" I'm trying to reach with these op/eds for them to fully absorb the implications of what I say here about the unicorn their leaders have been selling them and the horse that is the true story instead. Who wouldn't resist having to adjust to those implications? Who wouldn't be reluctant to face the reality that they've been had, that the people they thought they could trust have been willing to sacrifice their children's and grandchildren's future on behalf of the sociopathic mega-corporations that help keep them in office?

Changes of that sort take time. And they require a good deal more of such pressures to change than one such op/ed piece can apply. The nut might crack-- but only over a stretch of time, and after more repeated, and more powerful blows. Way more than a single voice in the comparative wilderness.

This next piece ran in the spring of 2014:

What Kind of Christianity is This?

In the past several decades, a major force has entered the American political arena under an explicitly Christian banner. I'm talking about the Christian Right, which has aligned itself with the Republican Party. Has this alliance advanced the values that Jesus taught?

Jesus advocated for the poor and the outcast, and castigated mostly the privileged and the mighty. Today's vociferous Christian political force supports the party that cuts programs to feed the hungry and to lift up the downtrodden, while protecting the interests of the fabulously wealthy.

When I hear Republicans talk about the poor in derogatory ways – lazy, slackers, etc.—I wonder, where in the Bible does Jesus show any such attitude toward the poor?

"Blessed are the peacemakers," Jesus said. But the party with which this Christian force is allied has made our politics into a kind of warfare. They disdain compromise, they treat their opponents without respect, and they fight even against ideas that they originated, once the other side proposes them.

At the heart of Jesus' teachings was an ethic of love. I'd like to ask the good Christians who support today's Republican Party: When was the last time your leaders have inspired you to love anyone or anything—except for an "Us" arrayed against a hated "Them"?

In the most powerful scene in which Jesus deals with issues of wrong-doing and punishment, the emphasis of his teaching is directed at the crowd that's ready to stone the adulteress. "Let him who is without sin cast the first stone," he says to the crowd, and then turns to the woman to deliver the caring message, "Go, and sin no more."

In the Republicans' way of dealing with issues of crime and punishment, can anyone point to a spirit of compassion and humility, rather than harsh punitiveness? Can one find "blessed are the merciful" in the main Republican attitude toward impoverished people who have sneaked across our borders?

I was not brought up in a Christian household, but got my first vivid sense of the Christian spirit from images in spectacular movies during the 1950s. These films—like *Quo Vadis, The Robe*, and *Ben Hur*—presented sharp contrasts between the brutality of the Romans and the beauty of spirit in the followers of Christ.

The Romans were all about power. They were harsh, contemptuous of those who did not live by the sword, taking pleasure in dominating and even in inflicting pain on the vulnerable. When the scene switched to the Christians, the spirit changed to gentleness, forgiveness of those who trespassed against them, generosity of spirit, and humility.

I took an interest in seeing what this teacher, Jesus, had said to bring forth such beauty in the human spirit.

Now I wonder how anyone who follows the teachings of Jesus could also follow even for a moment someone like Rush Limbaugh. Practically his every word violates what Jesus taught (Matthew 5: 22) against expressing contempt for one's brethren.

Something has gotten dangerously switched around, turning up into down and light into darkness.

When I was a candidate for Congress (2011-12), I traveled all around Virginia's 6th District, speaking with citizens of all kinds. In the process, I was privy to a variety of strains and disagreements and antagonisms. But among all these, one stood out dramatically.

There was one actor—one power—in the District that was regarded in a way like no other, with a kind of elemental repulsion and deep dread I'd never heard expressed in America before. The object of these extraordinary feelings was Liberty University, the Christian institution of higher education in Lynchburg, Virginia.

What does it mean for a Christian institution to be experienced that way by its neighbors? It hardly seems possible that following Jesus's teachings—"Love thy neighbor as thyself"—could give rise to such feelings.

And what does it mean for an institution that claims to be built to advance Christian values to be aligned with the Party that serves the mighty powers of Mammon, and that regularly preys on the lowly and vulnerable?

Many good Christians seem to have been led to believe that, if they give their support to politicians who oppose abortion and oppose recognizing rights for people with a different sexual orientation, they are serving the cause of Christian values in America.

But even if Jesus would agree on those two issues—and he had precious little to say about such things—his message was so much bigger. His teachings bore upon the entire spirit that infuses human affairs.

> It has long seemed to me that the world would be a much better place if people acted according to the spirit Jesus taught.
>
> What would Jesus do? One thing seems clear to me: in America today, he would not vote Republican.

This piece exemplifies a central part of my rhetorical strategy in my messages to the conservatives I'm able to reach with these op/ed pieces: I do not challenge their basic values. I embrace those values for the positive things I find in them, and try to show the discrepancy between their own deep values and the spirit that animates the force they support in the power arena.

This is not phony on my part. I genuinely do appreciate those values in their genuine form. In the 1990s, I did hundreds of radio shows engaging with the conservatives in my area on "the questions of meaning and value that we face in our lives." I framed my shows with the appeal that we talk with each other "in a spirit of mutual respect, as if we might actually learn from each other." And I meant it.

> (These conversations gave rise to my book, *Debating the Good Society: A Quest to Bridge America's Moral Divide* (from M.I.T. Press in 1999), in which I composed a fictional discussion among various liberal and conservative voices, trying to move toward a kind of truth in which the half-truths of each side might be integrated into a "higher wisdom" that resolved their apparent contradictions. I was a builder of bridges for decades before I became a wager of battles. What changed was not me but the political culture of the right, as this force—through the efforts of people like Karl Rove—made impossible the kind of constructive conversation that I had so much enjoyed for a whole decade.)

The effort in "What Kind of Christianity Is This?" is not to change these devout conservative Christians to abandon their faith, but to awaken them to the seduction to which they have been subjected by a force that only pretends to be in alignment with the better angels of their nature, while actually feeding their worst parts.

It is in that context that I took particular pleasure in this piece appearing in the *News & Advance*, the newspaper in Lynchburg, Virginia—the home of that very dark institution that, as I not only heard from others but also learned from my own first-hand experience, is animated by the very opposite of the Christian spirit it claims to represent.

This next piece ran in the newspapers in the fall of 2014:

Why the Republicans Love the Abortion Issue

How many Americans fit this profile?

- They are inclined to view politics in moral terms, and it is important to them to be one of the good people and not one of the bad people.
- Their understanding of the workings of the larger systems in their world—e.g. the US government, and the American and world economies—is limited.
- Having neither the time, interest, nor background to develop a complex picture of American politics, they welcome a simple way to exercise their duties as citizens. Finding a single issue that can define their political choices serves this purpose.

Millions, I would guess.

To lock in the support of such people, the issue of abortion is perfect.

Protecting the defenseless unborn can easily be cast as a high moral purpose. The issue arises on the human scale, no complex systems involved. It concerns family relationships, and also involves the consequences of sexual behavior, on which cultural traditions have had much to say.

The abortion issue creates the opportunity for a savvy political force to capture and hold those millions of single-issue voters. The Republican Party has seized that opportunity for decades, convincing those millions that they are the moral party and their opponents are immoral.

While Americans as a whole are not comfortable about abortion, it is only a minority who think it should be illegal in all circumstances. The Democratic Party has inevitably settled into representing the feelings of the American majority that does not want abortion banned outright.

Although the position the Democrats take on abortion—"safe, legal, and rare"—reflects the majority opinion in America, very few in that majority vote on that single issue. But, by targeting voters who meet the above profile, the Republican Party has been able over the decades to cultivate an important block of single-issue anti-abortion voting.

That's why the abortion issue has been a gold-mine for the Republicans. That's why as soon as the Republicans captured state governments in the 2010 elections, even though the nation was still in a deep economic recession, and the people were clamoring for programs to create jobs, in state after state the Republicans diverted attention away from the urgent economic issues and re-inflamed the political battles over abortion.

The Republicans have encouraged those single-issue millions to see abortion as defining political morality—a pure case of good vs. evil, with no moral ambiguities. With the Democrats locked into a non-absolutist position—abortion as regrettable but not to be prohibited by law—the idea can be established in people's minds, as I have heard on the campaign trail, that "one cannot be both a Christian and a Democrat."

But what makes this single-issue voting block a gold mine for Republicans also makes it a danger to the country.

When a political party can get millions of voters, who care about moral values, locked into seeing it as the defender of morality, it frees itself to engage in immoral conduct of all sorts without fear of losing those voters' support. And that is what has happened.

In America today, a great many immoral and unjust acts that have nothing to do with abortion are being carried out in our political arena—the preponderance of them by the same political force that has gained the permanent support of one-issue anti-abortion voters.

Abortion has the special appeal for today's Republican Party, that it is wholly disconnected from the quest for money and power that are the Party's real purposes.

> Those millions of single-issue pro-life voters are satisfied that they are supporting morality even though they vote for a political party that has been relentlessly transferring wealth and power from average Americans to the richest and mightiest few. With its right hand pointing to abortion, the Republican Party distracts attention from the large-scale acts of immorality being carried out by its left hand.
>
> In the Bible, while relatively little is said about the status of the unborn, the passages are many in which the prophets call for protecting "widows and orphans" and for giving justice to the weak.
>
> In a nation where the task of aligning power with the good and against the evil is far from simple, the simplification of the tasks of citizenship into a single test can play directly into the hands of the kind of evil power the prophets railed against.

Let me note first that my use of the word "evil" in the last line is quite atypical of my usual approach in speaking to the "good, decent conservatives" upon whose change of heart the future of America—the balance of power between the forces of good and evil—may ultimately depend.

The idea that "the Republican Party has become the instrument of an evil force" is, indeed, the content of the message that these people need to hear. But, unlike with the secular liberals to whom this book is mainly addressed, there's no need to use the word evil because it is already fully alive, as a concept, in their worldview.

They may have been deceived into a false picture of where the problem of evil is most concentrated in America today, but there's nothing to be gained by making the word "evil" part of the discussion. Indeed, the word is too strong to use in most cases.

What I usually try to do with conservatives is simply *show* the force and what it's doing, and let the picture speak for itself. In this instance, it is only because of the biblical reference to what the "prophets railed against" that I used the word that reinforces the heavy spiritual stakes involved.

Next, please note that once again I avoided challenging the conservative readers on the core value they see at stake in this issue. Nothing in this piece says either that they are right or wrong to oppose abortion.

(As a candidate also—e.g. in the answer I gave to a question on a Liberty University questionnaire to the candidates—I took a position, which I believe in, that goes to a different level: in this case, the level of "religious liberty." On the basis of the vital American value of religious freedom, I argued* that the coercive power of government should not be brought in to enforce the religious views of some on those who hold other views on an essentially religious question.)

It is the *use* of the issue that is my focus here. Continually putting the abortion issue at the center of our public discourse is part of the divide-and-conquer strategy of the force on the right. It is ideal for that purpose because it is one issue that will never bring Americans together, and so it keeps the citizenry involved in battles that neutralize the power of the people.

So the piece is intended to challenge my conservative readers not to change their views on the issue, but to broaden their vision of all the places where their (Christian) moral values are at stake in our politics, and to see through the manipulation.

> In op/eds, I have also addressed, in a kindred way, the other issue that has been cultivated to create single issue voters by distracting them away from the main action of our politics. I'm referring, of course, to the issue of gun rights. Here, the very force that has been working relentlessly to dismantle our democracy, and the liberties it protects, use fear-mongering lies to distract those worried about liberty to guard against a completely irrelevant and bogus threat—i.e.that America's armed citizens (who are supposedly the guardians of the nation's liberty) will be disarmed—while the real threat lies in what this right wing force (of which the NRA is an integral part) is doing to American democracy.

(Some other pieces* directed at the conservatives

- When Bad Politics Are Supported by Good People,
- No Real Patriots,
- An Attack on the System Our Founders Gave Us
- The Republicans' Shameful Divide and Conquer Strategy)

So what impact does my "calling out the evil" have on the conservatives of my region? Frankly, I don't know. And I wouldn't expect to know. Other than the right-wing trolls who jump in online to post comments typical of the genre—long on insults, and utterly devoid of substance—the conservatives are generally silent. (Occasionally I'll meet one who says that sometimes I make them think, or sometimes they like something I said.)

But I do know a fair amount about the impact these pieces are having on the liberals/Democrats in the area. I know because they tell me, coming up to me when they see me in public. Never before have writings of mine been greeted with so much enthusiasm—and gratitude—from a community of people.

It seems to energize and inspire them to see messages like these being delivered to their conservative neighbors. Which is encouraging in itself, whatever the long-term impact on the conservatives—encouraging because, given the two-sided nature of our sick political dynamic, rousing Liberal America for the battle is the other job that needs doing.

The Fire Still Unlit

My recent attempt to generate a "campaign" using a series of articles got lots of readers but generated no movement. More than my previous efforts, it left me with a feeling of failure.

But nothing in the large picture has changed. We are still losing.

I write this in early 2015, shortly after the American electorate handed more power to a Party that blatantly betrayed the nation, trampled on the ideals of our democracy, and showed its indifference to the public good with the power it had in the previous Congress. (See the Preface to Part I here.) The Democrats never even tried to help the American people see how the Republicans had betrayed and damaged America, although clearly that should have been the main issue for the American people to consider in electing a new Congress.

And so we continue to see the political conduct that would be punished in a healthy democracy instead rewarded and strengthened to inflict still more damage.

Meanwhile, that same spirit that has driven me for more than a decade continues to drive me to take the truth displayed in our political scene and use it to try to turn things around.

Why, after all this time, should I think that to be possible? As impelled as I still feel to work toward that end, I've been acutely aware of my marginality as a messenger, and of the consequent modesty of the impact of my efforts. Whatever good, for example, may be accomplished by my calling out the evil in my District's newspapers, it is but a drop in a small backwater of a bucket. What's needed is not an occasional op/ed but a barrage of such messages, and not just in one semiremote corner of the country but on the national stage.

The question is as it always has been: can the message take off, and become an instrument by which a "many" can become a *force*?

That is what I attempted to do in my main post-election effort, prior to undertaking this book. Having described the first three phases of my mission, I feel obliged to talk about the fourth, though I'd rather not. Because with this one, I swung for the fences yet again but I'm not sure I'm entitled to say that I hit even a single.

For this fourth effort, I prepared a series of articles which I described as part of "a campaign to light a fire in Liberal America." The title of the series was "Press the Battle." I had lined up access to major liberal/progressive websites—*Huffington Post, Daily Kos, Opednews*, and several others. And—with the help of a fine team of people who volunteered their talents and energy to help the "campaign" succeed—I prepared a series of articles to convey to people pretty much the same picture that this book contains. (Except that it was weighted much more toward America's national crisis and less toward the "integrative vision" that explains how the forces involved in this crisis work.)

Moreover, I front-loaded the series with the pieces that I thought would be most attention-getting: the more concrete, the more political, the more evocative.

The hope was that people would answer my call to battle, and help to make something happen. That did not come to pass.

I got readers, mostly appreciative. A few of my pieces got "Likes" in the thousands. But not once did anyone respond with a comment that indicated an interest in getting something to happen. Beyond the good little team that I'd formed, nothing more came together.

When it became clear that this series was not going to give rise to any kind of "Campaign"—and when I'd reached the point where it was time to present some of the bigger, more abstract ideas about how the human world works—I read the handwriting on the wall and simply stopped posting the series. I'm not sure that the readers—who seemed to be taking the articles one at a time, and not as pieces of a larger picture—even noticed that I did not complete the process I'd begun. (The entire series—those that were widely published, and those that were not—can be seen at www.pressthebattle.org.)

Despite all the readers, can I call that a single? It felt like a failure.

Regardless of the fate of the "Press the Battle" campaign, it had always been my intention to write this book. These ideas, I felt, might prove to have a long-term value, and it felt absolutely mandatory that I present what I'd seen about the human drama.

When the time came, however, it was not only about that long-term possibility that the spirit that's been driving me all this time spoke. In the important moments that governed my course, I continued to see scenarios—plausible-looking scenarios—in which this book succeeded where "Press the Battle" had failed.

Burning in my mind is an image of America coming to the "Emperor's New Clothes" moment it so badly needs. Not a "moment," of course, but a process of realization, as an organized campaign of impassioned people work, intelligently and diligently, to get a vital truth into the national conversation. As in the fairy tale, a truth is told that—while obvious and important—is not generally acknowledged. Suddenly the truth of it is seen, and acknowledged, and talked about: "the Republican Party has become the instrument of an evil force."

That Emperor, standing there stripped of its lies.

And so here it is, the fifth and probably last phase of my mission, providing in book form a call to battle and a set of ideas that people might use to strike a meaningful blow against the force that must be defeated.

What reason is there to believe this new scenario is plausible?

When It Comes to Forces of the Spirit, Expect the Unexpected

The destructive force on the right appears to have the advantage in terms of conventional kinds of power. It can be defeated, however, if the force of the spirit is tapped. When the spirit enters into human affairs, there is no predicting what can and cannot happen. It depends on the choices people make—like mine to write this book and yours how to make use of it.

What most needs to be said here is that we are dealing with an extraordinary period in American history, that this is a battle that takes place at the level of the spirit, and that when the spirit is involved, there is simply no way to predict, even within broad limits, what can or cannot happen.

I could also say that one keeps trying, like Thomas Edison, who came to his light bulb solution after trying hundreds, or thousands of approaches, and who is quoted as saying that he hadn't failed 10,000 times, but rather that he'd succeeded in eliminating 10,000 approaches that would not work.

I could also say that, by putting the whole picture together between two covers, this book might succeed in getting people to look at a vast and deep picture that could more readily escape notice when presented in pieces. And my own experience is that this vast and deep picture is one that can make the hairs on one's body stand on end, stir the heart, and move one's spirit to press the battle.

(Besides which, a book like this is more likely to find a readership prepared to take in the Big Picture than the audiences these ideas have encountered with other forums and other genres.)

But really, while there may be something to those notions, that's not really what brings this book forward. As I indicated in Interlude II, I enlisted in this mission, despite my reluctance to leave a more beautiful path, because I felt *called* to it. A call of that sort is a matter of the spirit.

And it seems that messages of the spirit always speak in terms of possibility. It always comes with a vision of how sacred values might prevail.

When, in the course of human events, the spirit gets tapped, quite astonishing things can happen. I wrote earlier in that vein about Gandhi and Mandela and Martin Luther King and Churchill. The same can be said, once in a while, about the impact of a book.

Did the writer and the publishers of *Uncle Tom's Cabin* have any way of knowing that Stowe's book would make history with its role in settling the spiritually (as well as politically) fraught question of slavery? Harriet Beecher Stowe put her novel out into the cultural stream at a time when political events were kindling passions in her region surrounding the very issue at the heart of her novel. She tied her narrative firmly into the spiritual/religious tradition of American civilization, making the character of Uncle Tom Christ-like in his virtue and his sacrifice. And she utilized the mode of sentimentality, then ascendant in the ways of her culture, and tapped into a deep current of emotional/moral energy. With winds like that blowing, and with Stowe raising such sails, the work traveled further into the hearts and minds of her countrymen than a work of fiction usually does, and the course of history was changed.

When Tom Paine's *Common Sense* was published in the mid-1770s, was there any way of knowing how it would catch fire in those revolutionary times, and how our history texts would still be talking about it more than two centuries later? In the years before *Common Sense* was published, a kind of spirit had arisen in the American colonies—a spirit that aspired to independence, a spirit sensitized to the sacred values of liberty and democratic justice. Paine spoke of the gathering American crisis in terms that resonated with so many of the aroused colonists that *Common Sense* helped bring to a head the very crisis that gave that pamphlet its significance.

This is the nature of how history gets made when the spirit is involved. Normal history is made along pre-established channels. It is at least somewhat predictable. But spirit moves outside those channels, and enormous force can be unleashed along unpredictable paths, depending on circumstances.

Who can predict where a bolt of lighting will appear in the sky? It depends on how turmoil in the atmosphere creates imbalances that seek to be discharged. When the moment is right, huge amounts of energy find their path.

During World War II, Joseph Stalin said, derisively, when asked about bringing the Pope in on negotiations, "How many divisions does he have?" Stalin understood raw power, and he was contemptuous of the Pope, who commanded no divisions. But some four decades later, a Polish pope—still having no divisions—helped spark a rising of the human spirit (in the Solidarity movement in Gdansk, Poland) that helped trigger the process that, within a decade, brought to an end the Soviet regime that Stalin had ruled.

It is on such unpredictable power that we Americans must rely if we are to protect our democracy, our planet, and a decent future for our children and grandchildren. From where else will come the necessary power to turn this national darkening around?

We will not be able to outspend the Koch Brothers and their ilk in their quest to buy our government. We will not out-organize the machinery that the right has assembled these past forty years. We will not be more eager to do battle than the wounded minions of the right, who have become so inflamed that conflict is the only social condition in which they feel at home. We will not be able to out-propagandize Rupert Murdock and the other denizens of the right-wing media. We will not be able to match the unity the right enforces with its coercive orthodoxy.

All we have that can turn this around is a moral and spiritual truth—aligned with the deepest values and interests of America—that can tap into the power of the spirit.

> [NOTE: This unpredictability of the spirit can cut both ways. In times of intense turmoil, dark forms of spirit can also cut through the usual channels and create dramatic and unexpected movement toward evil: consider what happened in Germany between the two World Wars.]

This book is my effort to provide a moral and spiritual truth that can help serve that end.

Do I think it *will* happen ("it" being that this book helps spark the kind of "prophetic movement" that strikes a meaningful blow in the battle)? No, it's not probable. But it *could* happen, and that scenario is plausible enough that—given what human history has displayed—it would not be weird if it did.

Can anyone point to anything else happening in the political arena that gives great promise of delivering the necessary blow to turn things around? I'm not seeing it. (Since I wrote those words, there have been encouraging developments, among them how Robert Reich has made his message so much more powerful, and how Bernie Sanders has drawn enthusiastic crowds for a message that at least points toward what we're up against.)

And those assessments are enough to drive me, heart and soul, into the fray.

Being *called* means taking all necessary risks.

In the next chapter, I will present an image—a fictional scenario—of how it could happen.

Chapter Twelve :

Excerpts from the (Fictitious) 2025 Article, "How 'The Emperor's New Clothes Project' Helped Rescue America"

Tenth Anniversary Commemoration

The success of this book depends on people stepping forward to make something happen.

Editor's note: 2025 being the 10th anniversary of the appearance of the book **What We're Up Against**, *we here at* **Prominent Publication** *decided to do a commemorative article about the well-known movement sparked by that book, the movement known as "The Emperor's New Clothes Project." As the name suggests, the idea behind the movement was that a kind of truth-telling would precipitate awareness of what was plain to see but not generally acknowledged. As in the fairy tale, the con artists should be exposed, and the naked truth laid bare.*

The author of **What We're Up Against** *had declared his hope that the book would be "the* **Uncle Tom's Cabin***" for this era. In other words, that it would help light a fire to impact the dangerous political situation in* *which the United States was then mired.*

Thanks to a group of able, motivated people, who read and were inspired by **What We're Up Against**, *that fire did get lit. As more and more Americans saw more clearly what it was that was damaging the country, the political dynamic in the country gradually shifted, and the United States began to repair its tattered civilization.*

Here are some excerpts from the interviews presented in that article.

How It Began: Growing Outward

> *What's vital here is not about this book itself, but more so about the central message of what it is we are up against, and still more than that about using that basic truth to change the national conversation and thereby to drain power from the force that is degrading our nation.*

I [reporter for *Prominent Publication*] sat down with several of the original group who responded to the book [*What We're Up Against*] by helping organize the movement that has done so much to restore decency and effectiveness to the American political process…

"When I read Schmookler saying that it 'might' happen, and that was good enough for him," said Person # 1, "I stopped and asked myself, is that good enough for me, too? If someone aflame with the spirit always focuses on 'possibility,' was I willing to listen to that 'spirit'? And I decided I was."

Here, Person # 2 broke in and added, "And there was that question, is there anything else happening in the system that looks promising to turn things around? This was right after that 2014 election where, after all the political atrocities from the right over the previous decade, the Democrats had not even ventured to talk about the elephant in the room, while cruising into an electoral disaster. If we were continuing to plunge downhill, I felt I had to do something. And since I didn't see anything more promising out there for me to join in, I decided I might as well give Schmookler's invitation a try."…

"Schmookler had set up an online forum [at whatweareupagainst.org]," Person # 3 chimed in, "where readers of the book could go to discuss not only the issues raised by the book, but also questions of how the overall strategy of 'See the evil, Call it out, Press the Battle' might be used to have a constructive impact on the political dynamic the book described... It turned out to be true that a nucleus of one or two dozen people willing to do the work of self-organizing a movement could get things rolling."

"It was important at the outset that we get beyond the talky-talky mode that predominates on most forums," Person # 2 told me. "Discussion of the ideas certainly had value. But that wasn't enough. The people in this room agreed from the outset that understanding had to be translated into action."

"We had to keep in front of us the question, 'Are we here just to vent and to get attention, or are we here to get something to happen?' Our first action, if I recall, was to create a separate forum on that website that was ONLY for practical discussions of strategy and for the communications necessary for us to self-organize in order to execute our strategies." That was Person # 2 again.

Person # 1 broke in, saying: "Yes, the self-organizing biz was a major point that Schmookler stressed to us from the beginning. He had a few ideas, but he wanted us to be asking ourselves, 'How can we make this happen?' and to take it upon ourselves to create the campaign. So we did. It took a while to develop a good process, create little teams, get good communication, etc. But once we took responsibility for the task at hand, instead of needing to be told what to do, we found we were perfectly capable of doing it."

"At first we focused a good deal of attention on how to get the book into the right hands," Person # 2 ventured. "So that some sort of buzz would get going. So we set up a networking process to call attention of the right target audience to the existence of this book. By right target audience, we meant people like us who would be able to register what it is that this book shows, and who cared about where the country was heading. We turned our friends onto it, and had them turn on their friends. We used social media. And we set up a publicity committee to work on getting the book reviewed, and getting interviews, etc."

"But we knew from the outset that it was **the central message, and not just the book**, that needed to get out there into the national conversation," Person # 4 shared. "There was no way that the book by itself was going to do that. The book was not written for a mass audience, and we wanted to build toward a mass movement."

"Right," Person # 3 said. "Elaborate and sophisticated argument doesn't reach all that many Americans. (Today in America, nobody could get the big national boost that Lincoln got by giving that Cooper's Union speech—with its compelling case for stopping the spread of slavery.)"

Then Person # 2 broke in: "Yeah, we recognized that, because of the intellectually dense nature of the book, we who read and responded to it were not a representative sample of the whole universe of people we'd want to reach and bring on board. So we knew that we needed to translate the book into other kinds of communication."

"In the book, Andy [Schmookler] had mentioned Tom Paine." This was Person # 4 again. "But part of the key to the success of Paine's *Common Sense* was that he wrote in plain, straight-forward language that was effective even with illiterate common people in the colonies, who needed it read to them. That's hardly the case with *What We're Up Against.* And *Common Sense* was a just a pamphlet, not a whole book. So we worked to bring into our movement people with those skills of popularization—plain and punchy writing, video-making, tweeting. The full catastrophe!"...

"We used Andy for some of that, especially at the beginning," Person # 1 explained, "as he'd developed some of those skills—radio, op/ed, etc. We worked to get him out into the media to talk about the book. But he was clear from the outset that it was important to get other people on board who were more skillful at the popular level, or who commanded a bigger platform (meaning audience), or both..."

"To bring people on board for whom the book wasn't the right vehicle, we worked to create a multi-layer approach," Person # 3 said. "Part of that involved getting credible people to testify that a legitimate case had been made for this and that proposition—like that it had been shown convincingly enough that forces worth calling 'evil' do operate in the human world, and that what's arisen on the right is a relatively pure case of such a thing. We found a few who 'got' the book, and were credible enough that their testimony made people who wouldn't follow the argument more open to adopting its conclusions."

"We found—perhaps it should not have been surprising—that once those ideas got enough momentum behind them in the culture, people started holding them in their minds," Person # 4 said. "They believed these things without having followed all the logic and evidence that had convinced us readers of the book. It started to FEEL true. By that means, the basic ideas of the book expanded their reach beyond the narrow field of the book's target audience.....

"It's interesting," Person # 1 said, "how ideas can percolate to become part of the common wisdom of a community of people. **The right-wing had demonstrated that the baldest lies can be made politically acceptable by coordinated trumpeting of them. We figured that it was high time that Liberal America demonstrate that the most vital political truth of our times could be made acceptable as well.**"

"At the beginning, our message—which challenged both the lying right and the denying left—was heard as kind of 'extreme' and 'harsh,'" Person # 2 related. "But as we gained in strength—as 'The Emperor's New Clothes Project' gained momentum—that same unacknowledged but blatant truth became increasingly acceptable."

"Like that saying," Person # 2 interjected, "'First they ignore it, then they laugh at it, then they say they knew it all along.'"

Gathering a Political Force

Progressive activist groups, regardless of their issues, are up against the same force. That by itself provides important commonness of purpose. United we stand.

"There was a political operation that we started fairly early," Person # 5 told me. "One big idea was that we could make a 'movement' by gathering together in common cause a whole spectrum of liberal/progressive activists and organizations whose main work was focused on particular issues. So many good people working for one cause or another—like getting money out of our politics, or combating climate change, protecting voters' rights, achieving economic fairness, resolving our festering immigration issue, etc. We saw a natural commonality of interest among these groups, and we saw advancing the strategy of 'See the evil etc.' as the perfect way for these already-existing groups to express that commonality of interest."

"Right," declared Person # 3. "For each one of these groups, the main barrier to their reaching their goals was **the same destructive force**—the same for each of them, and the same that we were taking on in a direct and comprehensive way. So for each of them, weakening that force opened the road to achieving their goals."

"Then all that remained," Person # 5 said, "was to persuade them that our movement was a promising way to weaken that force and open the way for their success. Not all of them got on board, but a goodly number did, at least to some extent."

"That greatly magnified our ability to get the word out, and to function as a more or less cohesive movement," Person # 3 said.

Heading into the Arena

Political candidates get listened to in special ways. And the many "safe" Republican seats offered a special opportunity to get the public to hear the message of the "Emperor's New Clothes" project.

I asked them how and when they started to get more directly involved in electoral politics...

"Already by the time the 2016 campaign was in full swing, we thought we could discern that our efforts and the beginnings of buzz about the book had led to some visible shift in the national conversation. Already there was more talk about how this 'outlier' of a political party was trampling on American political norms and ideals," Person # 2 said.

"And we could see that some Republicans were trying to look more responsible and constructive," Person # 5 added. This created a degree of tension, and occasionally outright strife, within the GOP, as cracks started to show up between those leaders who were wedded to the destructiveness, and those who had just gone along with the prevailing winds. Well, now the prevailing winds were shifting—and we were happy to give ourselves a bit of the credit for that."...

"I remember when and how we made the pivot to dealing more directly with the politicians," Person # 2 told me. "We'd been discussing why it was that Schmookler's campaign speech—the one whose video drew such an audience—had so much more dramatic impact on its audience than, say, the writings in his 'Press the Battle' series. We were discussing how the spoken word can be much more powerful than the written word, because so much of what we communicate is not contained in just the words. And then Schmookler said he thought that an essential part of the success of that speech was that he was delivering it not as a mere commentator, but as 'a warrior on the field of political battle.' In other words, as a candidate."

"For that audience, at that moment, Schmookler was their champion, doing combat on their behalf," Person # 3 elaborated. "He thought that it was the combination of the message itself, and the role he was playing at an event staged in the context of a hard-fought election."

"So then we figured," Person # 2 continued, "if we want this message of *What We're Up Against* (and 'See the evil. Call it out. Press the Battle.') to have its full impact, we needed to get some of these combatants—the politicians running for office—to deliver the message."

Person # 3 took this up. "At first there was limited receptivity. For one thing, a great many politicians didn't have much more insight into what was going on in our politics than the public—they're not there because they're great thinkers, after all. But even those who did agree with our message were often hesitant to adopt it. Understandably since, at that point, those 'prevailing winds' of public opinion had only begun to shift, and they didn't want to sound harsh or alarmist. Some of them did start to point more firmly in the right direction in their speeches, gently nudging their listeners to see how disgraceful the conduct of the Republicans had been. But only gently."

"So we turned to a particular subset of candidates," Person # 5 said, "to get our message into the electoral arena. We turned to those candidates running in congressional districts that are essentially unwinnable for any Democrat. We persuaded a number of them that they could be important players in the vital political battle of our times."

"This was an important strategic idea," Person # 2 commented. "In the short run, the political battle is over who will hold the offices where the laws get made. But in the long run, the battle is over shaping the public consciousness—because it is the people's consciousness that determines to whom the people will give that power. So good candidates, even in unwinnable races, are able to play an important educational role. We worked to get candidates to help the public recognize the paramount political reality of those dark times: the destructiveness and irresponsibility of what was driving the Republican Party. We encouraged them to tap into the powerful public discontent with Congress, and show them that the failure of Congress that enraged them was a deliberate political strategy of the GOP.'

"We tried with some success to build a network of these truth-warriors in very red districts," Person # 1 said. "We encouraged them to think of themselves as "behind enemy lines," with good access to the power base of the foe. Well-positioned to talk to Republican voters about their 'once-respectable' party."

"A whole cadre of such candidates could—and did!—become more than the sum of their parts," Person # 2 expanded on the story. "The coordinated message got amplified, for example, when the national press picked up on the national phenomenon of these powerful messages being delivered in these 'safe' Red districts."

"But not so safe anymore. Not after, with the help of these candidates, our movement started to make inroads into public awareness," Person # 2 said. "Maybe not enough to turn the Republicans out of those safe seats, but enough to move public opinion enough away from the Republican Party to change the outcome of some close races for Senate, and for electoral votes in the presidential election."

Shaping the Battle

An effective campaign can move from trying to persuade candidates to include the message about what we're up against to recruiting candidates who are good at delivering that message.

"And as our self-organizing continued to develop apace," Person # 1 said, "'The Emperor's New Clothes Project,' in affiliation with other activist groups who had seen our potential usefulness to them, began to play a more active role in determining which individuals actually would wield the power. We helped recruit candidates and helped some in primary battles to win their nominations. And as the winds shifted, we were able to get more politicians to see that they could help themselves by making our message—adapted into a form suitable for their electorate—a central part of their campaigns."

"'The truth is our weapon,' Schmookler had said in that semi-viral speech of his. Eventually, the message became a weapon not only around the campfires of Liberal America, and not only 'behind enemy lines,' but at center stage, where the candidates contended for the most powerful offices in the land," Person # 2 said.

"It was pretty thrilling for all of us," Person # 4 recalled. "By the time of the 2020 presidential election, a national force, armed with this message, had emerged with sufficient power that we now really could Press the Battle at the pinnacle of power. The Democrats nominated So-and-So, who had shown himself capable of speaking strong truths in unassailable ways. He was a good counter-puncher, too, so that when the Republicans struck back at his calling them out for the damage they were doing to the country, he invariably used their attacks effectively as an opportunity to make his case stick, thus further educating the public. And he won in a landslide."

"That was the last time the Republicans tried to defend the indefensible," add Person # 5. "From then on, the GOP started to morph back into the form of a normal major American political party. They saw the handwriting on the wall: they had either to change their ways, or be driven into political oblivion."

Person # 2 came in: "The Party gradually purged itself of some of the sociopathic people who had been so prominent during their era of destructiveness, and either could not hide their proclivities or carried so much baggage that they were a liability. Meanwhile, the mere opportunists who'd gone along for the ride simply took the opportunity to act like normal, reasonably constructive politicians. Some of them were punished by their electorates for what they had been and done. But most of them were able to re-align themselves with the new climate."

A Nation Moving Forward Again

There is a path by which wholeness can be restored to the American power system, the truth can regularly defeat the lie, and the nation can make constructive decisions to navigate its way into a good future for our children and grandchildren.

"With both major parties at last acting responsibly, and interested in getting things accomplished for the good of the nation, after the election of So-and-So [as president] in 2020, there was a wave of healing legislation," Person # 5 recalled. "The Congress and the new president went through the backlog of things that the 'Party of No' had obstructed. It was not quite up to the level of FDR's remarkable 100 days avalanche of legislation in 1933. But in fairly short order, the United States became the leader of the world's efforts to deal responsibly with climate change, passed a constitutional amendment that effectively replaced 'one dollar, one vote' with 'one person, one vote,' reformed the tax system to make it more progressive and fair, enacted legislation to create more equality of opportunity (including reforms in the financing of higher education so that the nation allowed its youth to make the most of their God-given gifts, and got service back from those youth in return), rebalanced the power ratio between workers and their corporate employers, and a host of other measures that repaired much of the damage that had been done to the nation during that dark era where the Lie defeated the truth."

"Yes, there was a new, far more favorable balance of power, e.g. between the truth and the lie," Person # 1 said. "Just as post-War Germany showed rather less tolerance than other nations for any kind of bigoted hate speech, so also—in the new political climate—politicians bent over backwards to be honest and straightforward. An Era of Honesty, one might say, set in. I don't expect it will last forever. But I don't think the generations now alive will ever again countenance anything like the dark era where an 'evil force' managed to get such a strong hand onto the helm of the United States of America."

I asked them about all those "good, decent conservatives" that Schmookler had written about in his book. What had happened to them?

"The diehards never changed. Nobody likes to be wrong, certainly not so very wrong as many of them were," Person # 2 answered. "But for some people, admitting such error comes harder than for others. (Think of how it has been possible for the South to maintain, for a century and a half, so many major lies about what their ancestors fought for in that noble 'Lost Cause.')"

"Besides, with many of these people on the right, their thought-processes are not, in general, big on self-corrective mechanisms," Person # 4 said. "It's a culture that places a lot more emphasis on the 'virtues' of undying loyalty to one's side and to consistency in one's beliefs. Better to be steadfast in error than wishy-washy in changing one's mind."

"But it isn't quite right to say that they didn't change," Person # 1 maintained. "My experience was that many of them re-wrote their own histories, and now see themselves as never having trusted the likes of Newt Gingrich or Rush Limbaugh or Karl Rove. And besides that, as their surrounding communities distanced themselves from the discredited, they all migrated together back toward a more normal kind of political consciousness. No outright moment of insight, no dramatic realization that they'd wrongly seen the Emperor as clothed in glory. But still, a turning away from the nakedness that had been exposed by our project and all its allies."

"It's not the diehards that changed the balance of power, however," Person # 3 said. "The shift came from those who were less wedded to the right-wing Lie, but rather had only been going with the common opinion of their communities. As opinions shifted, they easily moved away from the Republican Party in its newly-exposed ugliness. The less-aligned, and the less-informed, ceased to be a source of power for the ugly force on the right. And this set the stage for the eventual re-emergence of a genuine conservative American political party."

At which point, Person # 1 intoned: "And by this means was power drained away from the evil force, making a positive shift in the balance of power between good and evil in America. And by this means, was America saved."

Acknowledgments

Many people have given generously of their time, energy, and creativity along the way. With apologies to anyone I may unintentionally be leaving out, I would like to express my gratitude to Steve Busch, Barry Castleman, Greg Correll, Lowell Feld, Trevor Fitzgibbon, Lee Fuhr, David Groff, Sam Gruen, Dennis Hendrix, Michael Holmes, Forest Jones, David Landau, Noree Lee, Layne Longfellow, Diane Loomis, April Moore, Richard Randall, Aaron Schmookler, Ed Schmookler, David Spangler, Steven Stauffer, Clayton Steneroden, Brian Umana, Phil Zipin, and Danny Zwicker,

Made in the USA
Charleston, SC
12 November 2015